PSYCHOLOGICAL PERSPECTIVES ON FEAR OF FLYING

T0326189

Psychological Perspectives on Fear of Flying

Edited by
ROBERT BOR
LUCAS VAN GERWEN

 Routledge
Taylor & Francis Group

LONDON AND NEW YORK

First published 2003 by Ashgate Publishing

Published 2016 by Routledge
2 Park Square, Milton Park, Abingdon, Oxfordshire OX14 4RN
711 Third Avenue, New York, NY 10017, USA

First issued in paperback 2016

Routledge is an imprint of the Taylor & Francis Group, an informa business

British Library Cataloguing in Publication Data
Psychological perspectives on fear of flying
  1.Fear of flying - Psychological aspects
  I.Bor, Robert II.Gerwen, Lucas van
  616.8'5225

Library of Congress Control Number: 2003100754

ISBN 13: 978-1-138-24997-4 (pbk)
ISBN 13: 978-0-7546-0903-2 (hbk)

Contents

List of Figures

List of Tables

List of Contributors

Page L. Anderson, Ph.D, is an Assistant Professor in the Department of Psychology at Georgia State University. She conducts federally-funded clinical trials that examine the effectiveness of virtual reality in the treatment of anxiety and is interested in applying technology to self-help programmes for anxiety. She received the President's New Researcher Award from the Association for the Advancement of Behaviour Therapy. She earned a Ph.D in clinical psychology in 1998 at the University of Georgia and a postdoctoral fellowship at Emory University School of Medicine. She served as director of clinical services at Virtually Better, a clinic specialising in cognitive-behavioural treatment of anxiety using virtual reality technology.
Georgia State University MSC 2A1155 33, Gilmer Street, Unit 2, Atlanta, GA 30303-3082, USA
Tel: 404.651.2850
Fax: 404.651.1391
Email: psypxa@langate.gsu.edu

Johannes Arnesen graduated as a Pilot in 1988. An over-supply of pilots in civil air traffic at that time prompted him to enter a medical curriculum from which he graduated as a MD in 1998. He later gained his pilot's licence and is now an SAS pilot. During his medical curriculum, he completed a main subject on flight phobia. In recent years he has been working with the data analysis of the Braathens flight phobia treatment programme.
Department of Behavioural Sciences in Medicine, Box 1111, Blindern, 0317 Oslo, Norway

Josine Arondeus, Ph.D, is a Clinical Psychologist, Psychotherapist and EAAP member. She works as a senior fear of flying therapist for the VALK Foundation, a collaborative venture between the University of Leiden, KLM Royal Dutch Airlines and Amsterdam Airport Schiphol since 1993. She is engaged in individual and group treatment of flying phobics, of passengers dealing with the psychological aftermath of aircraft accidents, and of aircrew members with psychological problems. She was a member of the organising committee of the second International Fear of Flying conference held in Vienna in 2000 and is currently preparing the third conference in this field.
The VALK Foundation, PO Box 110, 2300 AC Leiden, The Netherlands

Tel: 00-31-71-5273733
Fax: 00-31-71-5273796
E-mail: info@valk.org

Robert Bor is a Consultant Clinical Psychologist at the Royal Free Hospital, London. He is Visiting Professor at City University, London, where he teaches on the MSc in Air Transport Management. He also teaches on the Diploma in Travel Health at the Royal Free and University College Medical School in the Academic Department of Travel Medicine and Vaccines. He holds an Honours degree in Psychology from the University of the Witwatersrand, Johannesburg, and a Clinical Psychology Masters and Doctorate from the University of South Africa. He is a Chartered Clinical, Counselling and Health Psychologist and qualified as a Systemic Therapist at the Tavistock Clinic, London. He has an interest in public health and also provides a specialist psychological consultation service for air crew and their families, airline managers and for passengers. He has set up a treatment service for passengers who have a fear of flying at two London travel health clinics. He is frequently interviewed for television and newspaper features on the psychology of travel. He serves on the editorial board of several leading international academic journals and has authored or co-authored numerous books and papers. He is a Fellow of the Royal Aeronautical Society and a Member of the European Association for Aviation Psychology and British Travel Health Association. He also has a pilot's licence. Robert Bor is a Churchill Fellow.

10th Floor, Royal Free Hospital, Pond Street, London NW3 2QG, England
Tel: 020 7830 2152
Email: robert.bor@rfh.nthames.nhs.uk
www.crewcare.org

Xavier Bornas, Ph.D, is Senior Lecturer in Behaviour Modification Techniques and Cognitive Therapies at the Department of Psychology, University of the Balearic Islands. He has directed the fear of flying research group at this university since 1993. He has published several scientific articles on this topic. The research group has developed the computer assisted fear of flying treatment (CAFFT), which is a simulated exposure technological tool. Dr. Bornas is now interested in Chaos theory as an alternative explanation for both the patterns of fear of flying and the CAFFT clinical results.

Department of Psychology, University of the Balaeric Islands, Cra. Valldemossa, km. 7,5, E 07071 Palma de Mallorca, Spain
Email: xavier.bornas@uib.es

Christelle Delorme, Ph.D, is a Clinical and Health Psychologist, and works as a junior fear of flying therapist. After enjoying a year practising travelling and flying herself, she now works for the VALK Foundation, a collaborative venture between the University of Leiden, KLM Royal Dutch Airlines and Amsterdam Airport Schiphol with the aim of helping people to overcome their fear of flying. She has conducted research on the relationship between personality pathology and fear of flying, which can be read about in her co-authored chapter on this topic.
The VALK Foundation, PO Box 110, 2300 AC Leiden, The Netherlands
Tel: 00-31-71-5273733
Fax: 00-31-71-5273796
E-mail: info@valk.org

Claudia de Zeeuw, Ph.D, is a Clinical Psychologist, Psychotherapist and works as a senior fear of flying therapist. She works for the VALK Foundation, a collaborative venture between the University of Leiden, KLM Royal Dutch Airlines and Amsterdam Airport Schipol with the aim of helping people to overcome their fear of flying. She has worked in this field for more than eight years at the VALK Foundation. The main goals of the Foundation are: to help prevent a fear of flying, to provide a facility for helping those affected overcome their fears and to work with other organisations to develop their own programmes. Together with the University of Leiden, she conducts research into the fear of flying, passenger behaviour. Dr de Zeeuw wrote a thesis on the topic of fear of flying and has published a paper in a scientific journal on treatment of fear of flying.
The VALK Foundation, as above.

Rene F.W. Diekstra works at the Municipal Health Department, Rotterdam, The Netherlands. He is a Chartered Clinical and Health Psychologist and is also a Registered Psychotherapist. He has authored and co-authored many books and published over 100 papers in peer review journals. He also serves on editorial boards of numerous academic journals. He was one of the co-founders of the First International Fear of Flying conference.
The VALK Foundation, as above.

Øivind Ekeberg is Professor in Behavioural Sciences in Medicine, University of Oslo, and Psychiatrist at the Department of Acute Medicine, Ulleval University Hospital, Oslo. Together with Ingerid Seeberg and Bjørg Bratsberg Ellertsen, MD, he initiated a treatment programme for flight phobia organised by the Braathens airline in 1983. He has been teaching during the courses since the beginning. Based on studies on flight phobia, he wrote his doctoral thesis: 'Flight Phobia: Prevalence, sympathetic responses and treatment', in 1991. Department of Behavioural Sciences in Medicine, Box 1111, Blindern, 0317 Oslo, Norway

Nadia Garnefski works as a Researcher and University Lecturer at the Clinical and Health Psychology Department of Leiden University in the Netherlands. She received her Ph.D from Leiden University in November 1997. The focus of her research is on the relationship between cognitive coping mechanisms and psychopathology in adolescents and adults.
Leiden University, Department of Clinical and Health Psychology, PO Box 9555, 2300 RB Leiden, The Netherlands
Tel: 00-31-71-5273733
Fax: 00-31-71-5273796
E-mail: info@valk.org

Larry F. Hodges, Ph.D, is an Associate Professor in the College of Computing and the head of the Virtual Environments Group in the Graphics, Visualisation and Usability Centre at the Georgia Institute of Technology. He is also co-founder of Virtually Better, a company that specialises in creating virtual environments for treating anxiety disorders. His research interests include all aspects of virtual reality and 3-D human-computer interaction. He received his Ph.D. from North Carolina State University in computer engineering in 1988. He is a senior editor of *Presence: Teleoperators and Virtual Environments*.
UNC-Charlotte, 9201 University Boulevard, Charlotte, NC 28223-0001, USA
Voice mail: 704 687-6128
Fax: 704 687-3516
Email: lfhodges@uncc.edu

Elaine Iljon Foreman, BA(Hons), MSc, AFBPsS, specialises in the treatment of fear of flying and other anxiety related problems. She holds an Honours Degree from Durham University, a Master's Degree from Aberdeen University, and is an Associate Fellow of the British Psychological Society. Her highly specialised treatment programme for fear of flying, is based on over 20 years of clinical experience, and on her ongoing research and development of cognitive behaviour therapy. She has researched the treatment of anxiety at Middlesex Hospital Medical School, and has created a brief, intensive therapy course for the fear of flying based on cognitive behavioural techniques. As well as being an invited expert on radio and TV programmes, her research results have been presented at international conferences in Europe, North America, the Far East and Australia.

Freedom to Fly, EIF Consulting Rooms, 21a Dean Road, London NW2 5AB, UK
Tel/Fax: 020 8459 3428
email: free2fly@dial.pipex.com
www.free2fly.dial.pipex.com

Vivian Kraaij works as a Postdoctoral Fellow at the Clinical and Health Psychology Department of Leiden University in the Netherlands. She received her Ph.D from Leiden University on research about negative life events in relation to mental health. The focus of her current research is on cognitive coping mechanisms in relation to various stressful events.
Leiden University, Department of Clinical and Health Psychology, PO Box 9555, 2300 RB Leiden, The Netherlands
Phone: 31 71 5273736
Fax: 31 71 5273619
E-mail: Kraaij@fsw.LeidenUniv.nl

Jordi Llabrés, Ph.D, is Assistant Professor at the Department of Psychology, University of the Balearic Islands. He teaches courses on Behaviour Disorders and New Technologies in Psychology. The author of numerous scientific articles on this topics, he has been involved in cognitive-behavioural assessment and treatment software development since 1995.
Department of Psychology, University of the Balaeric Islands, Cra. Valldemossa, km. 7,5, E 07071 Palma de Mallorca, Spain

Neil J. McLean is a Clinical Psychologist and Lecturer in Psychology at the University of Western Australia in Perth, Western Australia. In 1982, in collaboration with Ansett Australia, he developed a treatment programme for fear of flying which eventually came to be offered in eight cities across Australia. McLean was the national coordinator of this programme until the demise of Ansett Australia in 2001. In 1997 he developed a video-based self-help programme titled 'Conquer your Fear of Flying'. He has a special interest in the cognitive factors that are associated with risk perception and fear.
University of Western Australia, Perth, Australia
Email: neil@psy.uwa.edu.au

Richard J. Roberts, Ph.D, holds qualifications in psychology and clinical social work and is a Senior Lecturer in the School of Social Work, University of New South Wales, Sydney, Australia. He was psychologist and consultant to the Sydney Fear of Flying clinic for 10 years from 1981 to 1990.
School of Social Work, University of New South Wales, Sydney, NSW 2052, Australia
Tel: 61 (2) 9385 1959
Fax: 61 (2) 9662 8991
Email: r.roberts@unsw.edu.au

Barbara Olasov Rothbaum received her Ph.D in psychology in 1986 and is currently a tenured associate professor in psychiatry at the Emory School of Medicine in the Department of Psychiatry and Behavioural Sciences and director of the Trauma and Anxiety Recovery Programme at Emory. Dr Rotherbaum specialises in research on the treatment of individuals with anxiety disorders, particularly focusing on exposure therapy. She has won both state and national awards for two books, and received the Diplomate in Behavioural Psychology from the American Board of Professional Psychology. She is currently Associate Editor of the *Journal of Traumatic Stress* and on the Editorial Board for the journal *Cyber Psychology and Behaviour.* She is also co-founder with Dr Larry Hodges, a Georgia Tech computer scientist, of Virtually Better Inc., and together they have pioneered the application of virtual reality to the treatment of psychological disorders. Two patents have been granted, and they have received over $1,000,000 in research funding for this application of virtual reality.
Director, Trauma and Anxiety Recovery, Program Emory University School of Medicine, 1365 Clifton Road, NE, Atlanta, GA 30322, USA
Tel: (404) 778-3875
Fax: (404) 778-4655
Email: brothba@emory.edu

Ingerid Seeberg, after 38 years at Braathens, has now retired as the head nurse of the airline. She took the initiative to develop the flight phobia treatment programme in 1983, and was the main organiser until 2000. In addition to the course that was developed in Oslo, she also organised similar treatment programmes in other cities in Norway that were served by Braathens. She has been the 'mother' of the flight phobia treatment in Norway.
Braathens, 1330 Oslo Lufthavn, Norway

Philip Spinhoven is Professor of Psychology at the Clinical and Health Psychology Department of Leiden University in the Netherlands. He is a Chartered Clinical and Health Psychologist and is also a Registered Psychotherapist. He has co-authored or edited several books and published over 100 papers in peer review journals. His research interests include fear of flying, psychological problems. He is adviser of the board of the VALK Foundation and closely related to the research by the foundation on fear of flying.
Leiden University, Department of Clinical and Health Psychology, PO Box 9555, 2300 RB Leiden, The Netherlands
Tel: 00-31-71-5273733
Fax: 00-31-71-5273796
E-mail: info@valk.org

Kasia Szymanska is a Chartered Counselling Psychologist, a BABCP Accredited Psychotherapist, is UKCP Registered and an Associate of the British Psychological Society. She practises as a psychologist in central London for the Central Stress Management Unit, Psychiatric and Psychological Consultant Services, and is a senior lecturer at the University of East London on the MSc in Counselling Psychology. She is an Associate Director of the Centre for Stress Management, London, where she runs training programmes in problem focused psychotherapy and post-traumatic stress disorder and is the Director of the Distance Learning at the Centre for Coaching. She is also a Consultant Editor of *The Online Journal of Multimodal and Rational Emotive Therapy*. She has authored and co-authored articles and chapters on therapist-client sexual contact, cognitive behaviour therapy and other issues.
Centre for Stress Management, PO Box 26583, London SE3 7EZ, UK
Tel: 0208 318 5653
E mail: kasia.s@tinyonline.co.uk

Michael P. Tomaro, Ph.D has nearly three decades of experience as both a Clinical Psychologist and a pilot. As a Clinical Psychologist, he is a charter member of the National Register for Health Service Providers in Psychology and a certified member of the National Association for the Advancement of Psychoanalysis. As a pilot, Dr Tomaro holds commercial and instrument pilot qualification in both single and multiengine aircraft. He holds both primary, instrument and multi-engine instructor ratings and has been a member of the National Association of Flight Instructors for 14 years. Dr Tomaro has worked with fearful flyers at General Mitchell International Airport, Milwaukee,

Wisconsin, for 20 years. He has published the programme 'Flying in the Comfort Zone' in both book and video format.

Aviation Psychologist: General Mitchell International Airport, 923 E. Layton Avenue, Milwaukee, Wisconsin 53207
Tel: 414-769-8123
Email: cmfzne@fearofflyingdoctor.com

Miquel Tortella-Feliu, Ph.D, is Senior Lecturer in Behaviour Therapy and Psychopathology at the Department of Psychology, University of the Balearic Islands. He has been involved in fear of flying research since 1993. He has published more than a dozen scientific articles on this topic covering assessment, epidemiology, psychopathological features of flight phobics, treatment and outcome prediction. He is now working on the evaluation of a computer exposure software for flying phobia. Dr Tortella-Feliu has also conducted clinical work at the Clinical Psychology and Psychiatry Unit of the University of the Balearic Islands where he specialises in cognitive-behavioural treatment of anxiety disorders.

Department of Psychology, University of the Balaeric Islands, Cra. Valldemossa, km. 7,5, E 07071 Palma de Mallorca, Spain
Email: miquel.tortella@uib.es

Richard van Dyck is Professor of Psychiatry at the Vrije University, Amsterdam, The Netherlands. He is a Chartered Clinical and Behaviour Psychotherapist. He has co-authored or edited several books and published over 100 papers in peer review journals.

The VALK Foundation, as above.

Lucas van Gerwen, Ph.D, is a Clinical Psychologist, Psychotherapist and a professional Pilot. He works for the VALK Foundation, a collaborative venture between the University of Leiden, KLM Royal Dutch Airlines and Amsterdam Airport Schipol with the aim of helping people to overcome their fear of flying. He has worked in this field for more than 20 years, and 12 years for the VALK Foundation. The main goals of the Foundation are: to help prevent a fear of flying, to provide a facility for helping those affected overcome their fears and to work with other organisations to develop their own programmes. As an EAAP registered aviation psychologist, he provides stress management training for *ab initio* student pilots with the KLM flying school. Together with the University of Leiden, he conducts research into the fear of flying, passenger behaviour, psychological problems among aircrew and the psychological aftermath of aircraft accidents. He is also the organiser and founding father of the International World Conferences on Fear of Flying. Dr van Gerwen is the author of two books on the topic of fear of flying and has published numerous papers in scientific journals on assessment and treatment of the problem.

The VALK Foundation, as above.
Email: StichtingVALK@cs.com

Marco Verschragen, Ph.D, is an Educational Psychologist with a background as an aviation technologist and works as an fear of flying therapist for the VALK Foundation located in Leiden, The Netherlands. The VALK foundation is a collaborative venture between the University of Leiden, KLM Royal Dutch Airlines and Amsterdam Airport Schiphol. The main goal of the VALK Foundation is: the prevention and the treatment of fear of flying on a scientific based programme.

The VALK Foundation, as above.

Robert Wolfger, Ph.D, is a Clinical Psychologist working for Austrian Airlines since 1979. At present he is Head of Public Affairs at Austrian Airlines. Since 1979 he has organised Fear of Flying Seminars. As an EAAP member, he organised the EAAP congress 'Terror in the Air' in 1985. In cooperation with the VALK Foundation he organised the 2nd International Fear of Flying Conference Airborne 2000.

Austrian Airlines, Hauptburo, Fontanastrasse 1, A-1107 Wien, Austria
Tel: 43-5-1766-2310
Fax: 43-1-688-5501
Email: robert.wolfger@aua.com

Acknowledgements

A number of people have worked hard to ensure the efficient production of this book. In particular John Hindley and Carolyn Court of Ashgate Publishers offered guidance and support at all stages from the initial idea through to production. Brandon Storey provided extensive editorial assistance, while Pat FitzGerald converted the original text into camera-ready copy and also helped to edit the text.

A book on a specialist clinical subject such as that covered in this book could not be produced without the willingness of all of those people who have a fear of flying with whom we have had the privilege to work. We have learned an enormous amount about the challenges they have faced as well as which treatment methods are most helpful in overcoming the problem. We are grateful to them as well as to each of the contributors, and also to many people we have not mentioned, all of whom have helped to bring this project to fruition.

Foreword

Robert Wolfger and Josine Arondeus

It is a privilege to present a foreword for a new book. Learning theory, however, suggests that the first and last events capture the long-term memory no matter what happened during these events or what happened in between. Therefore it is not only a privilege but also a challenge.

When asked by a range of people – including those who never experienced a fear of flying or journalists who are simply curious about it – what fear of flying is, many of us who are so-called experts might not have a clear cut definition at hand. We start with descriptions, emotional states, clustering and differentiating from other fears. We explain which components are associated with such a fear, such as lack of knowledge, fear of turbulence, separation anxiety, claustrophobia, acrophobia, social phobia, agoraphobia, fear of losing control or having no control at all. In addition, we talk about the intensity of these states beginning with bearable tension and increasing to full-blown panic attacks which some of our clients have to endure. We describe the bodily sensations accompanying these emotional states, what they mean to the clients, how dangerous or harmless they are and how to overcome them.

When giving such an explanation we always feel somewhat uneasy about our explanations. Did we describe fear of flying or anxiety or fear in general, highlighting several circumstances under which such anxiety or fear may develop? Have we talked about common fear, phobia, panic attack and blended in some cognitive and emotional elements associated with flying? Is fear of flying really distinct from other phobias that have been experienced by millions of people for thousands of years? Is the cure for any phobia a simple exposure programme that has been tested? What about Demosthenes the well-known orator of ancient Greece, who was afraid to speak in public, but managed to overcome his fear? What about one of the greatest German poets, Johann Wolfgang von Goethe, who, about 200 years ago, prescribed himself an exposure programme in order to overcome his fear of heights (Markgraf and Schneider, 1996). Time and again he climbed up onto the Strassburg Münster church while it was under construction until his acrophobia subsided. Even Freud himself developed his well-known theory of anxiety neurosis because between the age of 30 and 40 he was subject to anxiety and panic attacks. He developed severe agoraphobia and was afraid of crossing the street or travelling by steam train (a common fear at that time). After trying to overcome these phobias through self-analysis, he had to accept that exposure was the most important therapeutic measure for such cases (Markgraf and Schneider, 1996). Are these examples of successful behavioural self-therapy or just expression of phylogenetic common sense? Do we need the complicated theoretical constructs of psychotherapeutic schools at all or just the common sense of repeated confrontation of fear? Is the focus on the symptoms of fear sufficient and are the symptoms even the cause? If the symptoms once feared no longer have a negative impact on someone's life, is the fear overcome, regardless of how? Accepting this implies that one also has to accept that any therapy that has a positive effect on lowering the intensity of the symptoms is a good therapy no matter what is behind the phobia and its causes. This concept of phobia led to a desire to classify different phobias. Sometimes, one comes across lists of up to 100 phobias that are considered to be distinct (Franke and Halter, 2000).

Internationally accepted classifications like the DSM IV restrict phobias to the well-known 11 discernible categories including: panic disorder without agoraphobia, panic disorder with agoraphobia, agoraphobia without history of panic disorder, specific phobia, social phobia, obsessive-compulsive disorder, post-traumatic stress disorder, acute stress disorder, generalised anxiety disorder, anxiety disorder due to a general medical condition, substance induced anxiety disorder and anxiety disorder not otherwise specified (APA, 1994). However, the desire to classify extends not only to the various disorders themselves, but also to the therapeutic schools, which all claim to be the most suitable solution to the problem. Are psychodynamic therapies effective for phobic patients; are patients better off with humanistic psychotherapy or family counselling or is behavioural modification (including systematic desensibilisation, cognitive restructuring, aversion or confrontation therapy, the training of social competence, etc.) the best way to overcome a phobia? One can only imagine how a client (or sometimes even a therapist) must feel 'being lost in a labyrinth' considering the possible combinations of 50 distinct phobias and 50 distinct therapeutic offers.

As researchers and clinicians working in the field of treating anxiety and phobias we have to address the following.

Firstly, we have to concentrate harder on the scientific control of the course of progress of the behavioural modification we claim to achieve. Simple questionnaires without probabilistic interpretations may not be sufficient. Clear definitions of what exactly was the problem, what was the target of the modification and what has been achieved within the framework of such problem or target is more necessary than ever. Therefore, we stress the importance of validation and reliable diagnostics and are happy that this book presents an entire chapter dealing with the development of a fear of flying questionnaire.

Secondly, we may have to accept that nature deserves more credit with respect to phobic developments. We also have to direct more of our interest to the above-mentioned research, which might make us understand more clearly expressions like 'gut decisions', or feeling 'butterflies in the stomach' when afraid. It can lead to more insight about the importance of breathing and relaxation exercises in phobia treatment. If research can prove that genetic predisposition explains between 40 to 50 per cent of the behaviour variations, then our therapeutic approach has to change drastically. Accepting the predisposition to feel more easily fearful (with all the positive consequences thereof as well) might be the right approach alongside confrontation, cognitive restructuring and basic explanation of facts outside and inside the trembling, sweating and pale body.

Thirdly, we might have to focus less on complex theories about why general and specific phobias develop and persist so easily. We have to swing the pendulum back from classification or discrimination of therapeutic approaches to integration based on such theories, and have to prove or to falsify them on basis of the outcome predictability (Popper, 1966). Is fear of flying rational within an evolutionary perspective? Is there a kind of technophobia associated with all forms of transportation? This book – one of the first on this topic – presents a scholarly understanding of the causes of fear of flying, and methods for treating this problem. As with all good textbooks, it seeks to answer some questions and raises many more. Hopefully, this will be the start of a series of books that examine this important topic.

References

American Psychiatric Association (1994), *Diagnostic and Statistical Manual of Mental Disorders* (4th edn), Washington, DC: American Psychiatric Association.
Franke, K. and Halter, H. (2000), 'Seelenheiler im Labyrinth', *Der Spiegel*, Vol. 36.
Markgraf, J. and Schneider, S. (1996), 'Paniksyndrom und Agoraphobia', in Markgraf, J. (ed.), *Lehrbuch der Verhaltenstherapie*, Berlin: Springer.
Popper, K.R. (1966), *Logik der Forschung*, Tübingen: Mohr.

Introduction

Robert Bor and Lucas van Gerwen

As air travel becomes more commonplace, an increasing number of people are exposed to stresses associated with it. Between 10 to 40 per cent of air travellers experience some kind of fear response to the air travel process, estimated at 10 to 40 per cent in the general population of industrialised countries (Agras, Sylvester and Oliveau, 1969; Dean and Whitaker, 1982; van Gerwen and Diekstra, 2000). Intensity of fears associated with flying may range from mild apprehension in some people to an incapacitating phobia in others. With increasing stress associated with flying and the 11 September 2001 terrorist attacks involving commercial aircraft still fresh in many passengers' minds, a fear of flying is not necessarily altogether irrational, even though statistically air travel remains the safest form of public transport. Fear of flying should not be lightly dismissed by health care professionals as the effects can wreak havoc on people's personal and professional lives. Furthermore, their fear of flying may also be indicative of anxiety-related problems in other areas of their lives.

Psychologists have been at the forefront of helping health care professionals and airline passengers to understand more about the onset, maintenance and resolution of a fear of flying. Assessment and treatment methods have been studied and documented, and there are now several well-established programmes available to those who are motivated to overcoming their problem. While there are a group of specialist psychologists world-wide who are extensively involved in research and practice pertaining to a fear of flying, the demand for this expertise extends far beyond these programmes. A wide range of health care providers (doctors, psychologists, nurses, counsellors, psychotherapists) working in a range of settings (e.g., travel health clinics, doctors' surgeries, psychology clinics), come into contact with this client group. A recent review showed that there are approximately 150 facilities with comprehensive programmes for treating fear of flying throughout the Western world (van Gerwen and Diekstra, 2000). Unfortunately, both specialists and non-specialist health care providers alike lack an authoritative textbook on topic of fear of flying as, to the best of our knowledge, none has yet been published.

This new text seeks to remedy this. The book is mainly intended for those who work in commercial, executive, military and private aviation. This includes aviation psychologists, aerospace medical/nursing personnel, flying instructors, clinical psychologists and psychiatrists, pilots, cabin crew staff, airport-based clergy and members of the rescue and police services. There is an increasing number of specialist facilities worldwide where passengers can seek help for their fear of flying and personnel involved in fear of flying programmes may find the ideas of specific relevance to them. A secondary audience includes researchers, therapists and psychologists with an interest in understanding and treating anxiety and phobias. Nurses and doctors working in travel health clinics will also find some of the contents relevant to their practice. Lastly, many people who experience psychological problems seek to learn more about their condition and how best to cope with it. Some airline passengers may therefore be interested in some of the perspectives described in this book.

The contents of this book include chapters on the extent and nature of the problem; understanding public perceptions of safety associated with flying; assessment of clients; psychological treatment approaches; use of specific interventions (e.g. virtual reality); and clinical case studies. The aim is to provide an up-to-date and authoritative handbook on the topic that covers theory, research and practice. The authors, drawn from different parts of the world, are all experienced researchers and clinicians, and are leaders in their respective fields. In a field that is as highly specialised as this, inevitably there is a certain amount of overlap between some chapters. For example, it is appropriate that when discussing assessment, there will also be reference to treatment and therapeutic approaches.

In Chapter 1, Lucas van Gerwen, Philip Spinhoven, Rene Diekstra and Richard Van Dyck consider what kind of people seek help for fear of flying. They describe the sociodemographic and clinical characteristics of patients who were self-referred to a treatment agency because of fear of flying. It is argued that the typology identified could have implications for the selection of treatment components. In Chapter 2, Neil McLean considers the influence of the media on perception of risk associated with flying. He argues that the media tend to present information on air safety issues in a way that highlights the negative aspects of flying. Coverage of aircraft crashes is presented vividly and in a way that may contribute to apprehension about flying. There is evidence to suggest that fearful flyers may be influenced by media coverage of aircraft incidents and accidents. This chapter sets out to describe how media stories influence perceptions of risk associated with flying.

Marco Verschragen, Claudia de Zeeuw and Lucas van Gerwen consider the effect of information about aviation on fearful flyers in Chapter 3. They report that levels of fear associated with a fear of flying can be mediated by a lack of information about flying and how to cope with anxiety. This chapter also examines the relationship between levels of anxiety and information in people who have a fear of flying. The results have implications for strategies for helping people cope with their fear of flying.

In Chapter 4, Lucas van Gerwen describes the importance and specific relevance of assessment techniques for a fear of flying, both for clinical practice and research. The content specifically highlights two different aspects of a fear of flying; anxiety related to flying experienced in different situations (flight anxiety modality questionnaire) and a measure of symptom modalities in which anxiety in flight situations is expressed (flight anxiety modality questionnaire). In the following section (Chapter 5), Christelle Delorme and Lucas van Gerwen address the prevalence of personality pathology among fearful flyers who seek treatment. The chapter also considers the relationship between personality pathology and treatment outcome for anxiety disorders. Vivian Kraaij and her colleagues have studied the relationship between cognitive factors and symptoms of anxiety and panic among people who have a fear of flying. In Chapter 6 they report the results of their research on the way in which people deal cognitively with their fear of flying. This has important implications for the treatment of fear of flying, a subject which is developed in the remaining chapters.

Multi-dimensional behavioural treatment methods are among the most effective for helping people with a fear of flying cope with the anticipated and actual negative experience some people associate with flying. In Chapter 7 Richard Roberts describes the specific stages and components used in a behavioural treatment approach. The issues raised in this chapter are developed further in the following chapter by Kasia Szymanska, who explains the application of rational emotive behaviour therapy for treating a fear of flying. Chapter 9, authored by Oivind Ekeberg and colleagues, presents a follow-up study of passengers who have undergone psychological treatment. The results reveal that on clinical parameters (standardised assessment methods) and behavioural indices (taking a flight), significant improvements were found for those who received treatment, while those in a control group did not demonstrate the desired changes.

Chapter 10, by Lucas van Gerwen describes a multimodal standardised treatment programme used by an agency specialising in the treatment of patients with fear of flying. It presents an evaluation of a programme of a facility in actual practice instead of a scientific institution. It demonstrates the procedures and outcomes of a well-established clinical programme, in particular with regard to the effectiveness of a two-day cognitive-behavioural group treatment and a one-day behavioural group treatment for flying phobics.

Mindful of context and limited resources, most health care professionals are aware of the need for brief forms of psychological treatment, a challenge taken up by Robert Bor in Chapter 11. The core skills and techniques for brief forms of intervention are described in this chapter. Case examples are included to illustrate the process. A list of self-help books dealing with the topic of fear of flying – and in a range of languages – is also included in this chapter.

Page Anderson and her colleagues explain that standard psychological therapy for coping with a fear of flying may not always include *in vivo* exposure to the noxious stimulus in Chapter 12. Cost, logistics and the intensity of fear are some reasons that might mitigate against such exposure. Virtual reality exposure offers an accessible and cost-effective alternative and has been unequivocally demonstrated to be an effective adjunct to therapy. This chapter describes the use of virtual reality exposure in treatment. In Chapter 13, Xavier Bornas and colleagues argue that computer-assisted therapy exposure offers an accessible and cost-effective alternative to both virtual reality exposure and *in vivo* exposure because of the low cost in instrumentation. This has been demonstrated to be an effective adjunct to therapy. This chapter describes the use of computer-assisted therapy in treatment.

While most people who want to overcome their fear of flying are likely to consult a psychologist, a proportion may instead prefer not to seek treatment. Instead, they might bury or ignore their anxiety and hope that they will be able to cope on their own. Air crew may then have to deal with a number of passengers who experience a panic attack while on board an aircraft. This chapter, written by Michael Tomaro, describes the theoretical issues relevant to understanding panic attacks and ways of managing these in flight. Finally, Elaine Iljon Foreman, explores the key elements perceived to account for therapeutic change in people who have suffered from a fear of flying in Chapter 15. This is considered relevant to understanding 'what works for whom' in treating people who suffer from a fear of flying. Cases are discussed and the results tested against a model accounting for the process of cognitive change.

We are grateful to all the authors who have brought their undoubted experience and expertise in actual clinical practice and research in the treatment of fear of flying to this book. All of the contributors submitted their chapters within the deadline and were enthusiastic about the project from the start. Now that the book is at hand, we hope that it will fulfil our aim to provide an authoritative text on psychological perspectives on fear of flying. It is fitting that this book should first appear in 2003, exactly 100 years after brothers Orville and Wilbur Wright pioneered the age of flight. This book may also prompt airlines and others in the aviation industry to take more seriously the plight and needs of those suffering from a fear of flying.

References

Agras S., Sylvester D. and Oliveau D. (1969), 'The Epidemiology of Common Fears and Phobias', *Comprehensive Psychiatry*, Vol. 2, pp. 151–6.

Dean, R.O. and Whitaker, N.M. (1982), 'Fear of Flying: Impact on the US air travel industry', *Journal of Travel Research*, June, pp. 7–17.

van Gerwen, L.J. and Diekstra, R.F.W. (2000), 'Fear of Flying Treatment Programs for Passengers: An international review', *Aviation, Space and Environmental Medicine*, Vol. 71, pp. 430–37.

Chapter 1

Sociodemographic and Clinical Characteristics of People who Self-refer for Treatment for their Fear of Flying

Lucas van Gerwen

This chapter reports on a study of sociodemographic and clinical characteristics of 419 patients who were self-referred to a treatment agency because of fear of flying. With the use of homogeneity analyses (PRINCALS) to explore the association between flight anxiety and different types of phobia, four specific subtypes of flying phobics were identified. The subtypes differed in terms of flight anxiety level, age, sex, complaints like fear of aircraft accidents, the need to have control over the situation or fear of losing control over themselves and phobias underlying their fear of flying, such as claustrophobia, acrophobia, social phobia and symptoms of panic attacks. It is argued that the typology identified could have implications for the selection of treatment components.

According to a number of studies, the prevalence of varying degrees of fear of flying is estimated at 10–40 per cent of the general population in industrialised countries (Agras et al., 1969; Arnarson, 1987; Arrindell, 1980; Dean and Whitaker, 1982; Ekeberg, 1991; Nordlund, 1983). Individuals affected by fear of flying can be divided into three groups: those who do not fly at all, those who restrict flying to an absolute minimum and experience considerable discomfort prior and/or during each flight, and those who show continuous mild or moderate apprehension about flying but do not avoid it, although it remains an unpleasant experience (Ekeberg et al., 1989). Fear of flying, whether experienced to a mild, moderate or high degree, usually affects functioning in one or more areas of life, e.g., professional life, social life and family life (van Gerwen, 1988). It may also affect marital or relationship satisfaction because of the fact that fear of flying hampers or restricts the partner's freedom of movement.

Despite its relatively high prevalence and the impact which flight anxiety has on the quality of life in general, well-structured programmes for the treatment of this phobia are scarce as are studies evaluating the effectiveness of such programmes, particularly when compared to the amount of research on the treatment of other phobias (Marks, 1987). A review of the literature based on psychological abstracts over a period of almost four decades (1960 to 1993) shows that there has not been any increase in studies on epidemiology, clinical characteristics and treatment of fear of flying. Most publications on the effects of fear of flying treatment programmes pertain to the use of behaviour therapy, mostly among military (Aitken, 1969), trained aircrew (Strongin, 1987) and only recently, among commercial airline passengers (Jansen et al., 1992).

Besides the paucity of studies on epidemiology and treatment of fear of flying, there is also a dearth of literature on the conceptualisation and classification/diagnosis of fear of flying. In DSM-III-R (APA, 1987), fear of flying was defined as a simple phobia. DSM-IV has revised fear of flying into the category of specific phobias (APA, 1994). Although there is little or no information in the literature on the demographic or clinical characteristics of patients with fear of flying, it is conceivable that fear of flying is composed of one or more other phobias, such as fear of confinement and claustrophobia. Alternatively, fear of flying can be the effect of generalisation of one or more natural environment phobias, as described in DSM-IV (APA, 1994), such as fear of heights, of falling, storms, water, instability, and others (Cleiren et al., 1994). This means that fear of flying might be an expression of several subtypes of phobias. Consequently, important conceptual and classification problems for fear of flying are not solved by DSM-IV.

This chapter addresses these issues using data from a large group of flying phobics who were self-referred to a special flying phobia treatment centre in the Netherlands. The purpose of this chapter is to explore the association of flight anxiety with different types of phobia and to present information on specific subtypes of flying phobics, in terms of both sociodemographic and clinical characteristics. It is hoped that these data will contribute to the classification and diagnosis of this disorder.

Method

Subjects

The data reported in this study were obtained from all subjects assessed at the VALK Foundation located in Leiden, the Netherlands, in the period from February 1990–January 1994. This agency is a joint enterprise of the University of Leiden, KLM Royal Dutch Airlines and Schiphol Airport Amsterdam. All participants sought treatment for fear of flying and came on their own to VALK. Self-referral was usually the result of asking an airline for information on treatment possibilities or through free publicity of the agency in newspapers, radio or television.

The group consisted of a total of 419 patients (183 men (43.7 per cent) and 236 women (56.3 per cent)). The participants' mean age was 40.9 years, SD = 10.4 (men M = 41.0, SD = 10.1; women M = 40.7, SD = 10.6) with a range of 17 to 73 years. The participants' educational level was relatively high. Thirty-nine per cent had higher education (higher professional or academic training), 20.3 per cent a medium level professional training and 41 per cent had elementary school education or lower professional training. Educational level did not significantly differ between the genders (chi-square = 7.6, df 3, NS), nor between the age groups (chi-square = 19.2, df 15, NS). Most participants were paid employees (51 per cent) while 27 per cent were self-employed, three participants (0.7 per cent) did volunteer work and 6 participants (1.4 per cent) attended school. Twenty-five per cent of all the women in the sample were not employed outside of the home. In contrast to educational level, the type of employment and profession differed for men and women. Almost half of the men worked in scientific or higher management jobs (vs 24 per cent of the women), 24 per cent in business (vs 15 per cent of the women) and 10 per cent were craftspeople or employed in industry (vs 2 per cent of the women). More women worked in service jobs (15 per cent vs 3 per cent of the men) and more often in clerical jobs (17 per cent vs 7 per cent of the men) or did not have a profession (25 per cent vs 4 per cent of the men).

Procedure

During the assessment phase that preceded the treatment programme, data were collected by standardised questionnaires and a one-and-half-hour interview. The Dutch version of Lazarus' 1989 multimodal life history inventory (Kwee and Roborgh, 1990) was used as a semi-structured interview to obtain information on the present situation and personal history of the participants and included questions about main phobic complaints, other than fear of flying, and present emotional state. Moreover, additional questions were included to assess the phenomenology and determinants of fear of flying and the flight history. Data collected by questionnaires included flight anxiety, fears and phobias, panic attacks and other somatic and psychological complaints. The assessment phase lasted an average of three hours. Interviewers were all certified psychologists.

Measures

1   Flight history and flight anxiety

Flight history During the semi-structured interview, information was collected on flying behaviour, such as the number of flights made by the participants during their lives, when they last flew, and whether they had received previous treatment for fear of flying.

Flight anxiety A visual analogue flight anxiety scale (VAFAS) was used. Each participant was asked to indicate the extent to which s/he was anxious about flying on a one-tailed VAFAS, ranging from 0 'No anxiety' to 10 'Terrified' or 'most extreme flight anxiety'.

The flight anxiety situations questionnaire (FAS) (van Gerwen et al., 1999)
Detailed psychometric properties of this questionnaire are reported elsewhere in this book but will be briefly summarised. The flight anxiety situations questionnaire is a 32 item self-report inventory with a five point Likert-type format ranging from 1='No anxiety' to 5='Extreme anxiety'. The factor structure of this questionnaire has been cross-validated and the internal consistency and external validity proved to be good. The questionnaire assessed characteristics related to anxiety experienced in different flight or flight-related situations, assessed via three subscales: 1) an anticipatory flight anxiety scale, which consists of 14 items that pertain to anxiety experienced when anticipating an aeroplane flight; 2) an in-flight anxiety scale consisting of 11 items pertaining to anxiety experienced during flight; and 3) a generalised-flight anxiety scale consisting of seven items referring to anxiety experienced in connection to aeroplanes in general, regardless of personal involvement in a flight situation. This form of anxiety possibly reflects the extent to which flight anxiety is generalised. The reliabilities of both the anticipatory flight anxiety and the in-flight anxiety scales were high, with a Cronbach's alpha of .96 and .93 respectively. The reliability of the generalised flight anxiety scale also proved to be good with a Cronbach's alpha of .84.

Avoidance of planes The first part of the fear questionnaire (Marks and Mathews, 1979) relates to the main target phobia which patients wants treated. In this study, participants rated their avoidance of planes on this single item scale of the fear questionnaire. (For further description of the scale see below.)

2   Other fear and phobic reactions

Interview Other fear and phobic reactions were assessed in the interview. Participants were asked to describe their main phobic complaints and fears underlying the fear of flying. We asked for specific reasons for the fear of flying. A maximum of two phobic reactions could be stated by each person. Participants themselves indicated what was the most important fear underlying the fear of flying. At the end of this study, the types of phobic reactions stated as reasons for fear of flying were classified into nine categories by the first author. The nine categories proved to be comprehensive and mutually exclusive. No inter-rater reliability data for this *post hoc* classification procedure are available.

Fear survey schedule – third revision (FSS-III) The Dutch version of the fear survey schedule, third revision (Wolpe and Lang, 1977) was used (Arrindell, 1980). The 76 items of the FSS-III aims to measure five types of phobia and the internal consistency of the subscales as assessed with Cronbach's alpha was satisfactory to good: 1) social phobia (13 items, .90); 2) agoraphobia (13 items, .79); 3) fear of disease, death and injury (12 items, .89); 4) fear of sex and aggression (eight items, .78); and 5) fear of living organisms (six items, .78).

The fear questionnaire In addition to the question related to the main phobia which participants want treated, this self-report questionnaire consists of two other parts (Marks and Mathews, 1979). The second part comprises 15 questions divided into three sub-scales, each five items, measuring the extent to which a person avoids certain situations: agoraphobia, fear of blood and injury, social phobia. The answer categories are from 1–9 on a Likert-type scale. The reliability of the agoraphobia scale was acceptable, with a Cronbach's alpha of .73. The reliability of the fear of blood and injury scale was relatively low, with a Cronbach's alpha of .61. Considering the small number of items, the reliability of the social phobia scale was acceptable, with a Cronbach's alpha of .60. The other part consist of five items related to anxiety/depression (five common non-phobic symptoms found in phobic patients, the presence of which indicates more general affect of disturbance). The reliability of the scale was good, with a Cronbach's alpha of .78.

3   Panic attack

The occurrence of panic attacks during a flight situation was assessed with a 13 item self-report checklist comprising the 13 symptom criteria for panic attacks as formulated in the DSM- III-R and DSM-IV (DSM-IV, APA, 1994). The severity of the symptoms was scored on a five point Likert-type scale. The presence of panic attacks was defined as the endorsement of four or more symptoms with a score larger than or equal to three (categories 'Quite strongly' and 'Very strongly'), (cf. panic attack questionnaire (PAQ) (Norton et al., 1992)). It is important to recognise that in this way only panic attacks during a flight situation were assessed which is different from cued or uncued panicking in general or the presence of a DSM panic disorder (DSM-IV, APA, 1994).

4   Somatic and psychological symptoms and complaints

The symptom check list-90 (SCL-90)   The symptom check list-90 (Derogatis, 1975) is a questionnaire which measures several kinds of psychopathology. The Dutch version of the SCL-90 is a 90 item self-report questionnaire which is answered on a five point scale (Arrindell and Ettema, 1986). Besides yielding a total score for psychoneuroticism, the inventory consists of eight subscales and the reliability as assessed with Cronbach's alpha was satisfactory to good: 1) agoraphobia (seven items, .80); 2) anxiety (10 items, .87); 3) depression (16 items, .90); 4) somatic complaints (12 items, .84), 5); insufficiency (nine items, .77); 6) sensitivity (18 items, .90); 7) hostility (six items, .77); 8) sleeping problems (three items, .71). The total scale reliability was excellent with a Cronbach's alpha of .97.

Results

1   Flight history and flight anxiety

Flight history   Table 1.1 shows the number of flights made before seeking therapy. The majority of participants had flown between 10 and 19 times, while only 10.7 per cent (45 patients) had never flown before. Of the participants who had flown before, 23 per cent had flown within 12 months of their application to the VALK Foundation. The majority, however, had not flown for more than two years, while 20 per cent had not flown for more than 10 years. The mean time between application for therapy and the last flight was 5.7 years (SD = 7.6). Ten per cent (42) of the participants had been treated previously for flight anxiety by another agency.

The majority of the participants knew people who fly often (350 patients, 83.5 per cent). A substantial number of them (250, 60 per cent) also knew other

Table 1.1 Flight history and results of the visual analogue flight anxiety scale (VAFAS) and questionnaire subscales for fear of flying patients

Questionnaire subscale	Valid no.	Mean	SD	Range
Flight history number of flights	419	33.08	57.19	0–254
VAFAS	419	8.17	1.54	4–10
Flight anxiety situations questionnaire				
Anticipatory anxiety	389	33.50	13.63	0–56
In-flight anxiety	389	29.74	10.19	0–44
Generalised flight anxiety	389	5.25	4.70	0–25
FSS-III				
Social phobia	413	23.46	7.99	13–50
Agoraphobia	413	25.13	7.08	13–54
Fear of illness and death	413	23.86	8.20	12–54
Fear of sex and aggression	413	12.48	3.89	8–28
Fear of living organisms	413	10.40	4.06	6–26
Fear questionnaire				
Agoraphobia	403	10.59	6.62	5–41
Fear of blood and injury	403	12.04	5.62	5–33
Social phobia	403	11.10	5.16	5–27
Anxiety and depression	403	14.80	6.56	5–40
Avoidance of aeroplanes	403	6.91	2.58	1–9
SCL-90				
Anxiety	402	18.48	6.69	10–46
Agoraphobia	402	10.78	4.44	7–35
Depression	402	25.17	8.70	16–67
Somatisation	402	18.46	6.08	12–47
Insufficiency	402	14.57	4.61	9–35
Sensitivity	402	26.71	8.61	18–74
Hostilty	402	8.01	2.64	6–26
Sleeping problems	402	5.06	2.37	3–15
Psychoneuroticism	402	139.65	37.65	90–308
Panic attack checklist	404	2.41	2.83	0–13

people who are afraid of flying. Almost one third of the sample (124, 30 per cent) knew someone who had been in an accident involving an aeroplane.

Level of anxiety   On the visual analogue flight anxiety scale (VAFAS), the majority of participants indicated suffering from severe to extreme anxiety at assessment. On this one-tailed VAFAS, 90 per cent of the women and 83 per cent of the men had a score between 7, 'severe anxiety' and 10, 'terrified/ panic'. Those with a relatively low score on this scale (4–6) mostly reported a specific flying situation of which they are afraid, e.g.,flying alone over water while it is dark or flying above the African continent.

The flight anxiety situations questionnaire (FAS)   This sample had a high score on anticipatory flight anxiety as well as on anxiety during a flight, and a relatively low score on generalised flight anxiety. The few participants who had a high generalised flight anxiety had witnessed a plane crash in which they were not involved. Thus, most patients who came for help did not generalise their fear to include everything connected with flying.

The fear questionnaire: avoidance of aeroplanes item   The high score on this item indicates that participants were also prone to avoiding aeroplanes to a high degree.

2   Fear and phobic reactions other than fear of flying

Fear survey schedule (FSS-III)   Not surprisingly for this sample, the item 'journeys by plane' had the highest score with a mean of 4.18 (range 1 to 5). Compared with a study from Wolpe and Lang (1977) with psychiatric patients, they found the highest score on the item 'losing control'. When we compared our sample with 703 members of a society for phobic patients (Arrindell, 1980), the flying phobics had a significantly ($p < .005$) lower score on all types of phobia scales (Cohen's *d* range between −.22 and −1.08). For the purpose of interpretation, Cohen (1977) considered $d = 0.20$ to be small, $d = 0.50$ to be medium and $d = 0.80$ to be large. But, compared with a group of 118 students (Arrindell, 1980), the flying phobics had a significantly ($p < .005$) higher score on all sub-scales except for the social anxiety scale (Cohen's *d* range between .16 and 1.34).

The fear questionnaire   In comparison with a phobic population (Marks and Mathews, 1979) the present sample scores were significantly lower with respect to agoraphobia (p < .005) with a Cohen's *d* value of −.94, fear of blood and injury (p < .05; Cohen's *d* = −.50) and social phobia (p < .005; Cohen's *d* = −.73).

Stated phobic reactions Table 1.2 shows that female patients stated as primary reason for their fear the chance of being involved in an aeroplane accident and for the males the greatest concern was not having control over the situation. In a plane the pilots are in control over the aircraft and those men also reported other situations where they wanted to stay in control, e.g.,they always wanted to drive their own car. As second reason, women reported confined places, claustrophobia (elevators, subways, tunnels), more often, while men feared losing control over themselves (starting to cry, going crazy, fainting, getting a heart attack, heart palpitations).

The following types of phobic reactions most often encountered were 'fear of an accident involving an aeroplane' (38 per cent), 'claustrophobia' (37 per cent) and the 'need for control over the situation' (36 per cent). When the primary and secondary reasons are collapsed for fear of flying, 'acrophobia' (heights) and fear of losing control over oneself were mentioned less often (28 per cent and 27 per cent, respectively), while fear of water was identified least often as a reason (5 per cent). There were some gender differences in the joint reasons (either listed as primary or secondary). 'acrophobia' (p = .014) and 'Need to be in control over the situation' (p = .009) were mentioned significantly more often by men than by women.

3 Panic attack

From 404 participants (15 less than the entire sample due to missing data), there were 151 (37.4 per cent) patients who experienced DSM-IV defined panic attacks during flight situation.

4 Somatic and psychological symptoms and complaints

The symptom check list-90 (SCL-90) When we compared the mean of the results with a phobic population, all scores were significantly lower (p < .005). The size effect is large as shown by the Cohen's *d* range between −.48 and −1.53. Compared with a normal population, our sample had a high score on anxiety, agoraphobia, depression, somatic complaints and on the total scale (p < .005) (Arrindell and Ettema, 1986). The Cohen's *d* shows that the scores are only slightly to moderately higher with a range between −.25 and .88.

Table 1.2   Stated phobic reasons for fear of flying

Stated phobic reason	Primary reason		Secondary reason		Joint reasons		
Sex	Males	Females	Males	Females	Males	Females	Total group
Valid no.	183	236	182	234	183	236	419
Fear of an accident	39	66	23	33	62	99	161
	21.3%	28.0%	12.6%	14.1%	33.9%	41.9%	38.4%
Claustrophobia	37	49	25	44	62	92	154
	20.2%	20.8%	13.7%	18.8%	33.9%	39.0%	36.8%
Acrophobia	37	32	26	22	63	54	117
	20.2%	13.6%	14.3%	9.4%	34.4%	22.9%	27.9%
Social anxiety	4	11	19	29	23	40	63
	2.2%	4.7%	10.4%	12.4%	12.6%	16.9%	15.0%
Loss of control	11	17	42	43	53	60	113
	6.0%	7.2%	23.1%	18.4%	29.0%	25.4%	27.0%
Need for control	43	37	34	35	77	72	149
	23.5%	15.7%	18.7%	15.0%	42.1%	30.5%	35.6%
Fear of water	3	2	5	11	8	13	21
	1.6%	0.8%	2.7%	4.7%	4.4%	5.5%	5.0%
Fear of darkness	0	1	5	12	5	13	18
	0%	0.4%	2.7%	5.1%	2.7%	5.5%	4.3%
Agoraphobia	9	21	3	5	12	26	38
	4.9%	8.9%	1.6%	2.1%	6.6%	11.0%	9.1%

The fear questionnaire: anxiety/depression subscale The mean of 14.80 (SD = 6.56) (see Table 1.1) is significantly lower (p < .005) than the mean reported for a phobic population (Marks and Mathews, 1979). The Cohen's *d* value shows a large effect: −1.08.

Typology of Flying Phobics

In order to assess associations of flight anxiety with different types of phobia and to develop a typology of flying phobics, a Principal Component Analysis by Alternating Least Squares (PRINCALS) was used.

As with normal Principal Components Analysis (PCA), PRINCALS is designed to represent the relationships between variables using a smaller number of components or dimensions. With the PRINCALS method, variables with different measurement levels (e.g., numerical, ordinal and nominal data) can be analysed at the same time (Gifi, 1991). Since in the present study many of the variables of interest were not measured on an interval level but on a nominal level (e.g., stated phobic reasons) PRINCALS instead of PCA was used. The values of these category quantifications can be plotted and examined in a visual way allowing an examination of the relationship between nominal, ordinal and numeric variables at the same time. (For more elaborate explanation and similarities or differences between a PCA and the PRINCALS technique, see Gifi (1991).) In this study, an interpretation of one of the results (a plot of category quantifications) is used to study a two-dimensional solution containing sociodemographic variables as well as the anxiety scales. First, an analysis on all scales was performed. To this end, the scales were analysed together and divided into three equal (33.3 per cent) percentile scores. The results of this analysis appear to be distorted to some extent by the fact that several scales measure the same (agoraphobia) or nearly the same constructs, so that these concepts are over-represented in the analysis. For this reason, we decided to carry on the analysis with only one representative scale for each concept: the FSS-III scale for agoraphobia was selected because it correlated most strongly with both the fear questionnaire and the SCL-90 scales for this construct. For the same reason also the FSS-III scale for social phobia was selected. Further scales selected for the analysis are; FSS-III fear of illness and death, fear of sex and aggression and fear of living organisms, SCL-90 anxiety, fear questionnaire avoidance of planes and the panic attack checklist. The flight anxiety scales were entered separately in the analysis instead of only a general sum score, in order to get more insight into the relationships between general phobia and anxiety scales, on the one hand, and flight anxiety, on the other.

other. Age and gender were added on a multiple nominal level. Age had been recoded into three age groups because it is not age in itself that is considered important but the life stage developmental aspect of age. The younger age group will probably be in a different social psychological situation to the middle aged and the older aged groups. Also, added to the analysis were the first (thus the foremost) of the two phobic fears stated as reasons for fear of flying. Seven of the nine categories were entered into the analysis because fear of darkness was only mentioned by one participant and agoraphobia was already represented by the FSS-III scale. Those categorical variables, (e.g., loss of control, social anxiety, fear of water) are marked by the triangular forms. Figure 1.1 gives the category plot of the PRINCALS analysis. The first dimension had an eigenvalue of .30, the second of .12. This may be considered sufficient for these types of exploratory analyses (Gifi, 1991). The categories of each scale are linked with lines to elucidate their position. The high loading scores are on the left side and the low scores on the right side of the x-axis.

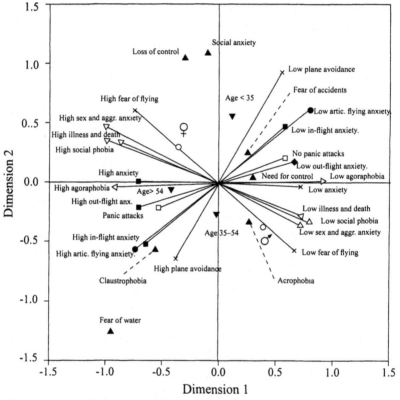

Figure 1.1   Typology of flying phobics

In Figure 1.1, we see the categories of the scales pertaining to different aspects of flight anxiety loading on a different dimension perpendicular to most phobia scales. The first dimension is best characterised by a combination of agoraphobia and general anxiety. The second is dominated by the flight anxiety scales and the phobic reactions stated as reasons for fear of flying (particularly contrasting 'loss of control over oneself' and 'fear of water'). The various reasons mentioned by the participants are less associated with the phobia dimension. Sociodemographic variables play a moderate role. Generally, there is a difference between men and women on the phobia dimension: women have higher scores for social phobia, fear of illness and death and fear of living organisms. Younger participants tend to evidence somewhat lower levels of flight anxiety.

The phobic fears that are most specifically associated with high levels of flight anxiety are in the first place claustrophobia and fear of water and secondly acrophobia. Social anxiety and fear of losing control over oneself are more closely related to high levels of other phobic fears. Claustrophobia is also moderately related to agoraphobia.

Considering the data, we can interpret each of the picture quadrants in terms of a typology. The upper right quadrant contains participants with relatively low to intermediate flight anxiety (in comparison to the rest of the sample), no avoiders, and few symptoms of panic attacks. These participants tend to be younger (under 35) and their problems are not closely related to a larger phobic complex. They have mentioned fear of an accident and the need to be in control over the situation as reasons for their fear of flying.

The fear of loss of control over oneself and social anxiety are mentioned by participants in the upper left quadrant. Here we more often find a cluster of monosymptomatic phobias (such as fear of living organisms, fear of sex and aggression and fear of illness and death). This is a group with a higher percentage of women, most of them also under 35 years old. These participants experience intermediate levels of flight anxiety.

The lower left quadrant contains participants who mainly experience high anxiety regarding aeroplanes, and have fear of water, claustrophobia or agoraphobia as a reason for their fear of flying. This is the group that exhibits panic attacks during a flight. Their anxiety in relation to anticipation of a flight and in-flight situations as well as their generalised flight situations is high. This is also the group that contains participants who are very prone to avoid flying. Most of the participants were above 54 years of age.

The lower right quadrant contains more men and those who report acrophobia as their main complaint. They show relatively lower scores on most phobic complexes and a medium to high score on flight anxiety. Their age is between 35 and 54 years.

Discussion

This chapter is one of the few research studies that provides data on demographic and clinical characteristics of people who apply for treatment to overcome their fear of flying. It is the only recent study that has examined a typology of such people.

The main outcome of our study is that flying phobics can be divided into four sub-classes. This distinction appears to have relevance for the identification of subtypes of flying phobias. The first subtype consists of those with relatively low to intermediate flight anxiety and no panic attack symptoms. They are relatively young (under 35 years) and their complaints are not closely related to any other phobic complaint. Often, they opt for therapy because of their fear of an aircraft accident and the need to be in control over the situation. They tend to interpret all sounds and movements of the plane in a way that provokes anxiety, as a sign that 'something is wrong'. The second subtype can be characterised by experiencing either fear of loss of control over themselves or social anxiety. In contrast to the first subgroup, this group comprises mostly women but is like the first subgroup also under 35 years. They experience moderate levels of flight anxiety. They are very aware of their somatic reactions and give these sensations a great deal of attention. The third subgroup mainly experience high anxiety regarding aeroplanes and have fear of water and/or claustrophobia as a main complaint underlying their fear. This is the group that reports panic attacks in anticipation of flights, during flights, and in relation to stimuli they associate with flying. It is important to emphasise that we only checked for the occurrence of panic attack associated with flying and were not assessing panic attacks in general or diagnosing a panic disorder. In this group are also the participants with agoraphobia. The fourth subgroup contains more men than the other subgroups and their main phobic complain is acrophobia. They show medium to high flight anxiety. They wanted help to overcome their fear of the height in a plane.

In accordance with earlier studies (Howard, Murphy and Clarke, 1983), fear of flying appears to be a heterogeneous problem and is not a unitary phenomenon. It can be conceptualised both as a situational phobia as well as the expression of other non-situational phobias. In the light of these findings, the DSM-IV classification of fear of flying within the category of specific phobias (APA, 1994) under the subtype of situational phobia seems to be debatable. Specifically, fear of flying might actually be the expression of phobias that are included within subtypes other than the 'situational subtype' such as fear of heights, which falls under the 'natural environment subtype'; or fear of injury, which falls under the 'blood-injection-injury subtype'; or fear of loss of control, which falls under the category of 'other subtype', or even a combination of these subtypes. Classifying fear of flying within the situational subtype, as subscribed in DSM-IV, is therefore rather arbitrary. It could be argued that any specific phobia has multiple determinants which could fall under different subtypes in the category of specific phobias. Moreover, especially in the subgroup of patients with high anxiety regarding aeroplanes and symptoms of panic and agoraphobia, fear of flying may be secondary to DSM panic disorder with or without agoraphobia. A limitation of the present study is that no standardised evaluation of psychiatric diagnoses has been performed. Consequently, in the absence of an index of primary diagnoses the issue of whether patients with fear of flying had primary specific phobia diagnoses or primary other anxiety diagnoses (especially panic disorder) remains unaddressed. Given the association of fear of flying with other anxiety measures for a substantial group of subjects, it seems warranted to conduct future studies into the comorbidity of anxiety disorders in subjects with fear of flying using standardised psychiatric assessment devices.

An important question is whether the identification of subtypes of patients with fear of flying has implications for treatment. There is much to say in favour of an answer in the affirmative to this question. If fear of flying, for example, mainly comprises the fear of an accident or crash while other phobic patterns such as panic attacks, agoraphobia, and generalised anxiety are not present, treatment can possibly be much more specific and focused upon flying behaviour or aeroplanes. In cases where flying phobia is an expression of other phobic patterns, such as agoraphobia, attention should probably be paid to these feared situations, apart from flight-related situations. Based on the PRINCALS analysis it is likely that a patient with severe fear of flying also has panic attacks during flights and suffers from claustrophobia or agoraphobia. The fact that many fear of flying treatment programmes (as offered by airlines internationally) are identical for all patients and usually given without proper diagnostic assessment, might therefore be problematic because they may be more tailored to some than to other sub-types of flying phobias as identified in this study. Further matching-treatment studies must show the benefits of the described subtypes for fear of flying.

It is an important focus for future research to establish whether indeed such differential effects exist. Flying phobics, though distinguished by their unique symptoms, are not all the same. How and in what way they differ can only be ascertained by careful exploration of their personal histories through interviews and questionnaires. A limitation of this study is the method in which we asked for and coded the specific reasons for the fear of flying. A maximum of two phobic reactions could be stated and we were able to classify the answers into nine categories. No data about inter-rater reliability are available. It may be helpful that we have developed those categories but future research is necessary to investigate whether phobic reactions can be classified into these categories in a reliable way.

This sample had a high score on anticipating flight anxiety as well as on anxiety during flight, and a relatively low score on associations about flying or planes. The few in this study who had a high generalised-flight score had witnessed a plane crash in which they were not involved. It is understandable that people who have a high generalised-flight (association) anxiety level avoid all flying stimuli, including a facility providing treatment for fear of flying. Future research can help to show whether the above findings of this study are representative for the total population of flying phobia patients (not only for patients who are self-referred) and have a bearing on clinical practice.

In our experience most of those who seek professional help for their fear of flying were aware of other problems, but did not consider themselves as 'patients'. This self-judgement has some empirical basis given the fact that in the present study in comparison with phobic patients, the flying phobics had substantiality lower scores on all types of phobia and anxiety scales. On the other hand, compared with a normal population, on most phobia and anxiety scales, the flying phobics obtained scores which were moderately higher. It seems that people who seek help for fear of flying are aware that fear of flying appears as a discrete symptom, but that it may be accompanied by additional phobic reactions. Typical of these are fear of death, travel, heights, confined spaces (elevators, subways, tunnels), crowds, 'going crazy', darkness, fire, thunderstorms, illness, heart attack, heart palpitations, blood, wounds, hospitals and bad weather.

References

Agras, S., Sylvester, D. and Oliveau, D. (1969), 'The Epidemiology of Common Fears and Phobias', *Comprehensive Psychiatry*, Vol. 2, pp. 151–6.

Aitken, R.C.B. (1969), 'Prevalence of Worry in Normal Aircrew', *British Journal of Medical Psychology*, Vol. 42, p. 283.

American Psychiatric Association (1987), 'Diagnostic and statistical manual of mental disorders' (3rd edn, rev.), Washington, DC: American Psychiatric Associations.

American Psychiatric Association (1994), 'Diagnostic and Statistical Manual of Mental Disorders' (4th edn, rev.), Washington, DC: American Psychiatric Association.

Arnarson, E.O. (1987), *The Prevalence of Flight Phobia among Icelanders*, abstract presented at the First Nordic Meeting, Aviation and Space Medicine, Oslo, Norway.

Arrindell, W.A. (1980), 'Dimensional Structure and Psychopathology Correlates of the Fear Survey Schedule (FSS-III) in a Phobic Population. A Factorial Definition of Agoraphobia', *Behaviour Research and Therapy*, Vol. 18, pp. 229–42.

Arrindell, W.A. and Ettema, J.H.M. (1987), *SCL-90; Handleiding bij een Multidimensionele psychopathologie indicator* [*Manual for a Multi-dimensional Psychopathology-indicator*], Lisse: Zwets en Zeitlinger B.V.

Cleiren, M., van Gerwen, L.J., Diekstra, R.F.W., van Dyck, R., Spinhoven, Ph. and Brinkhuysen, P. (1994), *No more Fear of Flying. An Evaluation of the Effects of the VALK Therapy Program*, Rijks Universiteit Leiden.

Cohen, J. (1977), *Statistical Power Analysis for the Behavioral Sciences*, New York: Academic Press.

Dean, R.O. and Whitaker, N.M. (1982), 'Fear of Flying: Impact on the U.S. air travel industry', *Journal of Travel Research*, June, pp. 7–17.

Derogatis, L.R., Lipman, R.S., and Covi, L. (1973), 'SCL-90: an outpatient psychiatric rating scale – preliminary report' *Psychopharmacology Bulletin*, Vol. 9, pp. 13–27.

Ekeberg, Ø. (1991), *Flight Phobia: Prevalence, sympathetic responses and treatment*, Department of Internal Medicine, Ulleval Hospital, University of Oslo, Norway.

Ekeberg, Ø., Seeberg, I. and Ellertsen, B.B. (1989), 'The Prevalence of Flight Anxiety in Norway', *Norsk Psykiatrisk Tidsskrist*, Vol. 43, pp. 443–8.

Gifi, A. (1991), *Nonlinear Multivariate Analysis*, Chichester: Wiley and Sons.

Howard, W.A., Murphy, S.M. and Clarke, J.C. (1983), 'The Nature and Treatment of Fear of Flying: A controlled Investigation', *Behavior Therapy*, Vol. 14, pp. 557–67.

Jansen, M., van Gerwen, L.J. and Diekstra, R.F.W. (1992), 'Vliegangst; kenmerken van vliegangstigen. Een kwantitatieve analyse' ['Fear of Flying; Characteristics of people who are afraid to fly. A quantitative analysis'], unpublished master's thesis, Rijks Universiteit Leiden, Leiden, The Netherlands.

Kwee, M.G.T. and Roborgh, M.R.H.M. (1990), *Multimodale Anamnese Psychotherapie. Handleiding* [*Multi-modal Life History Inventory Psychotherapy. Manual*], Lisse: Swets en Zeitlinger.

Lazarus, A.A. (1989), *The Practice of Multi-modal Therapy*, Baltimore, MD: Johns Hopkins University Press.

Marks, I.M. (1987), *Fears, Phobias, and Rituals, Panic, Anxiety, and Their Disorders*, New York/Oxford: Oxford University Press.

Marks, I.M. and Mathews, A.M. (1979), 'Case Histories and Shorter Communications. Brief Standard Self-rating for Phobic Patients', *Behaviour Research and Therapy*, Vol. 17, pp. 263–7.

Nordlund, C.L. (1983), 'A Questionnaire of Swedes' Fear of Flying', *Scandinavian Journal of Behaviour Therapy*, Vol. 12, pp. 150–68.

Norton, G.R., Cox, B.J. and Malan, J. (1992), 'Nonclinical Panickers: A critical review', *Clinical Psychology Review*, Vol. 12, pp. 121–39.

Strongin, T.S. (1987), 'A Historical Review of the Fear of Flying among Aircrewmen', *Aviation, Space and Environmental Medicine*, March, Vol. 58, No. 3, pp. 263–7.

van Gerwen, L.J. (1988), *Vliegangst, oorzaken, gevolgen en remedie [Fear of Flying, Reasons, Effects and Remedy]*, Baarn: Ambo.

van Gerwen, L.J., Spinhoven, Ph., Van Dyck, R. and Diekstra, R.F.W. (1999), 'Construction and Psychometric Characteristics of Two Self-report Questionnaires for the Assessment of Fear of Flying', *Psychological Assessment*, Vol. 11, pp. 146–58.

Wolpe, J. and Lang, P.J. (1977), *Manual for the Fear Survey Schedule*, San Diego: Edits.

Chapter 2

The Influence of the Media on Perception of Risk Associated with Flying

Neil J. McLean

Fear of flying is common. Epidemiological studies (Agras, Sylvester and Oliveau ,1969) indicate that approximately 20 per cent of the adult population have a fear of flying, making this one of the most common fears. That fear of flying is so common seems a paradox given the safety record of commercial aviation. In Australia there has not been a fatality on commercial jet aircraft and this safety record stretches over 25 years. To put this figure into perspective, in that same time period over 50,000 people have been killed on Australian roads (McLean, 1997). Yet despite these figures, fear of flying is widespread, whereas there is relatively little apprehension about the dangers associated with road travel.

Given the safety record of commercial aviation, why do so many people have a fear of flying and what are the aetiological factors that give rise to this fear? Early behavioural theories worked from the premise that an initial traumatic experience was at the core of phobic anxiety reactions. According to these theories a phobia develops when an association is set up between a particular stimulus event (e.g., a flight) and the experience of anxiety. In this way anxiety becomes a conditioned response that is activated whenever the individual confronts an event or situation similar (i.e., flight related) to that which triggered the original experience of anxiety.

However, the behavioural theory has significant flaws. It is apparent that not all individuals with a phobia have had a traumatic encounter with the situation, event or object that they come to fear. A small percentage (around 10 per cent) of those with a fear of flying have never flown before (McLean, 1996) so people in this group, by definition, developed their fear with no direct exposure to the experience of flight. Even amongst those who have flown, very few can recall a flight experience that they believe triggered their fear (McLean, 1996). This is hardly surprising given the safety record of flying and the uneventful nature of most flights.

The inability of simple associationist theories to explain the aetiology of fear has led to the development of more cognitively based theories. Bandura (1965) was one of the first to suggest that individuals do not need direct traumatic exposure to an event to develop a fear. He argued that fear can be learned by vicarious means, such as observation of the fear response of others, with this response acting as a model and influencing the observer to develop similar fear reactions. It is not uncommon for those in treatment for fear of flying to note that one or both of their parents had similar fears. While this may suggest a genetic vulnerability, it is also possible that parental reactions to flying act as a model and a source of vicarious learning.

More recently, cognitive theories (e.g., Beck, Emery and Greenberg, 1985) have focused on an individual's perception of risk or threat as a central factor in the development and experience of fear. According to this view, anxiety stems from an individual's perception that a situation or object represents a threat or danger. Hence a person will develop a fear of flying if they perceive one or more aspects of flying as posing some form of threat to their personal safety or well being.

There is evidence that indicates that individuals with a fear of flying do overestimate the level of threat associated with flying. Davis (1993) asked fearful flyers to rate the level of danger associated with a range of aspects of flight (e.g., take-off; turbulence) and found that these ratings were significantly higher than ratings made by a non-fearful control group. Given the objective safety of commercial aviation why do people come to view flying as a dangerous activity? As noted, parental modelling can be one factor shaping perceptions, but parental input is just one source of information and social influence. Teachers, peers and friends are others who have the potential to influence attitudes, beliefs and more specifically, perceptions of risk. But in a world with ever-increasing access to a range of media sources, it is not surprising that the influence of the media in shaping attitudes and perceptions has received considerable attention. The role of the media in the aetiology of fear of flying is the focus of this chapter.

There is anecdotal and qualitative evidence to suggest that media depictions of flying do influence individuals in their assessment of flying related risks. Participants in a fear of flying treatment programme (McLean, 1995) are asked as part of their initial assessment to describe the onset of their problem and to note the factors they believe to have contributed to this onset. Comments such as 'It happened gradually [with] lots of publicity of plane crashes' and 'Seeing plane crashes on the news' suggest that at least some fearful flyers believe that media reports were a factor in the aetiology of their fear. However anecdotal and retrospective reports such as these provide only limited support for the role of media messages in the aetiology of fear, and indeed it is not immediately apparent how the media could influence an individual to develop a fear of flying. If the media were to accurately represent the safety record of commercial aviation then it would be expected that this message would give rise to confidence rather than concern.

In recent years research on media effects has become increasingly sophisticated, moving from simple correlational studies looking at the relationships between media exposure (e.g., time spent watching television) and patterns of behaviour (e.g., violence), to more complex analyses of the characteristics of the media messages, the processing idiosyncrasies of the individuals receiving the messages, and the behavioural, cognitive and affective responses to media messages.

Studies focusing on the content of information conveyed via media news reports point to a strong editorial influence that significantly shapes the information made available to the media consumer. It is further suggested that this selective presentation of information can influence the way individuals perceive and process their social world.

Combs and Slovic (1979) examined the way newspapers reported stories relating to death. As they had predicted, newspaper reporting of the pattern of mortality in a community was characterised by significant attentional biases. Deaths resulting from violence (e.g., homicide), natural disasters (e.g., tornadoes; floods) and accidents (e.g., drownings; motor vehicle accidents) were much more frequently reported than deaths arising from illnesses, such as diabetes and cancer. In fact, death by illness is 15 times more likely than death by accident, yet newspaper articles on accidental deaths far outnumbered (by a factor of three) articles reporting deaths by illness.

It is apparent, and probably not surprising, that newspapers pay disproportionate attention to mortality events and do not provide a veridical reflection of the pattern of mortality in a community. Events that are commonplace are generally seen as less newsworthy than events that are unusual or spectacular in nature. What effect does this selective pattern of reporting have on the public perception of mortality? Combs and Slovic (1979) suggest that public perception of mortality risk largely mirrors the way deaths are reported in the newspapers. They asked their research participants to estimate mortality risk and found that spectacular or unusual causes of death were seen to be far more common than less dramatic but significantly more frequent causes of death. For example, death caused by diabetes is more than twice as common as death by homicide, but this was not the public perception, with participants rating the mortality risk of homicide as four times greater than diabetes-related mortality. Newspapers monitored in two locations across a period of 12 months reported 528 stories of death by homicide but just one article reporting a death arising from diabetes.

This study suggests that there is a link between media reporting of events and public perception of these events, although the causal direction of this effect has not been established. However, it is clear that the newspapers monitored in this study were selective in their focus and did not provide an accurate picture of the mortality profile of the community. Do similar biases occur in the reporting of aviation safety? While this has yet to be studied systematically, there is some evidence that this may be the case.

In April 1994, *The West Australian*, a daily paper in Perth, Western Australia, carried in some detail the story of an aircraft crash near Amsterdam in which three people were killed ('Three die in KLM crash', 1994). As far as could be seen, the airline involved and the people who lost their lives had no particular connection with Perth, or Australia in general. Of course Australian daily newspapers cover world events that may not have direct associations with Australia but it is extremely unlikely that a triple fatality in an automobile accident on a motorway in the Netherlands would have attracted the same interest in an Australian newspaper. In fact an article ('New South Wales deaths push road toll to 30', 1994) in the same newspaper just the day before, reporting the loss of thirty lives on Australian roads the previous holiday weekend, received considerably less print space than the article on the triple fatality air crash near Amsterdam. This seems to be suggestive of a pattern of reporting similar to that identified by Combs and Slovic (1979) in which statistically uncommon events such as homicide and aircraft crashes receive disproportionately more media attention than more commonplace events such as car accidents and illness related deaths.

It is apparent that the media is selective in what is reported and biased in the attention paid to certain types of events, but it is important to look not only at what is reported but how information is reported. Editorial decisions and journalistic styles can significantly influence the emphasis of a story and the way the information is presented and conveyed. The information contained in a newspaper report can be coloured by the use of dramatic eye-catching headlines and graphic photographs. A television report can use visual images in a way that emphasises certain aspects of a story.

Gibson and Zillman (1994) examined the use of exemplars in media reporting and how these exemplars or case studies influenced reader or viewer perceptions. Media reports of social issues frequently use case studies that purport to illustrate the key points of the story but may do so at the expense of providing a more balanced representation of the issues in question. Gibson and Zillman (1994) argued that the use of exemplars in this way might be misleading if the case study does not provide an accurate reflection of the issue and if the article does not place the exemplar in an appropriate perspective. They examined the impact of exemplars on media consumers by experimentally manipulating the way information on the risks of carjacking was presented. All participants received accurate information about the base rate likelihood of being injured in a car jacking but were then exposed to stories of carjackings which differed in the degree of violence involved. Participants exposed to more violent versions of the story subsequently overrated the significance of carjacking as a national problem, They were also much more likely to see carjacking as being associated with extreme levels of violence even though they had been informed of the actual risks of violence associated with this crime. Gibson and Zillman (1994) concluded that judgements are susceptible to the influence of vivid case studies, however unrepresentative these may be, and that this influence operates even when accurate but less dramatic base rate information is available.

These findings are not surprising given the wealth of evidence (e.g., Kahneman, Slovic and Tversky, 1982; Slovic, 2000) that points to the frailty of human judgements and the biases that operate to distort judgement. It is apparent that individuals all too rarely make careful, balanced and data driven assessments of risk and danger. Instead, they are inclined to use heuristics or mental 'rules of thumb' which can lead to judgements biased by the relative availability and accessibility of information. The availability heuristic refers to the tendency for individuals to make assessments of risk or probability that are influenced by the ease with which instances or exemplars can be brought to mind. For example, an individual with a friend in the last stages of incurable stomach cancer may be much more likely to see his own stomach pain as symptomatic of cancer than if he had not had recent vicarious exposure to the disease.

As Combs and Slovic (1979) demonstrated, editorial decisions determine media focus, which in turn can influence the relative availability of information to the media consumer. And as noted earlier, many people with a fear of flying have no direct experience of flying, or relatively limited experience, which means they must rely on information sources such as the media when they attempt to assess the risks associated with flying. Distortions of judgement may arise however, if the information made available by the media does not represent a balanced picture of aviation safety, or if it is presented in other ways that can influence risk assessments.

As Gibson and Zillman (1994) indicated, information that is presented vividly is more likely to have an impact on assessment of risk than more accurate but less vivid or emotionally dramatic material. According to Nisbett and Ross (1980) the cognitive processes underlying this effect are relatively straightforward: vividly presented information is more likely to be attended to, more likely to be stored, and more likely to be remembered than more pallid information. Information that is stored in this way remains available to the individual and hence forms part of the information 'data bank' which drives future decision making and risk assessment. Conversely, more accurate but less remarkable information is less likely to be stored and therefore less likely to be available and influential when future risk assessments are made.

The vividness of information is thought to be determined by several factors including its emotional appeal to the individual, the degree to which the information is concrete and capable of provoking imagery, and the sensory, temporal and spatial proximity of events from which the information is gleaned.

Clinical and anecdotal evidence suggests that media reporting of aviation safety can make a vivid impact and this vividness is determined by factors such as personal relevance, proximity and imaginability. For example, participants in fear of flying treatment groups held throughout Australia, seemed less affected by the crash of an Air France Concorde jet over Europe than the demise of a Singapore Airlines jet at Taiwan airport. Even though the video and photographic images of the Concorde crash were highly dramatic and vivid it seemed that few participants identified with the experience of supersonic travel and thus were relatively unaffected by the images of the Concorde on fire. Conversely many Australians fly with Singapore Airlines, and this physical and personal proximity appeared to increase the salience of information describing this event, even though the visual images associated with this crash were arguably less dramatic than those of the stricken Concorde. While this evidence is largely anecdotal there is also experimental evidence that points to the impact of media representations of aviation on risk perceptions.

Lowe (1996) recruited university undergraduates with high and low scores on a fear of flying scale and exposed them to one of three alternative packages of articles related to aviation taken from magazines and newspapers. Two of the packages focused on stories describing aircraft accidents and incidents (crashes; turbulence causing injury; fire on board an aircraft) while the other package contained articles related to aviation but focusing on aspects unrelated to dangers of flight (airline competition on particular routes; airline staffing policies; and cabin designs). The two packages depicting accidents and incidents were identical in content but varied in the vividness of presentation; the 'vivid' articles included headlines (e.g., 320 IN JUMBO CRASH TERROR) and photographs, whereas the 'non-vivid' versions carried the same articles but without the headlines and photographs.

After reading the articles participants were instructed to imagine that they were about to take a long international flight and then were asked to rate the likelihood of certain negative events (e.g., crashing; encountering severe turbulence; running out of fuel) occurring during this flight. As expected, the risk ratings of those participants reading the articles highlighting the dangers of flight were significantly higher than the risk ratings of those exposed to the neutral flight material. This effect was most evident in the 'vivid' condition where those participants with a fear of flying exposed to the vivid version of the accident/incident stories recorded the highest risk ratings.

Lowe's (1996) findings suggest that exposure to material highlighting the dangers associated with flying does influence the perception of flight related risk. It was also of note that this influence was most pronounced when the materials highlighting flight dangers were presented to individuals who already harboured some apprehension about flying. Individuals with no fear of flying were relatively unaffected by the material they had read. So are the messages about flight danger that are conveyed by the media instrumental in the development of fear of flying or do they simply act to exacerbate the anxiety in those who have already developed a fear of flying? In attempting to understand the impact of media messages it is important to recognise (Coleman, 1993; Dunwoody and Neuwirth, 1991) that individuals are not passive recipients of media messages but that they actively filter and process the messages conveyed by the various media outlets. As noted by Dunwoody and Neuwirth (1991, p. 15):

> individuals are active selectors and processors of information; they use different information channels for different purposes; they attend to information in those channels with different intensity; [and] they may interpret information available in different channels as differentially applicable to self or society.

It is likely that cognitive processes frequently associated with anxiety may make those with a fear of flying particularly vulnerable to the impact of media messages which highlight flight dangers.

Beck et al. (1985) noted that individuals tend to selectively attend to events and information that are in accord with their existing beliefs. He termed this process selective abstraction. According to Beck, an individual with a fear of flying will tend to pay particular attention to information that is in accord with his original premises about flying but will be likely to ignore information at odds with these premises. It is as if a person has antennae that allow them to receive only certain channels of information. In the case of those with a fear of flying, any information that points to flying as a dangerous activity receives full attention, whereas information that attests to the safety of air travel may, at best, receive cursory attention but more commonly is ignored. This may well explain why individuals with a fear of flying are generally very well aware of any aviation accident or incident that has occurred and are able to recount the media reports of these events in great detail!

This process of selective abstraction is magnified by the tendency of media outlets to pay disproportionate attention to the dangers rather than the safety of aviation. It might be argued that the media tend to provide information that the fearful flyer is expecting and looking for. In this way, media messages can serve to consolidate and exacerbate the anxiety of the fearful flyer.

The role of media messages in the aetiology of fear is less clear. While it appears that media messages can and do exert an influence on perception of risk, this effect appears to be more pronounced in assessment of societal risks than personal risk (Dunwoody and Neuwirth, 1991). This so called 'impersonal impact hypothesis' suggests that while media messages can heighten an overall sense of risk or danger in a situation, there is less tendency to see this heightened risk as personally applicable. This notion of personal invulnerability may help explain why individuals with no fear of flying appear to remain relatively impervious to media messages which highlight the danger associated with aviation. It appears that for these people, media stories that focus on the dangers of aviation carry little personal relevance, and hence have little impact on their perception of personal risk.

There is only limited research focusing directly on the capacity of the media to influence the types of risk perception that are thought to be at the core of phobic reactions such as fear of flying. Much of what has been discussed in this chapter has been extrapolated from general research on media effects and from what is known about the cognitive processes underlying anxiety.

There is evidence to suggest that individuals who have already developed a fear of flying attend to media stories on aviation accidents and incidents in a way that exacerbates their fear. Beyond this many questions remain unanswered. Do media messages play a role in the aetiology of fear of flying and if so under what circumstances? Are there personal characteristics such as empathy, suggestibility, capacity to visualise and trait anxiety that render some individuals particularly vulnerable to media messages? Does personal experience of flying moderate the impact of media messages on risk perception? We live in a world with unprecedented access to information but the impact of this information on the cognitive processes and products associated with fear has received little attention.

References

Agras, S., Sylvester, D and Oliveau, D. (1969), 'The Epidemiology of Common Fears and Phobias', *Comprehensive Psychiatry*, Vol. 10, No. 2, pp. 151–6.

Bandura, A. (1965), 'Vicarious Processes: A case of no-trial learning', in Berkowitz, L. (ed.), *Advances in experimental social psychology: vol. 2*, New York: Academic Press, pp. 1–55.

Beck, A.T., Emery, G. and Greenberg, R. (1985), *Anxiety Disorders and Phobias: A cognitive perspective*, New York: Basic Books.

Coleman, C.-L. (1993), 'The Influence of Mass Media and Interpersonal Communication on Societal and Personal Risk Judgements', *Communication Research*, Vol. 20, No. 4, pp. 611–19.

Combs, B., and Slovic, P. (1979), 'Causes of Death: Biased newspaper coverage and biased judgements', *Journalism Quarterly*, Vol. 56, No. 4, pp. 837–43, 849.

Davis, M. (1993), *Worry and the Availability Heuristic: The role of explanations in the pessimism of worriers and fearful flyers*, unpublished honours thesis, University of Western Australia, Perth, Australia.

Dunwoody, S. and Neuwirth, K. (1991), 'Coming to Terms with the Impact of Communication on Scientific and Technological Risk Judgements', in Wilkins, L. and Patterson, P. (eds), *Risky Business: Communicating issues of science, risk and public policy*, New York: Greenwood Press.

Gibson, R. and Zillman, D. (1994), 'Exaggerated versus Representative Exemplification in News Reports', *Communication Research*, Vol. 21, No. 5, pp. 603–25.

Kahneman, D., Slovic, P. and Tversky, A. (eds) (1982), *Judgement under Uncertainty: Heuristics and biases*, New York: Cambridge University Press.

Lowe, P.J. (1996), *The Availability Heuristic: Influence of vivid and non-vivid information on risk judgements by fearful and non-fearful fliers*, unpublished master's dissertation, University of Western Australia, Perth, Australia.

McLean, N.J. (1995), 'Cognitive Processes underlying Fear of Flying', paper presented at the annual meeting of the Australian Psychological Society, Perth, Australia.

McLean, N.J. (1996), 'Ansett Fear of Flying Program', paper presented at the First International Fear of Flying Conference, Valk Foundation, Tarrytown, NY.

McLean, N.J. (presenter) and Duncan, P. (producer) (1997), *Conquer your Fear of Flying* [videotape] (available from Stellan Holdings, 166 Broome St, Cottesloe, Australia, 6011).

Nisbett, R.E. and Ross, L. (1980), *Human Inference: Strategies and shortcomings of social judgement*, Englewood Cliffs, NJ: Prentice-Hall.

Slovic, P. (2000), *The Perception of Risk*, London: Earthscan Publications Ltd.

The West Australian (1994), 'New South Wales Deaths push Easter Road Toll to Thirty', 5 April, p. 7.

The West Australian (1994), 'Three Die in KLM City Shuttle Crash', 6 April, p. 9.

Chapter 3

The Effect of Information about Aviation on Fearful Flyers

Marco Verschragen, Claudia de Zeeuw and Lucas van Gerwen

Introduction

In many fear of flying treatment programmes, the provision of information about aviation and psycho-education are important components of treatment. Like the therapeutic flight, the provision of information is a major part of all fear of flying treatment programmes that participated in the Tarry Town conference in New York in 1996 (van Gerwen and Diekstra, 2000).

The object of this study was to gain insight in the effect of information about aviation on fearful flyers. The effect was measured by a change in the intensity of fear of flying. We also examined whether the effect of information on fearful flyers is different for people with a monitor coping style than for people with a blunting coping style, as defined in the theory of Miller and Mangan (1983).

Monitoring and Blunting

Miller and Mangan (1983) suggested that information must have certain features in order to be reassuring. Also, individual differences exist to the extent to which people gain from information. Miller (1979, in Miller and Mangan, 1983) argued that information reduces arousal when a person has control or a choice in the given situation. This is described by Miller as the instrumental value of information. Laboratory research has shown that participants prefer to have information if they can use this to control the aversive situation (Averill and Rosenn, 1972; Averill, O'Brien and DeWitt, 1977). If information has no instrumental value, according to Miller, it can even lead to an increase of the fear.

Miller and Mangan (1983) also argued that individual differences influence the effect of information. In stressful situations, people tend to choose from one of these two coping strategies: 1) monitoring; the search for information about the stressor, and 2) blunting; the avoidance of information about the stressor. According to Miller and Mangan, people have a disposition for a certain coping strategy which is stable over various situations. They examined the effect of one's coping strategy when information was given or withheld. Forty women undergoing a medical examination (colposcopy) were divided in one group with monitoring coping strategy (monitors, n = 20) and one with blunting coping strategy (blunters, n = 20), using the Miller Behavioral Style Scale (MBSS) (Miller, 1987) (see 'Measures' section for details on MBSS). In both groups, half of the women were provided with detailed information about the examination, the other half were given little information.

Before, after and during the examination muscular tension, heartbeat and mood were rated (the latter by self-rating). Among other results, it was found that monitors who received detailed information and blunters who received little information had lower heartbeats after the examination than monitors who received little information and blunters who received detailed information. Gatusso, Litt and Fitzgerald (1992) also found an interaction effect of information and coping strategy. Forty-eight men undergoing medical examination (endoscopy) were subjected to four conditions: 1) no preparation at all; 2) information about the procedure; 3) relaxation exercise; and 4) relaxation exercise plus positive feedback on the relaxation skills. During the examination, monitors in condition 1) and blunters in condition 2) were most tense. Both monitors and blunters in condition 3) gained from the relaxation and for the monitors in condition 4) the positive feedback had an extra relaxing effect.

Method

Participants

Forty-five adults (26 female and 19 male) participated, with an average age of 40.13 years (17 to 64, SD = 11.75). All participants came to the VALK Foundation on their own initiative to overcome their fear of flying. Participants were randomly assigned to the test and control groups. Of the 45 participants, only 10 were assigned to the control group. This number was deliberately kept small because this condition, not reading the book, meant deprivation of an important part of the treatment.

Measures

Three tests were used in this study. The flight anxiety situations questionnaire (FAS) and the visual analogue flight anxiety scale (VAFAS) were used to determine the intensity of the fear of flying (van Gerwen, Spinhoven, Van Dyck and Diekstra, 1999). The Miller Behavioural Style Scale, or Monitor Blunter Style Scale (MBSS) was used to predict the participants' coping strategy. The VAFAS consists of one self-rating scale for the intensity of fear of flying from 0 (no fear at all) to 10 (panic). The FAS is a questionnaire comprising 32 items. Answers are given on a five point Likert scale varying from no fear to intense fear. The FAS results in scores on three subscales: 1) the anticipation score indicates fear before the actual flight; 2) the in-flight score indicates the fear during several typical flying events such as take-off and turbulence; 3) the association score indicates the extent to which people experience fear when they are faced with flying, but are not actually flying, for example when they see or hear planes or have to go to the airport. The FAS association score is left out of consideration in this study. Reliability and validity of the FAS are good to excellent. Internal consistence of the three subscales is high, with Cronbach alpha's of .88, .95 and .97. Test-retest correlations were .90, .92 and .90 respectively.

The MBSS aims to predict what coping strategy people will choose in a threatening situation. Will they look for information about the stressor or will they look for a distraction? The MBSS consists of four different situations, each with eight statements. Four out of the eight statements correspond to a monitoring strategy and the other four correspond to a blunting strategy. Participants are required to choose those statements that are most applicable to them. The difference in number of monitoring and blunting statements chosen is the overall MBSS score. It depends on the mean MBSS score of all subjects, whether a subject is a monitor or a blunter. When someone's score is higher than the mean score, he or she will be judged to be a monitor, when the score is lower than the mean score, he or she will be judged to be a blunter (Miller, 1987).

The technical information given appears in *Help, I've Got to Fly* (van Gerwen and Diekstra, 1996). The book explains fear of flying and provides a cognitive-behavioural method to overcome this. Firstly, information about aviation is given. Flight safety, pilot training, cabin crew training, aerodynamics and aircraft maintenance, are all discussed. Secondly, psycho-education is given about fear and anxiety, and relaxation exercises are provided as are hints for distraction and a method for rational self analysis are explained.

Procedure

The design for this study was a quasi experimental, pretest/post-test control group design. The test group comprised 35 subjects and the control group consisted of 10 subjects. Subjects were assigned to the test or control group (only test group got to read the book), and also classified according to their coping strategy; monitoring or blunting. The design gives two independent variables with each two conditions. The dependent variables are the fear of flying intensity measured with FAS and VAFAS. The experimental design is shown in Table 3.1.

Table 3.1   Experimental design

	Monitors	**Blunters**
Test (information)	n =17	n =18
Control (no information)	n = 5	n = 5

In both test and control group, MBSS, FAS and VAFAS were presented to the participants at their first visit to the VALK Foundation, followed by an diagnostic interview. In the interview, the genesis and the nature of the fear of flying were discussed, as well as the number of previous flights, the avoidance behaviour, and relevant aspects of the course of life. After the diagnostic interview, the participants from the test group took the book *Help, I've Got to Fly* home. They were instructed to read the whole book. After an average of two to three weeks they returned for the final measurement of this study; again FAS and VAFAS were presented. After this, the participants continued their actual treatment, which was not the subject of this study.

Results

Of the participants in the test group, 29 out of 35 read the whole book (83 per cent). Of the monitors, 15 out of 17 (88 per cent) and of the blunters, 14 out of 18 (78 per cent) read the book. The drop out rate was 6.25 per cent (three subjects), for unknown reasons. Two of the drop-outs were blunters. The main component in their fear of flying was need for control (twice) and fear of loss of control (once). The intensity of fear of flying as measured with the VAFAS was no higher than the average of the other subjects. Blunters seemed to be a little more avoidant than monitors. On average, before treatment, blunters had not flown for 5.5 years (SD = 8.50) and monitors had not flown for 5 years (SD = 4.35). This difference is not statistically significant. Monitors and blunters had made almost the same amount of flights before treatment, respectively 13.95 flights (SD = 15.18) and 13.70 flights (SD = 13.57).

Effect of Information on the Intensity of Fear

After reading the book, subjects from the test group showed a slight decrease in the FAS anticipation score from 64 to 60. FAS scores are always shown in percentile score with a maximum value of 100. The control group showed an increase on the FAS anticipation score from 47 to 58. Repeated measures variance analysis (with test condition and coping strategy as between subjects-factors and moment of measurement (before or after reading the book) as within subjects-factor) shows a significant difference in FAS anticipation scores between test and control group ($F(1.41) = 6.09, p < .05$). Table 3.2 shows the average fear intensities and standard deviations at baseline and after reading the information of the participants from test and control group. Control group subjects had a lower FAS anticipation score at the first measurement, than the test group subjects ($F(43) = 1.03, p = .05$). This also accounts for FAS in-flight scale and VAFAS but here the differences are not significant.

Table 3.2   **Average fear intensities (in percentiles) and standard deviations on FAS anticipation scale at baseline and after reading the information, for both control and test group (maximum scale value = 100)**

	No.	Before Mean	S.D.	After Mean	S.D.
Test	35	64.00	23.59	60.23	19.00
Control	10	47.30	21.21	58.40	20.99

Monitors had higher average fear intensities on VAFAS and FAS in-flight scale than blunters at first assessment. At the start, monitors had an average score of 8.27 on the VAFAS and blunters had an average score of 7.26 (maximum scale value = 10). T-test analysis shows a significant difference in fear intensity at the start ($t(43) = 2.24, p < .05$). On the FAS in-flight scale, monitors scored an average of 77.64 at baseline and blunters 68.74 (percentile scores). Table 3.3 shows these averages and standard deviations.

Table 3.3   Fear intensities at first assessment on VAFAS and FAS in-flight scale (in percentiles) for monitors and blunters (maximum scale value VAFAS = 10, FAS in-flight score = 100)

	No.	VAFAS Mean	S.D.	FAS in-flight Mean	S.D.
Fear intensities at baseline					
Monitors	22	8.27	1.45	77.64	17.91
Blunters	23	7.26	1.57	68.74	18.76

The fear intensity on the VAFAS decreased after information in the monitors test group from 8.53 to 7.53. Monitors from the control group (no information) showed an increase in fear intensity on the VAFAS from 7.40 to 7.80. This is a statistically significant difference for this condition $(F(1.20) = 11.47, p < .05)$. For blunters there was little effect on this condition, whether or not they received the information. In the test group, blunters increased from 7.28 to 7.33 and in the control group the intensity remained the same at 7.20. A small interaction-effect was found between condition and coping strategy $(F(1.41) = 3.51, p = .068)$. This effect is shown in Figure 3.1. In Table 3.4 the corresponding averages and standard deviations are shown.

Table 3.4   Fear intensities on the VAFAS, for the two conditions and coping strategies (maximum scale value = 10)

	No.	Before Mean	S.D.	After Mean	S.D.
Test					
Monitors	17	8.53	1.07	7.53	1.55
Blunters	18	7.28	1.64	7.33	1.19
Control					
Monitors	5	7.40	2.30	7.80	1.92
Blunters	5	7.20	1.48	7.20	1.48

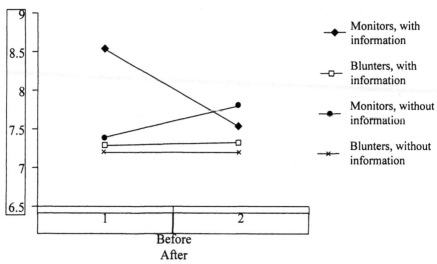

Figure 3.1   Interaction effect between coping style and condition, fear intensities at baseline and after the information, on the VAFAS (maximum scale value = 10)

Fear intensity on the FAS in-flight scale also decreased for the monitors in the test group. Their fear intensity decreased from 80 to 66 (percentile score). The fear intensity in the control group scarcely changed from 69.20 to 69.60. This is a statistically significant difference for this condition ($F(1.20) = 6.01$, $p < .05$). Both in test and control group, blunters showed a slight decrease in fear intensities on FAS in-flight scale, respectively from 71 to 68 and from 60 to 56. There is no statistically significant difference for the condition. Neither is the interaction-effect between condition and coping strategy. Table 3.5 shows the average fear intensities and standard deviations at baseline and after reading the information.

Effect of Type of Fear of Flying on the Fear Intensity

For this analysis, the participants were divided into groups according to the main component in their fear of flying, namely fear of an accident, need for control, claustrophobia, fear of heights, or fear to loose control. With repeated measures variance analysis (with test condition and nature of fear of flying as between subjects-factors and moment of measurement (before or after reading the book) as within subjects-factor), we examined whether the nature of fear of flying had an effect on the fear intensity as measured with the VAFAS and the FAS anticipatory and in-flight scale.

Table 3.5   Fear intensities on the FAS in-flight scale (in percentiles), for the two conditions and coping strategies (maximum scale value = 100)

	No.	Before		After	
		Mean	*S.D.*	*Mean*	*S.D.*
Test					
Monitors	17	80.12	17.61	66.12	20.44
Blunters	18	71.06	19.90	68.50	12.42
Control					
Monitors	5	69.20	18.16	69.60	15.06
Blunters	5	60.40	11.87	56.00	7.62

For almost all types of fear of flying in the test group, the fear intensity on the FAS anticipatory scale decreased after reading the information. Only for those participants who had a fear of losing control as a main component of their fear of flying, the fear intensity increased from 60 to 68 (percentile scores). A further test within the test group (no participants in the control group had a fear of losing control as a main component) compared fear of losing control with the other components of fear of flying. The results revealed a significant difference in fear intensities ($F(1.42) = 7.56$, $p < .05$). In the control group the fear intensity increased for all types of fear of flying.

On FAS in-flight scale the fear intensity also increased for participants with fear of losing control in the test group (from 73 to 80, percentile scores). The other participants showed a reduction in fear. A further test within the test group compared a fear of losing control with the other components of fear of flying and revealed a significant difference in fear intensities ($F(1.42) = 4.89$, $p < .05$). In the control group, the fear intensity increased for participants with a need for control and claustrophobia. Participants with fear of an accident in the control group showed little change in fear intensity.

On the VAFAS, the fear intensity increased for all types of fear of flying in the test group as well as for participants with fear of losing control as main component. In the control group, the fear intensity increased for participants with a need for control and remained constant for all other types of fear.

Correlation between VAFAS and FAS

Table 3.6 shows the correlation between the VAFAS and the FAS scales. All correlations are statistically significant. Correlations are calculated with Pearson-correlation coefficients.

Table 3.6   Pearson-correlation coefficients for the fear of flying tests

	VAFAS	FAS anticipatory	FAS in-flight
VAFAS	1.00	0.38*	0.37*
FAS anticipatory	–	1.00	0.39**
FAS in-flight	–	–	1.00

*   Correlation is significant for $p < 0.05$ (two-sided).
**   Correlation is significant for $p < 0.01$ (two-sided).

Discussion

The most important results we found were:

1) the information given to the participants in the test group resulted in a slight decrease in anticipatory fear. Fearful flyers in the control group who did not receive this information showed an increase in anticipatory fear;
2) with information, monitors showed a greater decrease in fear (on the VAFAS and FAS in-flight scale) than did blunters. Monitors who did not receive the information showed an increase in fear on the VAFAS. A marginal interaction effect was found between coping strategy (monitoring and blunting) and condition (information or none);
3) with information, participants with fear of losing control as main component of their fear of flying, showed an increased in fear on FAS anticipatory and in-flight scales.

No differences were found between monitors and blunters with regard to the number of flights previously made and avoidance behaviour. It should be noted that all participants voluntarily came to the VALK Foundation for a fear of flying treatment. The number of flights and the avoidance behaviour could be different for fearful flyers who do not seek professional treatment. They may have been more avoidant, or may have had lower scores on MBSS which could mean that more monitors than blunters apply for a treatment for their fear of flying.

Effect of Information on the Fear Intensity

Participants from the test group showed a slight decrease in score on the FAS anticipatory fear after reading the book from 64.0 to 60.2. This confirms the hypothesis that giving information has a fear reducing effect, provided that the information has an instrumental value (Miller and Mangan, 1983). In the control group, both monitors and blunters showed an increase in anticipatory fear. It would be interesting to know why blunters showed an increased anticipatory fear when they received no information. However, the analysis of the data shows that the increase in anticipatory fear is small for the blunters and that the major increase in fear intensity was caused by the monitors who had a lower anticipatory fear at baseline. The increase in anticipatory fear for monitors and blunters in the control group ranged respectively from 34.4 to 49.8 and from 60.2 to 67.0. The increase in anticipatory fear for monitors and blunters shows a significant difference for test and control groups.

At baseline, monitors had higher fear intensities on VAFAS and FAS in-flight scales than blunters. One reason for this difference might be that VAFAS and FAS are self-rating questionnaires and therefore more subjective. Monitors and blunters may differ in the way they experience fear. Recording of heartbeat during a flight could be an objective measure to determine whether monitors and blunters differ in their physiological response. There was no difference in anticipatory fear at baseline between monitors and blunters.

We have found an interaction-effect between coping strategy and condition (test or control group). Monitors gained more from the information provided about fear of flying than blunters (on VAFAS and FAS in-flight scale). Monitors also showed an increase in fear intensity (on VAFAS) when the information was withheld. This is consistent with Miller and Mangan's (1983) theory. The information had little effect on blunters in the test group. Apparently, the information had sufficient instrumental value (Miller and Mangan, 1983) not to cause an increase of the fear. A wide range of issues was dealt with in the book used in this study. As well as aviation information, some relaxation exercises (breathing and progressive relaxation) and advice for distraction from distressing thoughts were given. The latter topics especially also have instrumental value for blunters. The fear intensity of blunters in the control group showed little or no change. In the study by Miller and Mangan (1983), the tension decreased for the blunters when they were shown a film that had no relation to and was a distraction from the stressor. Such a film might have also had a fear reducing effect on the blunters in our study.

Effect of Type of Fear of Flying on the Fear Intensity

The intensity of fear of the participants who had a fear of losing control as a major component in their fear of flying increased after they had read the information. All other participants showed a decrease after reading the book. Perhaps these fearful flyers who are afraid of losing control over their own body are more prone to panic attacks. The study conducted by van Gerwen et al. (1997) demonstrated that the intensity of fear of flying is generally higher when fearful flyers also suffer from panic attacks. It could be that this group gains less from information and are candidates for more intensive therapeutic help. This finding may explain why the type of fear of flying influences the effect of information.

Implications of the Study

The study has some shortcomings. Firstly, we had a small number of participants in the study. This made it difficult to design a study that could show an interaction effect between condition, coping strategy and type of fear. To achieve this, the study should be done over a larger period of time. Secondly, the control group was small (10 in total). This was partly due to the small total number of participants, and partly because this condition implicated less preparation to the rest of the treatment. Thirdly, the internal consistency of the MBSS was moderate for this type of research. We are unclear as to whether the MBSS is the best instrument to use for fearful flyers. In future research, other coping questionnaires should be taken into consideration. Furthermore, test and control group differed at baseline in intensity of fear on all three scales; the test group scored higher at baseline than the control group. We can not explain this difference or tell if this fact influenced the results of the study. Finally, the effect of information was measured two to three weeks after baseline. There was no way to measure long-term effects because such an effect could interfere with other parts of the treatment.

Despite these shortcomings, the study has resulted in some important findings. Information was a useful part of the treatment both for monitors and blunters. For all monitors the information had a fear reducing effect. Withholding information even led to an increased fear. Blunters also gained from the information, as we may conclude from the decreased anticipatory fear. Only in fearful flyers who have a fear of losing control as a main component of their fear did the information lead to an increased fear. At first glance, it seems that this sub-group of fearful flyers should not receive information, but that is not necessarily the case. Information has three other functions apart from fear reduction, namely: 1) information forms the basic knowledge that is later used in the treatment to challenge irrational ideas; 2) information forms the first step in exposure; often after years of avoidance the information is the first confrontation with the distressing stimulus 'flying'; and 3) the information can lead to an increased motivation for treatment. The results of this study are preliminary, but promising. Further research is needed to confirm these results.

References

Averill, J.R. and Rossenn, M. (1972), 'Vigilant and Nonvigilant Coping Strategies and Psychophysiological Stress Reactions during the Anticipation of an Electric Shock', *Journal of Personality and Social Psychology*, Vol. 23, pp. 128–41.

Averill, J.R., O'Brien, L. and DeWitt, C.W. (1977), 'The Influence of Response Effectiveness on the Preference for Warning and on Psychophysiological Stress Reactions', *Journal of Personality*, Vol. 45, pp. 395–418.

Gatusso, S.M., Litt, M.D. and Fitzgerald, T.E. (1992), 'Coping with Gastrointestinal Endoscopy: Self-efficacy enhancement and coping style', *Journal of Consulting and Clinical Psychology*, Vol. 60, No. 1, pp. 133–9.

Miller, S.M. and Mangan, C.E. (1983), 'Interacting Effects of Information and Coping Style in Adapting to Gynecologic Stress: Should the doctor tell all?', *Journal of Personality and Social Psychology*, Vol. 45, No. 1, pp. 223–36.

Miller, S.M. (1987), 'Monitoring and Blunting: Validation of a questionnaire to assess styles of information seeking under threat', *Journal of Personality and Social Psychology*, Vol. 52, No. 2, pp. 345–53.

van Gerwen, L.J. and Diekstra, R.F.W. (1996), *Help ik moet vliegen!* [*Help, I've Got to Fly!*], Utrecht: Bruna.

van Gerwen, L.J., Spinhoven, P., Van Dyck, R. and Diekstra, R.F.W. (1997), 'People who Seek Help for Fear of Flying: Typology of flying phobics', *Behavior Therapy*, Vol. 28, pp. 237–51.

van Gerwen, L.J., Spinhoven, P., Dyck, R. van and Diekstra, R.F.W. (1999), 'Construction and Psychometric Characteristics of Two Self-report Questionnaires for the Assessment of Fear of Flying', *Psychological Assessment*, Vol. 11, No. 2, pp. 146–58.

van Gerwen, L.J. and Diekstra, R.F.W. (2000), 'Fear of Flying Treatment Programs for Passengers: An international review', *Aviation, Space and Environmental Medicine*, Vol. 71, No. 4, pp. 430–37.

Verschragen, M.J. (2000), 'A Study on the Effect of Information Provided to People with Fear of Flying', unpublished master's thesis, Leiden University.

Chapter 4

Construction and Psychometric Characteristics of Two Self-report Questionnaires for the Assessment of Fear of Flying

Lucas van Gerwen, Philip Spinhoven, Richard van Dyck and
Rene F.W. Diekstra

Despite the prevalence of fear of flying, clinical frequency and accompanying social and professional impairment, well-designed and controlled treatment outcome studies are scarce. Research reports are limited by the absence of appropriate and validated assessment tools, which makes evaluation of treatment outcomes and identification of effective elements of treatment programmes difficult. The first international conference on fear-of-flying treatment modalities in February 1996 in Tarrytown, NY, attended by participants from over 12 countries, clarified that different kinds of unvalidated fear-of-flying self-report measures are used all over the world (van Gerwen and Diekstra, 2000).

In addition, most fear-of-flying treatment programmes use a behavioural avoidance test (BAT): patients may or may not take a test flight. A behavioural avoidance test does not necessarily reflect the 'real' (are patients less afraid before and during a flight) efficacy of treatments unless accompanied by thought-sampling techniques or physiological measures, such as heart rate or galvanic skin responses (e.g., heart rate was continuously recorded during the behavioural test in a study by Haug et al., 1987). Fear of flying does not always imply behavioural avoidance of the phobic stimulus and therefore its different response modes should be taken into account (van Gerwen et al., 1997). Patients do not (cannot) always avoid the feared stimulus and eventually face their flying with high distress (Howard, Murphy and Clarke, 1983).

The population affected by fear of flying can be divided into several subgroups, consisting of: a) those who do not fly at all; b) those who restrict flying to an absolute minimum and experience considerable discomfort on each flight and; c) those who have continuous mild or moderate apprehension about flying but who do not avoid it. This latter group (those who do not avoid flying, although it remains unpleasant) constitutes 20 per cent of the total flying population (Ekeberg, Seeberg and Ellertsen, 1989). In this context, BATs would be useful for the group whose fear of flying has caused a stop to flying, but it would tell very little about the effects of treatment for those who have continued to fly in spite of high distress.

A literature survey, using psychological abstracts from 1978 to 1997, revealed that there have been very few focused attempts to develop reliable and validated instruments for measuring fear of flying. Besides measurement methods using videotapes (Capafons et al., 1997) or pictures presented with a backward masking technique (Amner, 1997; Andersson, 1989), very few studies have reported the psychometric properties of self-report scales (Bornas and Tortella-Feliu, 1995; Gursky and Reiss, 1987; Haug et al., 1987; Howard et al., 1983; Johnsen and Hugdahl, 1990). For further psychometric characteristics, Howard et al. (1983) referred to an unpublished manuscript by Howard, Mattick and Clarke (1982). With the exception of a study by Sosa et al. (1995), there is very limited data on factor structure, reliability and validity. Moreover, some studies mention the use of fear-of-flying self-report scales adapted from previous studies but do not give psychometric characteristics (Beckham et al., 1990; Light, 1983; Muret de Morges, 1982). This also applies to the various self-report measures included in a number of popular scientific self-help books (e.g., Braunburg and Pieritz, 1979; Forgione and Bauer, 1980; Yaffé, 1987). In conclusion, the few existing measures have serious shortcomings, of which the most significant are unknown or poor psychometric properties, lack of specificity and coverage of only certain aspects or modalities of fear of flying. Consequently, most of the few publications that do report the effects of treatment programmes do not use validated fear-of-flying questionnaires.

The development of measures that assess patients' feelings, attitudes and cognition's about specific flying-related events may be particularly important in light of advances in cognitive-behavioural therapies. Measures should be useful for cognitive-behavioural treatment plans and for assessing specific treatment effects. Support for the validity of such measures should be correlation between the questionnaires and subscales, although not too high; correlation between questionnaires or subscales and a visual analogue flight anxiety scale, fear-of-flying items in other questionnaires and some correlation with a BAT. There should also be divergent validity with scales that measure other anxieties, such as fear-of-living organisms.

A Guiding Conceptualisation of Flight Anxiety

Fear of flying appears to be heterogeneous and not a unitary phenomenon (Howard et al., 1983; van Gerwen et al., 1997). It can be conceptualised both as a situational phobia as well as the expression of other nonsituational phobias. It could be the expression of other phobias such as fear of heights, fear of injury, fear of confinement, claustrophobia, fear of loss of control, or even a combination of these. It is conceivable that fear of flying consists of one or more other phobias. Alternatively, fear of flying can also be the effect of generalization of one or more natural environment phobias as described in DSM-IV (APA, 1994), such as fear of heights, falling, storms, water, instability and so forth (Cleiren et al., 1994). Accordingly, the events on a flight that produce fear can be part of the above phobias (e.g., a plane flies high, you cannot open the doors while flying, turbulence gives a feeling of instability, etc.). There are different cues at different times that trigger fear of flying. Anticipation of danger motivates people to avoid stimuli associated with possible harm from the external, physical, or social environment (e.g., fear that a plane will crash). Anticipation of anxiety motivates people to avoid stimuli associated with their experience of anxiety. It is related to concern about the personal consequences of an involuntary anxious reaction to the stimulus (Gursky and Reiss, 1987). Theorists generally agree that responses to fear of flying comprise three components: behaviour, physiology and cognitions. Although fear-of-flying treatment facilities mainly report behaviour (BAT), it is also important to measure the other two aspects of cognitive and somatic responses. For this, we developed two questionnaires that cover different and complementary aspects of fear of flying. One concerns anxiety-provoking stimuli, to measure the level of anxiety produced by specific situations related to flying, distinguishing between the preliminary phase (e.g., planning a trip, boarding the plane) and the actual flight (e.g., different situations in flight). This scale should cover a wide variety of situations related to the flight, which will allow detailed assessment of the most relevant phobic stimuli for each patient. The other questionnaire focuses on anxiety responses, on the assessment of thoughts related to the danger of flying and to the physiological sensations of anxiety while flying.

The primary aim of this chapter was to show the development and validation of two self-report tools for assessing different aspects of fear of flying, tools that are also sensitive to change for assessing differential treatment effects. Several studies were conducted over a 10-year period. In this chapter, seven studies are presented. Study 1 presents the development and content validity of the flight anxiety situations questionnaire (FAS) and the flight anxiety modality questionnaire (FAM). In Study 2, the items are refined and further selected. Study 3 gives the factor structure of the items initially selected from both questionnaires. Study 4 provides the factor structure and internal consistency of the final versions. Also, quantitative evidence of the relevance and representativeness for the construct it is designed to measure is provided. Study 5 shows the reliability and test-retest reliability of the FAS and FAM scales. Study 6 contains the convergent and divergent validity of the FAS and FAM. Study 7 presents the sensitivity to change of the FAS and FAM scales.

Study 1

Overview

The purpose of Study 1 was to formulate the domain of the questionnaires, to identify dimensions and to generate items for the FAS and FAM. Items were derived from multiple sources. The content of the FAS and the FAM was described consistently with recommendations on content validation guidelines by Haynes, Richard and Kubany (1995).

Method

The initial selection of items for the FAS started in 1986 with a description of chronological events on a flight and by interviewing patients with flight phobia as research for a book on fear of flying (van Gerwen, 1988). The study of the FAM on cognitions and physiological sensations started a bit later in 1988. For both, the literature was reviewed and analysed. Previously published scales were reviewed and examined. Relevant areas and items were obtained from interviews with pilots ($N = 3$, all men), cabin crew ($N = 4$, all women) and therapists ($N = 5$, three women and two men) who do clinical work with patients with fear of flying.

Those 12 experts were asked the following questions:

a) based on your experience, what situations are relevant and typical in acting as anxiety-provoking stimuli in fear of flying patients during a flight and in anticipation of a flight;

b) based on your experience, what thoughts go through these patients' minds when anticipating a flight or in a flight situation; and

c) what specific symptoms of anxiety have you observed in these patients when anticipating a flight or during a real flight?

Twenty-six patients (10 men and 16 women) with fear of flying received a structured interview (designed by Lucas J. van Gerwen and Ben Arts). The interview format was as follows: patients were asked several open questions, such as the following:

a) 'What situations can you mention that are relevant and representative during a flight and in anticipation of a flight that provoke anxiety?';
b) 'What thoughts go through your mind when you are anticipating a flight or when you are in a flight situation?'; and
c) 'What somatic symptoms of anxiety do you experience in anticipation of a flight or during a real flight?' (Questions were also asked during an actual flight.)

Forty-nine situations, 31 thoughts and 26 symptoms were compiled from both groups of experts and patients. With five national experts, answers of both experts and patients were checked to see whether the items remained within the domain of the questionnaires. Initial items were developed and reformulated several times. Items were tested in clinical work with patients with a fear of flying by asking the patients ($N = 12$, four men and eight women) to comment on them in a clinical interview. In open-ended questions, we asked whether items fit within the domains of the questionnaires and whether there were omissions or redundant items.

Results

The domain of an FAS questionnaire should include situations relevant to a journey by plane and generally connected with planes that can provoke anxiety. It should exclude situations that are extraordinary on a normal flight. The intended function of the instrument is to make a diagnostic self-report that is fast and easy to administer and can be used for designing intervention programmes and evaluating treatment effects. The instrument should be a diagnostic tool for referring patients to the most appropriate treatment programme.

The methods just outlined resulted in the identification of the following two situational dimensions and refinement of the items in a 40-item version: a) *anticipation anxiety* – anxiety occurring when a person anticipates going on a flight (20 items); and b) *in-flight anxiety* – anxiety experienced during a flight (20 items).

The domain of a FAM questionnaire is to assess different distressing thoughts and symptoms of anxiety or anticipatory anxiety in flight situations. The intended function is to make a diagnostic self-report instrument that is fast and easy to score for designing intervention programmes and evaluating treatment effects. The instrument should be a diagnostic tool for referring patients to the most appropriate treatment programme. It should indicate whether patients are more aware of their cognitions or whether they pay more attention to their somatic complaints.

Refinement of the items resulted in a 44-item preliminary version of the FAM. Twenty-four items covered the somatic modality dimension and 20 items covered the cognitive modality dimension.

Study 2

Overview

The purpose of Study 2 was to refine items for the FAS and FAM.

Method

Participants Participants were involved in various seminars that do not deal with fear of flying, except for one. We recruited people through an advertisement in a local newspaper for a lecture on fear of flying. This resulted in a large group of Dutch people ($N = 433$), 191 of whom were not afraid to fly and 242 who experienced fear of flying. The sample was collected in 1990.

Procedure Before the seminars started, participants were asked to fill out two visual analogue scales and a preliminary version of the FAS and FAM. Instructions for the FAS questionnaire were as follows: 'Circle Yes or No for every situation', where 'No' means *no anxiety* and 'Yes' *slight to overwhelming anxiety*. This was followed by a list of statements pertaining to specific situations related to flying and aeroplanes. Instructions for the FAM questionnaire were as follows: 'Circle Yes or No for each symptom', where 'No' means *not at all* and 'Yes' *moderately to very intensely*. The first visual analogue scale was the visual analogue flight anxiety scale (VAFAS). Participants were requested to answer the following question using a one-tailed

VAFAS, ranging from 0 (no anxiety) to 10 (terrified): 'Please indicate how anxious you are about flying at present'. On the second visual analogue scale, ranging from 0 (no enjoyment at all) to 10 (very much enjoyment), participants were asked to: 'Please indicate how much you enjoy flying at present'. The entire group ($N = 433$) filled out the FAS, FAM and VAFAS scales.

Results

The visual analogue scales enabled us to determine the number of participants who were afraid to fly. The questionnaires of those who had no problem with flying did not contain additional information because all items were marked *No*. Items never marked *Yes* by the flight anxiety group were reformulated or deleted. The remaining items were discussed with five experts and those suffering from fear of flying. Refinement of items resulted in a 32-item version of the FAS and a 40-item version of the FAM. It was also decided to change the scoring of the items to Likert-type scale, ranging from 0 to 4.

Participants in the above group with fear of flying were asked to fill out the questionnaires again on the Likert-type scale and to mail them back. Of the 242 requests, 98 were returned and results were again discussed with pilots, cabin crew, therapists, experts and people with flying phobia. After that, we reformulated only a few items.

Study 3

Overview

The purpose of Study 3 was to explore the structure of the initially selected items and possibly to further refine items for the FAS and FAM.

Method

Participants Participants consisted of people consecutively referred to the VALK (*Vlieg*Angstbestrijding *Leidse* universiteit *KLM*) Foundation, located in Leiden, the Netherlands. VALK is a training centre for treating people with fear of flying. It is a joint enterprise of Leiden University, KLM Royal Dutch Airlines and Amsterdam Airport Schiphol. All participants were patients who were afraid to fly.

The sample ($N = 136$) was collected from 1990 to 1991. The group consisted of 44 per cent men and 56 per cent women. The mean age of these patients was 40.8 years (SD = 10.4).

Statistical analyses An explorative principal-components analysis with varimax rotation was performed to explore the structure of the initially selected items for the FAS and FAM questionnaires. All participants completed the FAS and FAM.

Procedure The FAS questionnaire consists of 32 items for assessing anxiety produced by different situations related to air travel. The introduction to the questionnaire is as follows: 'Circle the number which corresponds to your level of anxiety in the situations mentioned. The numbers range from 1 to 5, where 1 is *no anxiety*, 2 is *slight anxiety*, 3 is *moderate anxiety*, 4 is *considerable anxiety* and 5 is *overwhelming anxiety*'. This is followed by a list of statements pertaining to specific situations related to flying and planes.

The FAM questionnaire has 40 items. Its aim is to inquire about symptoms of anxiety or anticipated anxiety in flight situations. The patient indicates an answer for each symptom on a scale with the following categories: 0 (*not at all*), 1 (*a little bit*), 2 (*moderately*), 3 (*intensely*), 4 (*very intensely*). The questionnaire was hypothesised to have the following two subscales relevant to the modalities in which anxiety is expressed: (a) the somatic modality scale (20 items), pertaining to physical symptoms; and (b) the cognition scale (20 items), which assesses the presence of distressing cognitions.

Results

In the FAS; the scree test (Cattel, 1966) showed a break between the steep slope of the first three factors and a gradual trailing of the remaining factors. The three-factor solution explained 64 per cent of the variance. To attain higher specificity, we changed items that loaded equally high on two factors after discussion with patients, therapists and experts. Finally, 32 items remained for this study (Cleiren et al., 1994).

Scale construction for the FAS anticipatory anxiety scale The anticipatory anxiety scale has 14 items that pertain to the anxiety of anticipating a flight. The scale scores for the anticipatory anxiety scale range from 0 (*no anxiety*) to 56 (*extreme anxiety*). Scale reliability was high, with a Cronbach's alpha of .96. Item 6, 'You decide to take a plane', and Item 21, 'The engines roar at high speed before the start', belong conceptually to this scale, but their low item-total correlations reflect their transitory positions between this and the generalised flight anxiety and anticipatory anxiety scales. Scale distribution is somewhat flat, with a platykurtosis (kurtosis = −0.44). The skewness of the distribution is slightly to the left (skewness = −0.43), with 90 per cent of the scores between 0 and 50. The scale mean is 33.52 and the standard deviation is 13.69. Accordingly, scale distribution is close to normal, with a very good spread around the mean and it shows a high internal consistency with a good additivity of items.

Scale construction for the FAS in-flight anxiety scale The FAS in-flight anxiety scale consists of 11 items pertaining to anxiety experienced in flight situations. The possible scale scores range from 0 (*no anxiety*) to 44 (*extreme anxiety*). The reliability of the scale was high, with a Cronbach's alpha of .93. Item 22, 'You are being pushed into your chair', shows a relatively low corrected item-total correlation. This item reflects the moment of takeoff. Conceptually, it overlaps somewhat with the anticipatory anxiety scale, because it concerns the moments preceding lifting off from the ground. Examining the pattern of correlations, it appears that the scale is determined more by direct sensory contact with plane movement (particularly Items 24, 25, 31, 28, 27 and 23) than by information given on the flight (Items 29, 32 and 26). The peakedness of the scale is normal (kurtosis = 0.05). The skewness of the distribution is negative (skewness = −0.71) with 90 per cent of the scores between 0 and 42. The mean is 29.68 and the standard deviation is 10.20. Accordingly, scale distribution is close to normal, although the scores tend toward the scale maximum, which is not surprising for this sample. The variance is satisfactory and there is high internal consistency with a good additivity of the items.

Scale construction for the FAS generalised flight anxiety scale The FAS generalised flight anxiety scale has seven items. They refer to anxiety generally experienced in connection with aeroplanes, usually experienced when seeing or hearing planes, regardless of personal involvement in a flight. This type of anxiety possibly reflects the extent to which anxiety is generalised or has become more strongly conditioned. Possible scale scores range from 0 (*no generalised flight anxiety*) to 28 (*extreme generalised flight anxiety*). Scale reliability is satisfactory, with a Cronbach's alpha of .84 and scale distribution is peaked (kurtosis = 1.35). The skewness of the distribution is strongly to the right (skewness = 1.05), indicating that a majority of the sample scores fall in the lower range and a limited number have considerably higher scores: 91 per cent of the scores are between value 0 and 12. The mean score is 5.21 and the standard deviation is 4.69.

Evaluating the factor structure of the original FAM Factor analyses on the 40 items of the FAM (principal-component analysis) showed 10 factors with an eigenvalue greater than one. The three-factor structure with eigenvalues of 11.0, 4.2 and 2.1 explained 43 per cent of the variance. In the varimax-rotated solution, the first factor contained items primarily related to panic disorder, with a mix of somatic and cognitive reactions. The second factor was clearly somatic, whereas the third factor uniquely reflected cognitive reactions.

It was, however, clear that the two-factor structure better differentiated somatic and cognitive components. This still explained 38 per cent of the variance. The first factor is predominantly somatic and the second one pertains to cognitive symptoms. A considerable number of items loaded moderately on both factors. Item 40, 'I think I will faint from fear', loaded much higher on the somatic than on the cognitive factor to which it was originally assigned. This is understandable in view that its content specifically refers to a physical symptom.

Scale construction for the FAM The initial, conceptually formed scales came out with reasonable reliability (Cronbach's alpha = .91 for the somatic scale and .86 for the cognitive scale). However, specificity of these scales was insufficient. Correlation between the scales was higher ($r = .67$) than the mean correlation between the items: .32 for the somatic scale and .29 for the cognitive scale. Besides, Cronbach's alpha was relatively low in view of the number of items. Because of this (Cleiren et al., 1994), it was decided to select only items that loaded independently on each of the factors (on the basis of the preceding two-component principal-component analysis). To attain higher specificity, all items that loaded lower than .50 on one factor scale as well as those that loaded equally high on both factors were dropped. Subsequently, a factor analysis was conducted on the remaining items. The factorial structure is now more clearly defined. This resulted in a somatic modality scale reduced to 11 items and a cognitive modality scale with eight items.

The reliability of the resulting scales was then evaluated. The somatic modality scale, in this form, had a reliability coefficient of .89 and further removal of items was unnecessary. Analysis showed that the reliability of the cognitive modality scale was improved by removing Item 18. After removal of this item, the alpha for the cognitive modality scale was also .89. Specificity of the resulting scales was now much better ($r = .22$), whereas at the same time the mean interim correlation in each scale was higher (mean $r = .42$ for the somatic and .53 for the cognitive scales). It was decided to use the newly formed scales in future analysis. This resulted in an item pool of 18 items.

The FAM somatic modality scale　The FAM somatic modality scale is formed by recoding raw scores, so that no symptoms correspond to 0 or to a low score and many symptoms correspond to a high score.

The FAM somatic modality scale consists of 11 items that assess the extent to which anxiety is expressed in physical symptoms. Possible scores range from 0 (*no physical distress symptoms*) to 44 (*extreme physical distress symptoms*). The range observed in the present sample runs from a minimum of 0 to a maximum of 43. The reliability of the scale was high, with a Cronbach's alpha of .89.

Distribution of the FAM somatic modality scale is as follows: $M = 15.80$ and SD = 10.80. Scale distribution is flat (a platykurtosis of -0.68). Distribution skewness is somewhat to the right (skewness = .60), with relatively more cases scoring under the mean in the lower regions of the scale. Scores range from 0 to 43.

The FAM cognitive modality scale　The cognitive modality scale has seven items that deal with cognitive aspects of flight anxiety. It assesses various distressing thoughts related to the anxiety. Possible scores range from 0 (*no cognitive distress symptoms*) to 28 (*extreme cognitive distress symptoms*). This scale may be considered to reflect the extent to which anxious cognitions are present in flight situations. Scale reliability was high, with a Cronbach's alpha of .86.

The distribution of the FAM cognitive modality scale is as follows: $M = 17.30$ and SD = 7.70. Scale distribution is quite flat (a platykurtosis of -0.93). The skewness of the distribution is somewhat to the left (skewness is -0.41), with relatively more cases above the mean in the higher regions of the scale.

Study 4

Overview

The purpose of Study 4 was to explore the structure of the final versions of the FAS and FAM items and the robustness of the factor structure obtained in Study 3. Additionally, quantitative evidence of the relevance and representativeness of the final versions of the FAS and FAM for the construct they are designed to measure was collected from five experts in the field of fear of flying.

Method

Participants Participants in Study 4 also consisted of people consecutively referred to the VALK Foundation. All were patients who had a fear of flying and who participated in the assessment phase prior to cognitive-behavioural group treatment.

The sample for the FAS ($N = 746$) was collected from 1992 to 1996 and the sample for the FAM was collected from 1993 to 1996 ($N = 497$). The group consisted of 42 per cent men and 58 per cent women. The mean age was 41.0 years (SD = 10.5). Educational level of the sample was relatively high. Thirty-nine per cent had a higher education (higher professional or academic training) and 20 per cent had medium level (professional) education. Forty-one per cent completed elementary school education or lower professional training.

Measures Different measures were completed in the assessment phase, of which the following are relevant to this study:

1   *the flight anxiety situations questionnaire* – the final version of the FAS questionnaire has 32 items consisting of three subscales: a) anxiety experienced when a person anticipates flying, up to the time the flight actually starts (take-off is announced); b) anxiety experienced during a flight (from start until landing); c) anxiety experienced in general in connection with planes, regardless of personal involvement in a flight. The instructions for the questionnaire are described in Study 3;
2   *the flight anxiety modality questionnaire* – the final version of the FAM questionnaire has 18 items designed to measure the following modalities: a) somatic modality, pertaining to physical symptoms; and b) cognitive modality, related to the presence of distressing cognitions. For instructions see Study 3.

Procedure During the assessment phase (T1), self-report instruments were completed by all the patients (referrals with fear of flying). Following assessment, patients were treated in a multicomponent programme (see Study 7).

Statistical analyses Principal-components analysis was used to investigate the optimal dimensional structure of the FAS and FAM for two randomly selected subsamples. It was executed on the correlation matrix of the FAS and FAM items with orthogonal rotation using the varimax procedure. This procedure was used in two randomly selected subgroups to cross-validate the factor structure. The number of factors was determined with a scree test (Cattel, 1966).

Results

For the FAS; in both random subsamples, a three-factor solution emerged, which can be clearly interpreted and explains 70 per cent of the variance in the first sample and 72 per cent in the second sample. Three scales were constructed:

a) anticipation flight anxiety scale (12 items), Items 6–11, 14–18 and 20. Anticipation flight anxiety (pre-flight) is experienced when anticipating a flight. The items refer to anticipation anxiety up to just before the flight actually starts (takeoff is announced);

b) in-flight anxiety scale (10 items), Items 22–25 and 27–32. In-flight anxiety is experienced during a flight (from the start of the engines and subsequent events until landing);

c) generalised flight anxiety scale (seven items), Items 1–5, 12 and 13. Generalised flight anxiety is generally experienced in connection with planes and when seeing or hearing them, regardless of personal involvement in a flight. It reflects the extent to which anxiety is generalised.

Three of the 32 items did not meet the criteria of loading at least .40 on their corresponding factor and a difference in loading of at least .15 with dissimilar factors and consequently were not included in the FAS subscales (Table 4.1). The factor structure of the FAS had the robustness obtained in Study 3.

For the FAM; in both random subsamples, a two-factor solution emerged explaining 56 per cent of the variance in the first sample and 54 per cent in the second sample. Two scales were constructed: a) the FAM somatic modality scale, which consists of 11 items assessing the extent to which anxiety is expressed somatically; b) the FAM cognitive modality scale, which consists of seven items related to the cognitive aspects of flight anxiety. The content of this scale is considered to reflect the extent to which anxious cognitions occur in flight situations. All items met the criteria of loading at least .40 on their corresponding factor with a difference in loading of at least .15 with the other factor and consequently were included in the FAM subscales (Table 4.2). Also the factor structure of the FAS had the robustness obtained in Study 3.

To assess the relevance and representativeness of the resulting questionnaire items as identified for the domains, we asked experts ($N = 5$) working with

Table 4.1   Factors and factor loadings of the flight anxiety situations questionnaire items

Item	*Loading*	
Factor 1: generalised flight anxiety	*First sample*	*Second sample*
1 You see an aeroplane	.72	.81
2 You hear the sounds of planes	.77	.82
3 You read a report about a flight	.70	.75
4 You bring someone to the airport	.69	.71
5 Friends tell you about a flight	.74	.70
12 You see planes taking off and landing	.55	.66
13 You hear the sound/noises of jet engines	.57	.64
Factor 2: anticipatory flight anxiety		
6 You decide to take a plane	.66	.63
7 You buy a ticket	.72	.69
8 You are on the way to the airport	.81	.80
9 You enter the departure hall	.83	.80
10 You are going through customs for a passport check	.85	.84
11 You are waiting for the boarding call	.87	.86
14 You are walking in the direction of the gate	.86	.83
15 You are going through the security check	.84	.81
16 You are going through the gate	.87	.85
17 You enter the flight cabin	.87	.81
18 The doors are being closed	.79	.77
20 The take off is announced	.73	.69
Factor 3: in-flight anxiety		
22 You are pushed back into your seat	.63	.71
23 You hear some noises during the flight	.78	.81
24 The plane banks left or right	.81	.81
25 The wings of the plane are moving, shaking	.84	.83
27 The sound of the engines decreases	.76	.74
28 The plane starts the descent	.73	.75
29 Air turbulence is announced	.78	.79
30 You are shaken	.81	.78
31 The sound of the engine gets louder again	.80	.79
32 The landing is announced	.71	.67

Note: FAS items that loaded >.40 on one of the three corresponding factors and with a difference of >.15, with dissimilar factors for the data of two random samples from a total of 746 patients.

fear of flying patients to assess the items for relevance and representativeness on a five point scale. The experts indicated a rating for each item on a scale with the following categories: 1 (*not at all relevant or representative*), 3 (*neutral*), 5 (*very relevant and representative*). The total scores for each item range from 5 (*not at all relevant or representative*) to 25 (*very relevant and representative*). Using content validity procedures described by Haynes et al. (1995), we asked whether items fit within the domains of the questionnaires and whether there were omissions or redundant items. Generally, the subscale items of both questionnaires were considered to be relevant and representative for the domains they are supposed to measure (range of scores 21–25). Only one item on the FAS (Item 10) and two items on the FAM (Items 7 and 12) received a mean score of 4.2 (*satisfactory*), whereas the remaining items were considered very relevant and representative (MS 4.4). Consequently, the items were considered to form the final versions of the FAS and FAM scales on the basis of the results of Study 4 (see Appendix A and B).

Study 5

Overview

The purpose of Study 5 was to examine the reliability, internal consistency and test-retest reliability of the final versions of the FAS and FAM scales.

Method

Participants Participants were consecutively referred to the VALK Foundation as described in Study 4. The FAS was filled out by 746 participants and the FAM by 497 participants. In addition, data from a group of 54 patients on a waiting list (22 men and 32 women, age 39.8 [SD = 10]) were collected. In the waiting list group, the FAS and FAM were measured three months before the assessment phase (T0) and during the assessment phase (T1). The interval between T0 and T1 (the waiting list group) is equal to the interval between T1 and T2 (treatment until follow-up).

Statistical analyses Cronbach's alpha coefficients were calculated to assess internal consistency and Pearson product-moment correlation coefficients to assess test-retest reliability of the FAS and FAM subscales.

Table 4.2   Factors and factor loadings of the flight anxiety modality questionnaire items

Item	Loading	
Factor 1: somatic modality	*First sample*	*Second sample*
13 I am short of breath	.81	.86
11 I feel dizzy or I have the feeling that I am going to faint	.82	.79
14 I have the feeling that I am going to choke	.82	.82
18 I think that I will faint from fear	.80	.78
7 The tension makes me clumsy and things fall out of my hands	.52	.58
1 I notice numbness in my limbs	.70	.66
3 I feel pain in the region of my chest	.71	.62
5 I feel palpitations of the heart or a quicker heartbeat	.63	.69
17 I feel suddenly warm or cold	.57	.63
12 My limbs are tense and cramped, so I feel the urge to move or walk	.53	.56
15 I have a dry mouth	.58	.59
Factor 2: cognitive modality		
16 I think the particular plane I am on will crash	.85	.83
9 I attend to every sound or movement of the plane and wonder whether everything is fine	.87	.84
10 I continuously pay attention to the faces and behaviour of the cabin crew	.82	.79
6 The idea that something will go wrong is constantly in my mind	.83	.82
8 I can't concentrate because I am preoccupied with thoughts about horrible flight situations	.74	.70
2 I have a fear of dying	.74	.65
4 I can't tell what is going to happen and that makes me feel very anxious	.64	.62

Note: FAM items that loaded >.40 on their corresponding factor and with a difference in loading of >.15, with the dissimilar factor of two random samples from a total of 497 patients.

Results

The internal consistency (Cronbach's alpha) of the FAS and FAM subscales is shown in Table 4.3. Cronbach's alphas are good to excellent, ranging from .88 to .97 (Nunnally, 1978). The high Cronbach's alphas of generalised flight anxiety (.97) on a relatively short scale indicate that items can be seen as parallel tests. But because of discussions with patients and experts, we decided to keep all the items in order to cover the entire domain.

The test-retest reliability of the FAS and FAM scales were also good to excellent, ranging from .79 to .92.

Table 4.3   Reliabilities, internal consistency and test-retest reliability coefficient of the flight anxiety situations questionnaire subscales and the flight anxiety modality questionnaire subscales

Scale	Cronbach's alpha	r
FAS	*(N = 746)*	*(N = 54)*
Generalised flight	.97	.90
In-flight	.95	.92
Anticipation	.88	.90
FAM	*(N = 497)*	*(N = 54)*
Somatic	.89	.79
Cognitive	.89	.84

Note: p < .000 for all scales.

Study 6

Overview

The purpose of Study 6 was to examine the convergent and divergent validity of the FAS and FAM scales.

Method

Participants Participants were consecutively referred to the VALK Foundation as described in Study 4.

Measures Different measures were completed in the assessment phase, of which the following are relevant to this study:

1   the flight anxiety situations questionnaire;
2   the flight anxiety modality questionnaire as described in Study 4;
3   fear survey schedule (FSS-III) (Wolpe and Lang, 1977). Regarding the Dutch version of the FSS-III (Arrindel, 1980), we only discuss the fear-of-aeroplanes item and the items from the subscale dealing with fear of living organisms. Items were scored on a five point scale, ranging from 0 to 4 (from *none* to *very much anxiety*);
4   avoidance of planes. The first part of the fear questionnaire (Marks and Mathews, 1979) relates to the main target phobia for which patients want to be treated. In this study, patients rated their avoidance of planes on this single-item scale. In this item, the answer categories are numbered from 1 to 9 with labels for every two categories: 1 (*I don't avoid*), 3 (*I sometimes avoid*), 5 (*I often avoid*), 7 (*I almost always avoid*) and 9 (*I always avoid*). 382 participants in our study sample filled out this questionnaire;
5   the visual analogue flight anxiety scale is already described in Study 2. The majority of the patients indicated severe to extreme anxiety. Ninety per cent of the women and 83 per cent of the men had a score between 7 (*severe anxiety*) and 10 (*terrified/panic*).

With respect to the FSS-III and Fear Questionnaire single-item scales for fear, specifically of avoidance of aeroplanes, were chosen as criterion measures for convergent validity because no other validated multi-item scales for these constructs are available.

Procedure During the assessment phase (T1), self-report instruments were filled out by all patients (referrals with fear of flying). Following assessment, patients were treated in a multicomponent programme (see Study 7).

Statistical analyses To assess convergent and divergent validity of the FAS and FAM, we correlated the subscales with each other, with the scores of the FSS-III, with the fear questionnaire item (that assesses avoidance of planes) and with the VAFAS. To determine the convergent validity (the correlation between two or more measures of the same theoretical construct) of the FAS and FAM subscales, we correlated the FAS and FAM and with the VAFAS, one item in the fear questionnaire assessing the avoidance of planes and the relevant flying item in the FSS-III. To determine divergent validity, we also correlated the FAS and FAM subscales with the fear of living organisms subscale of the FSS-III. The VAFAS and FAS were completed by 746 participants and the FAM was completed by 497. Because of missing values, we report only 743 cases on the FSS-III. We report 381 participants on the fear questionnaire because this questionnaire was only collected in the period between 1992 to 1994.

Results

As Table 4.4 shows, almost all correlations were significant at a .001 level. Most of the intercorrelations between FAS and FAM subscales were moderate to strong. The FAS in-flight anxiety and the cognitive scale of the FAM are especially closely related ($r = .66, p = .000$). This is understandable because both subscales are specifically related to anxiety experienced during flight. Also, FAS anticipation anxiety is closely related to FAS in-flight anxiety ($r = .57, p = .000$) and FAS generalised flight anxiety ($r = .53, p = .000$). This is also understandable because when anticipatory anxiety is high, in-flight anxiety will also be high. Correlations between FAS and FAM subscales were moderate to strong with the VAFAS (ranging from .29 to .45, $p = .000$) and the FSS-III fear-of-flying item (ranging from .29 to .46, $p = .000$). The FAS anticipation scale shares most variance with all other scales pertaining to flight anxiety. Taken together, these results suggest sufficient convergent validity of the subscales. The avoidance-of-planes item on the fear questionnaire shows significant association with the FAS and FAM subscales (except for the cognitive scale of the FAM). However, the significance of this association is less pronounced than that of the VAFAS and FSS-III. These results could be interpreted as an indication that the FAS and FAM scales measure other, more specific aspects of fear of flying than self-reported avoidance. As we argued in the introduction, fear of flying does not always imply absolute avoidance of flying; it is expressed variously.

To determine divergent validity, we correlated the FAS and FAM subscales with the Fear of Living Organisms subscale of the FSS-III. Except for Generalised Flight Anxiety ($r = .32, p < .001$), all correlations are low, ranging from .09 to .27. This suggests divergent validity of the FAS and FAM subscales in comparison to a measure of phobic stimuli not conceptually related to fear of flying (Table 4.4).

Table 4.4   Correlation coefficients, number of cases and 2-tailed significance for the FAS and FAM subscales, the visual analogue flight anxiety scale (VAFAS), the fear questionnaire avoidance item, the FSS-III item about flying and the FSS-III subscale fear of living organisms

Scales	FAS anticipation	FAS in-flight	FAS generalised	FAM somatic	FAM cognitive
FAS in-flight	.57 (746) p = .000				
FAS generalised	.53 (746) p = .000	.44 (746) p = .000			
FAM somatic	.49 (495) p = .000	.36 (495) p = .000	.36 (495) p = .000		
FAM cognitive	.42 (495) p = .000	.66 (495) p = .000	.36 (495) p = .005	.32 (496) p = .017	
VAFAS	.45 (745) p = .000	.35 (745) p = .000	.29 (745) p = .000	.40 (495) p = .000	.35 (495) p = .000
FQ-avoidance	.43 (381) p = .000	.28 (381) p = .000	.14 (381) p = .005	.32 (138) p = .000	.10 (138) p = .225
FSS-III item	.46 (743) p = .000	.40 (743) p = .000	.29 (743) p = .000	.38 (495) p = .000	.46 (495) p = .000
FSS-III living organisms	.19 (743) p = .000	.23 (743) p = .000	.32 (743) p = .000	.27 (495) p = .000	.27 (495) p = .000

Study 7

Overview

The purpose of Study 7 was to assess the sensitivity to change of the FAS and FAM subscales.

Method

Participants Pre-treatment measurements during the assessment phase (T1) and post-treatment measurements, three months after treatment (T2), of 80 randomly selected patients out of the total sample on the FAS and FAM were taken to assess the sensitivity to change of the FAS and FAM scales ($N = 80$, 35 men and 45 women, age 42.3, SD = 9.3). We collected the post-treatment measures three months after treatment instead of immediately after the therapeutic test flight to avoid euphoric scores. There is considerable anecdotal evidence that patients score better directly after a test flight due to euphoric moods. However, no systematic empirical data are available.

The 54 patients in the waiting list group (22 men and 32 women, age 39.8 [SD = 10]) are described in Study 5. In the waiting list group, the FAS and FAM were measured three months before the assessment phase (T0) and during the assessment phase (T1). The interval between T0 and T1 is the same as the interval between T1 and T2.

Procedure During the assessment phase (T1), self-report instruments were completed by all patients (referrals with fear of flying). Following assessment, patients were treated in a multicomponent programme with an individualised treatment preparation phase (two hour), a group treatment phase (two days, 21 hour) and a follow-up phase after three months (three hour) on the basis of a standarised treatment manual (van Gerwen, 1992). The treatment phase has seven components, as follows: a) information on anxiety; stress; phobias; flying; aviation in general; pilot and cabin crew training; sensory experiences; and personal hygiene (nutrition, exercise, etc.); b) relaxation training; c) distraction training; d) controlling upsetting thoughts (i.e., learning how to control and modify negative thoughts with cognitive-behavioural methods); e) panic management; f) exposure or graded practice; and g) a test flight (van Gerwen et al., 2002). All patients in our study made the test flight. The length of treatment, the time between the assessment phase and the test flight are approximately two weeks. Trainers are certified psychologists.

Statistical analyses To assess the sensitivity to change of the FAS and FAM subscales, we analysed differences in pre-treatment (assessment) and follow-up measurements three months after treatment on the FAS and FAM with paired *t* tests. The sensitivity to change was also determined by analysing differences in FAS and FAM scores during a waiting list period versus a treatment period of about the same duration with paired *t* tests. Moreover, to evaluate the degree of change, we calculated Cohen's *d* effect sizes within groups. Finally, to obtain more insight into the reliability of change, we calculated reliable change indices for the FAS and FAM subscales (Jacobson and Truax, 1991). The proportion of patients showing a reliable change was assessed with these indices.

Results

Table 4.5 shows that the FAS and FAM scales appear to be sensitive to change. On all scales, the difference between pre- and post-treatment scores has a very high effect size (Cohen's *d* ranged between 0.91 and 2.42). In contrast, FAS and FAM scores of patients on a waiting list did not change significantly (Cohen's *d* ranged between 0.08 and 0.22). For the purpose of interpretation, Cohen (1977) considered *d* = .20 to be small, *d* = .50 to be medium and *d* = .80 to be large.

According to Jacobson and Truax's (1991) procedure, the proportion of patients manifesting a reliable change was 41 per cent for the FAM somatic subscale, 81 per cent for the FAM cognitive subscale, 73 per cent for the FAS anticipation anxiety subscale, 84 per cent for the FAS in-flight anxiety subscale and 39 per cent for the FAS generalised flight anxiety subscale.

General Discussion

As pointed out at the beginning of this chapter, although fear of flying pertains to a specific situation, it is still a complex phenomenon. Using a test for behavioural avoidance as the only treatment outcome measure can be misleading because many phobics do not completely avoid the feared stimulus. The fact that the self-reported avoidance of planes on the fear questionnaire shows a relatively low association with FAM cognitive and FAS generalised flight anxiety scores supports this statement. To obtain a comprehensive picture of fear of flying, it is necessary to construct reliable and validated measures reflecting its complex structure. This is the first study on the dimensional structure of two instruments for assessing fear of flying based on data from large groups of patients with this problem. The study shows several strengths but also weaknesses.

The results also show that different measures are necessary to measure fear of flying comprehensively. One measure is related to the level of anxiety produced by different air travel situations and the other to the modality in which anxiety is experienced. Being invariant across two separate randomly

Table 4.5   Mean scores on scales at pre-treatment test and post-treatment test (N = 80)

Scale	Pre-test (T1)	Post-test (T2)	T-value	Cohen's d
VAFAS	8.73 (1.33)	3.55 (2.72)	16.75*	2.42
FAM somatic	17.34 (10.36)	5.86 (6.53)	8.83*	1.33
FAM cognitive	18.81 (7.19)	5.15 (5.67)	13.26*	2.11
FAS anticipation	28.38 (11.69)	9.94 (9.30)	11.51*	1.75
FAS in-flight	28.71 (9.51)	8.76 (6.97)	15.74*	2.39
FAS generalised flight	5.75 (5.03)	1.94 (3.15)	6.68*	0.91

* $p < .001$

Table 4.6   Mean scores on scales at pretest 1 (T0) and pretest 2 (T1) before treatment (N = 54)

Scale	Pretest (T0)	Pretest 2 (T1)	T-value	Cohen's d
FAM somatic	16.17 (9.85)	13.93 (10.43)	1.15 ns	.22
FAM cognitive	19.15 (7.45)	18.54 (7.62)	0.42 ns	.08
FAS anticipation	29.37 (11.81)	27.63 (12.73)	0.74 ns	.14
FAS in-flight	29.37 (9.73)	27.88 (10.22)	0.77 ns	.15
FAS generalised flight	6.44 (5.87)	5.61 (5.56)	0.56 ns	.15

selected subsamples, the factorial structure of the FAS indicates that flight anxiety is specifically related to different situations connected with air travel. The invariant structure of the FAM shows that it is worthwhile to differentiate between cognitive and somatic modalities in flying phobia. Most of the intercorrelations between FAS and FAM subscales were moderately strong, indicating both sufficient factorial specificity and convergent validity. Most of the correlations between FAS and FAM subscales and the FSS-III scale for fear of living organisms were low, suggesting divergent validity. Moreover, the internal consistency and test-retest reliability of the FAS and FAM subscales proved to be good to excellent. Finally, the subscales of the FAS and FAM were found to be sensitive to change in measuring treatment outcomes. In accordance with expectations, the waiting list group did not show a significant change.

It should be noted that a weakness of the study is its lack of physiological measurements. Consequently, we do not know the extent to which the self-reports actually reflect what happens physiologically. There is reason to assume, however, that it also does reflect physiologically effects, because patients reported several flights without problems after treatment (van Gerwen et al., 1999). Reliance on retrospective self-reports alone as an indication of change after treatment is, of course, not identical with a behavioural or nonreactive measure. Therefore, we can only state that the FAS and FAM questionnaires are sensitive to change insofar as self-reports manifest change and should be taken together with a BAT.

The results suggest that together, the FAS and FAM may be helpful for measuring different aspects of fear of flying and assessing treatment effects. Because the FAS and FAM comprehensively measure relevant aspects of fear of flying, these scales can be used to measure differential effects of treatment. It is advisable to use the FAS and FAM in combination to measure stimulus as well as response aspects comprehensively. Moreover, the ability to establish a difference between components of fear of flying will help us to measure differential treatment effects on specific aspects of the phobic complaints.

Future research must show whether the above findings of this study have a bearing on clinical practice and convergent and divergent validity should be determined with other questionnaires.

References

American Psychiatric Association (1994), *Diagnostic and Statistical Manual of Mental Disorders* (4th edn), Washington, DC: American Psychiatric Association.

Amner, G. (1997), 'Fear of Flying in Civil Airline Passengers. A Manifold Phenomenon with Various Motivational Roots', unpublished doctoral dissertation; Department of Psychology, Lund University, Sweden.

Andersson, G. (1989), 'A Psychodynamic Approach to Flight Phobia: Evaluation of a New Percept-genetic Instrument', *Pscychological Research Bulletin*, Vol. 29.

Arrindell, W.A. (1980), 'Dimensional Structure and Psychopathology Correlates of the Fear Survey Schedule (Ffs-iii) in a Phobic Population. A Factorial Definition of Agoraphobia', *Behaviour Research and Therapy*, Vol. 18, pp. 229–42.

Beckham, J.C., Vrana, S.R., May, J.G., Gustafson, D.J. and Smith G.R. (1990), 'Emotional Processing and Fear Measurement Synchrony as Indicators of Treatment Outcome in Fear of Flying', *Journal of Behavior Therapy and Experimental Psychiatry*, Vol. 21, pp. 152–62.

Bornas, X. and Tortella-Feliu, M. (1995), 'Descripcion y analisis psicometrico de un instrumento de autoinforme para la evaluacion del miedo a volar' ['Description and Psychometric Properties of a Self-report Assessment Measure for Fear of Flying'], *Psicologia-Conductual*, Vol. 3, pp. 67–86.

Braunburg, R. and Pieritz, R.J. (1979), *Keine Angst vor Fliegen* [*No Fear of Flying*], Niederhausen, Deutschland: Falken Verlag.

Capafons, J.I., Sosa, C.D., Herrero, M. and Viña, C. (1997), 'The Assessment of Fear of Flying: Elaboration and validitation of a videotape as an analogous situation of a flight', *European Journal of Psychological Assessment*, Vol. 13, pp. 118–30.

Cattel, R.B. (1966), 'The Scree Test for the Number of Factors', *Multivariate Behavioral Research*, Vol. 1, pp. 245–76.

Cleiren, M.P.H.D., van Gerwen, L.J., Diekstra, R.F.W., Van Dyck, R., Spinhoven, Ph. and Brinkhuysen, P. (1994), *No More Fear of Flying. An Evaluation of the Effects of the VALK Therapy Program*, Leiden, The Netherlands: Leiden University.

Cohen, J. (1977), *Statistical Power Analysis for the Behavioral Sciences*, New York: Academic Press.

Ekeberg, Ø., Seeberg, I. and Ellertsen, B.B. (1989), 'The Prevalence of Flight Anxiety in Norway', *Nordisk Psykiatrusk Tidsskrift*, Vol. 43, pp. 443–8.

Forgione, A.G. and Bauer, F.M. (1980), *Fearless Flying. The Complete Program for Relaxed Air Travel*, Boston: Houghton Mifflin.

Gursky, D.M. and Reiss, S. (1987), 'Identifying Danger and Anxiety Expectancies as Components of Common Fears', *Journal of Behavior Therapy and Experimental Psychiatry*, Vol. 18, pp. 317–24.

Haug, T., Brenne, L., Johnsen, B.H., Berntzen, D., Gotestam, K.G. and Hugdahl, K. (1987), 'A Three-systems Analysis of Fear of Flying: A comparison of a consonant vs. a non-consonant treatment method', *Behaviour Research and Therapy*, Vol. 25, pp. 187–94.

Haynes, S.N., Richard, D.C.S. and Kubany, E.S. (1995), 'Content Validity in Psychological Assessment: A functional approach to concepts and methods', *Psychological Assessment*, Vol. 7, pp. 238–47.

Howard, W.A., Mattick, R.P. and Clarke, J. C. (1982), *The nature of fear of flying*. Unpublished manuscript, University of New South Wales, Sydney, Australia.

Howard, W.A., Murphy, S.M. and Clarke, J.C. (1983), 'The Nature and Treatment of Fear of Flying: A controlled investigation', *Behavior Therapy*, Vol. 14, pp. 557–67.

Jacobson, N.S. and Truax, P. (1991), 'Clinical Significance: A statistical approach to defining meaningful change in psychotherapy research', *Journal of Consulting and Clinical Psychology*, Vol. 59, pp. 12–19.

Johnsen, B.H. and Hugdahl, K. (1990), 'Fear Questionnaires for Simple Phobias: Psychometric evaluations for a Norwegian sample', *Scandinavian Journal of Psychology*, 31, pp. 42–8.

Light, R.H. (1983), 'Understanding Airphobia. Cognitive, Emotional and Personality Aspects', unpublished doctoral dissertation, California School of Professional Psychology, San Diego, CA.

Marks, I.M. and Mathews, A.M. (1979), 'Brief Standard Self-rating for Phobic Patients', *Behaviour Research and Therapy*, Vol. 17, pp. 263–7.

Muret de Morges, D.G. (1982), *La peur de voler en avion* [*The Fear of Flying by Plane*], Geneva: University of Geneva.

Nunnally, J.C. (1978), *Psychometric Theory* (2nd edn), New York: McGraw-Hill.

Sosa, C.E., Capafons, J.I., Viña, C. and Herrero, M. (1995), 'La evaluacion del miedo a viajar en avion: estudio psicometrico de dos instrumentos de tipo autoinforme' ['Assessing Fear of Flying: Psychometric analysis of two self-report instruments', *Psicologia-Conductual*, Vol. 3, pp. 133–58.

van Gerwen, L.J. (1988), *Vliegangst, oorzaken, gevolgen en remedie* [*Fear of Flying, Reasons, Effects and Remedies*], Baarn, The Netherlands: Ambo.

van Gerwen, L.J. (1992), *Vliegangst behandelings draaiboek* [*Fear of Flying Treatment Manual*], Leiden, The Netherlands: VALK Foundation.

van Gerwen, L.J. and Diekstra, R.F.W. (2000), 'Fear of Flying Treatment Programs for Passengers: An international review', *Aviation, Space and Environmental Medicine*, Vol. 71, pp. 430–37.

van Gerwen, L.J., Spinhoven, Ph., Diekstra, R.F.W. and Van Dyck, R. (1997), 'People who Seek Help for Fear of Flying: Typology of flying phobics', *Behavior Therapy*, Vol. 28, pp. 237–51.

van Gerwen, L.J., Spinhoven, Ph., Van Dyck, R. and Diekstra, R.F.W. (2002), 'Multi-component Standardized Intervention for Fear of Flying: Description and effectiveness', *Cognitive and Behavioral Practice*, Vol. 9, pp. 138–49.

Wolpe, J. and Lang, P.J. (1977), *Manual for the Fear Survey Schedule*, San Diego, CA: Educational and Industrial Testing Service.

Yaffé, M. (1987), *Taking the Fear out of Flying*, London: Graham Tarrant, Newton Abbot, David and Charles Publishers.

Appendix A

Flight Anxiety Situations Questionnaire (FAS): Quantification of Fear in Various Flight Situations

---
Name: Sex:
Date: Research number:

Circle the number which corresponds to your level of anxiety in the situations mentioned. The numbers range from 1 to 5, where 1 = no anxiety, 2 = slight anxiety, 3 = moderate anxiety, 4 = considerable anxiety and 5 = overwhelming anxiety.

Item		No anxiety	Slight anxiety	Moderate anxiety	Consid-erable anxiety	Over-whelming anxiety
1	You see an airplane	1	2	3	4	5
2	You hear the sounds of planes	1	2	3	4	5
3	You read a report about a flight	1	2	3	4	5
4	You bring someone to the airport	1	2	3	4	5
5	Friends tell you about a flight	1	2	3	4	5
6	You decide to take a plane	1	2	3	4	5
7	You buy a ticket	1	2	3	4	5
8	You are on the way to the airport	1	2	3	4	5
9	You enter the departure hall	1	2	3	4	5
10	You are going through customs for a passport check	1	2	3	4	5
11	You are waiting for the boarding call	1	2	3	4	5
12	You see planes taking off and landing	1	2	3	4	5
13	You hear the sound/noises of jet engines	1	2	3	4	5
14	You are walking in the direction of the gate	1	2	3	4	5
15	You are going through the security check	1	2	3	4	5
16	You are going through the gate	1	2	3	4	5
17	You enter the flight cabin	1	2	3	4	5
18	The doors are being closed	1	2	3	4	5
19	You are informed of the flight safety regulations by the cabin crew	1	2	3	4	5
20	The take-off is announced	1	2	3	4	5
21	The engines give full power before take-off	1	2	3	4	5
22	You are pushed back into your seat	1	2	3	4	5

Item	No anxiety	Slight anxiety	Moderate anxiety	Consid- erable anxiety	Over- whelming anxiety
23 You hear some noises during the flight	1	2	3	4	5
24 The airplane banks left or right	1	2	3	4	5
25 The wings of the plane are moving, shaking	1	2	3	4	5
26 The cockpit informs you of the actual altitude or flight-level	1	2	3	4	5
27 The sound of the engines decreases	1	2	3	4	5
28 The plane starts the descent	1	2	3	4	5
29 Air turbulence is announced	1	2	3	4	5
30 You are shaken	1	2	3	4	5
31 The sound of the engine gets louder again	1	2	3	4	5
32 The landing is announced	1	2	3	4	5

Appendix B

Flight Anxiety Modality Questionnaire (FAM)

How Do I Express My Fear?

Circle the number which corresponds to the intenslty of your reaction during a flight, or what you think the intensity of your reaction will be. The numbers range from 1 to 5, where 1 = no reaction, 2 = a little reaction, 3 = moderate reaction, 4 = intense reaction and 5 = very intense reaction.

Item	Not at all	A little bit	Moderately	Intensely	Very intensely
1 I notice numbness in my limbs	1	2	3	4	5
2 I have a fear of dying	1	2	3	4	5
3 I feel pain in the region of my chest	1	2	3	4	5
4 I can't tell what is going to happen and that makes me feel very anxious	1	2	3	4	5
5 I feel palpitations of the heart or a quicker heartbeat	1	2	3	4	5
6 The idea that something will go wrong is constantly in my mind	1	2	3	4	5
7 The tension makes me clumsy and things fall out of my hands	1	2	3	4	5
8 I can't concentrate because I am preoccupied with thoughts about horrible flight situations	1	2	3	4	5
9 I attend to every sound or movement of the plane and wonder whether everything is fine	1	2	3	4	5
10 I continuously pay attention to the faces and behaviour of the cabin crew	1	2	3	4	5
11 I feel dizzy or I have the feeling that I'm going to faint	1	2	3	4	5
12 My limbs are tense and cramped, so I feel the urge to move or walk	1	2	3	4	5
13 I am short of breath	1	2	3	4	5
14 I have the feeling that I am going to choke	1	2	3	4	5
15 I have a dry mouth	1	2	3	4	5
16 I think the particular plane I am on will crash	1	2	3	4	5
17 I feel suddenly warm or cold	1	2	3	4	5
18 I think that I will faint from fear	1	2	3	4	5

Chapter 5

Personality Pathology and Fear of Flying: Cognitive-behavioural Treatment Outcome

Christelle Delorme and Lucas van Gerwen

Since the publication of DSM III, attention focused on personality pathology has greatly increased. This is evidenced by the number of scientific publications in this area and the development of a wide range of structured and semistructured assessment methods for enhancing the reliability and validity of diagnoses (Zimmerman, 1994; Verheul et al., 2000). Recently, a number of review studies have appeared in which the effects of personality pathology on the treatment of psychological syndromes, particularly anxiety disorders, have been examined (Arntz, 1999; Reich and Green, 1991; Reich and Vasile, 1993; Dreessen and Arntz, 1998; Menning and Heimberg, 2000). It is generally assumed that individuals with personality pathology benefit less from treatment for anxiety disorders. Possible problems such as low tolerance for strong emotions, poor compliance with homework assignments, questionable motivation for change and relational difficulties in the therapeutic setting might obstruct the therapeutic process.

Dreessen and Arntz (1998) show in their review study that empirical research does not consistently support this assumption. It can only be hypothesised that some specific personality disorders or traits have a negative impact on the results of treatment for anxiety disorders. The impact of personality pathology specifically on the results of fear of flying treatment has never been studied.

The literature contains various definitions of personality and personality traits (Derksen, 1995). Personality is the totality of an individual's characteristic behaviours, feelings and thinking patterns, which are manifested in characteristic ways of relating to the environment and others, in lifestyle, attitudes and dealing with feelings. These traits are developed in a complex interaction of early (social) environmental, biological and genetic factors, education and experience (Millon and Davis, 1996). Imitation, identification and learning processes play a significant role in personality development.

Personality is the socialised pattern of interacting personal and environmental factors, which assumes a more fixed form after adolescence (Derksen, 1995).

According to Brink (1987), personality disorders include pathological personality traits, a disturbance in interpersonal relations or social and/or professional dysfunction, and subjective suffering. For those with a personality disorder, the balance in the transaction between personal and environmental factors is moved to the personality traits side.

The two most widely accepted definitions of a personality disorder are provided by the *International Classification of Diseases* (ICD) from the World Health Organisation (WHO) and the *Diagnostic and Statistical Manual of Mental Disorders* (DSM) from the American Psychiatric Association (APA). Both of these systems were developed for the classification of psychological disorders and are used worldwide. Several revisions have been issued for both systems. Currently, DSM-IV (APA, 1994) and ICD-10 (WHO, 1992) are being used. ICD-10 diagnoses (WHO, 1993) were used in this study, and they closely correspond to DSM-III-R diagnoses.

ICD-10 (WHO, 1992) defines a personality disorder as a severe, long-term disorder in an individual's characterological constitution and behavioural tendencies, which usually extends to various aspects of the personality and is nearly always associated with or results in serious personal and social disturbance. ICD-10 describes nine personality disorders and a remaining category; personality disorders not otherwise specified (NOS). DSM uses three clusters to order the personality disorders and for the purpose of this study, the diagnoses according to the ICD-10 were also ordered in those clusters.

The present study reported in this chapter is unique because it is the only one that reports on personality pathology in actual clinical practice of a fear of flying treatment programme (Sedere and Dickey, 1996). The object of this study is to find an answer to the question, 'What is the relationship between fear of flying and personality pathology?' Three sub-questions are being posed: 1) what percentage of the fear of flying population studied has a personality disorder and which are those personality disorders; 2) is there a relation between fear of flying and personality pathology; 3) does personality pathology affect treatment results in the short and long term?

Method

Participants

The data reported in this study were obtained from 922 participants, 558 women (60.5 per cent) and 364 men (39.5 per cent), who were assessed and treated from January 1993 to January 1999 by a facility that is specialised in treating flying phobics. The average age of participants was 40.3 years (SD = 10.6) with a distribution ranging from 13 to 76 years (women 40 years, SD = 10.7 and men 40.8 years SD = 10.7). Participants were referred from a range of sources, such as health care agencies, health professionals, company health programmes, though most were self-referrals.

Sociodemographic data assessed show that the subjects' educational level was relatively high: 36.7 per cent received higher education (higher professional or academic training) and 14.8 per cent upper secondary vocational education, 35.2 per cent had elementary school education with lower vocational training, while 13.2 per cent had only elementary school.

In terms of avoidance behaviour, only 9.3 per cent of the participants had never flown, the majority (72.3 per cent), took their last flight more than two years before their application for treatment. The most commonly reported complaints underlying fear of flying were fear of an accident (34.7 per cent), need to have control of the situation (25.3 per cent), claustrophobia (15.9 per cent), fear of loss of control (fear of losing control of their body) (12.1 per cent), and fear of heights (7.3 per cent). van Gerwen et al. (1997) report a detailed description of the diagnostic, demographic and clinical characteristics of participants referred to the VALK Foundation.

Measures

The following measures were selected from a more extensive assessment battery that is regularly used to assess participants. Here, we describe the fear of flying assessments and the self-report questionnaire that provides the ICD-10 diagnoses of personality disorders.

The flight anxiety situations (FAS) questionnaire (van Gerwen et al., 1999) is a 32-item self-report inventory with a five point Likert-type answering format, ranging from 1 = 'No anxiety' to 5 = 'Overwhelming anxiety'. The questionnaire assesses characteristics related to anxiety experienced in different flight or flight-related situations and consists of three subscales:

1) an anticipatory flight anxiety scale, containing 14 items that pertain to anxiety experienced when anticipating a flight;
2) an in-flight anxiety scale, containing 11 items pertaining to anxiety experienced during a flight; and
3) a generalised flight anxiety scale, containing seven items referring to anxiety experienced in connection with aeroplanes in general, regardless of personal involvement in a flight situation.

The psychometric properties of the FAS proved to be excellent (van Gerwen et al., 1999). This study showed an empirically divided factor structure, explaining 72 per cent of the variance, an internal consistency of subscales varying between .88 and .97, and test-retest reliability measured with Pearson product moment correlation coefficients, ranging from .90–.92.

The flight anxiety modality (FAM) questionnaire (van Gerwen et al., 1999) is an 18-item questionnaire for measuring the symptoms of (anticipatory) anxiety in flight situations. Each symptom is rated on a Likert-type scale with the following categories: 1 = 'Not at all', 2 = 'A little bit', 3 = 'Moderately', 4 = 'Intensely', 5 = 'Very intensely'. The FAM was designed to assess the following modalities in which anxiety in flight situations may be expressed: 1) somatic modality, pertaining to physical symptoms; and (2) cognitive modality, related to the presence of distressing cognitions. The psychometric properties of the FAM proved to be good to excellent (van Gerwen et al.,1999). The study showed an empirically divided factor structure, explaining 56 per cent of the variance. The internal consistencies of subscales was .89 for both subscales, and the test-retest reliability was .79 for the somatic modality and .84 for the cognitive modality.

A visual analogue flight anxiety scale (VAFAS) enabled participants to indicate the extent to which they were anxious about flying on a one-tailed visual analogue scale. This scale ranges from 0, 'No flight anxiety' to 10, 'Terrified'.

The questionnaire on personality traits (Vragenlijst voor Kenmerken van de Persoonlijkheid) (VKP) is a self-report questionnaire used to determine the presence of personality pathology (Duijsens et al., 1996). The VKP has been derived from the international personality disorder examination (IPDE), a semistructured interview developed by the World Health Organisation (WHO) to diagnose personality disorders. The VKP consists of 174 questions, categorised into seven areas: work, self, affects, interpersonal relationships, reality testing, impulse control and behaviour before the age of 15 years. The VKP is scored on a three-point scale: 0 (false), 1 (uncertain?) and 2 (true). In addition to a categorial diagnosis and a 'probable diagnosis', the VKP also provides a dimensional score. The categorical diagnosis indicates whether the subject has a personality disorder, which is the case when at least a minimum number of required criteria are confirmed. A probable diagnosis is indicated when a subject has one criterion less than the minimum number required for diagnosis. The dimensional score is a total score for each disorder, in which both the confirmed and uncertain scored criteria are included in the calculation. ICD-10 distinguishes nine disorders: paranoid, schizoid, antisocial, impulsive, borderline, histrionic, anankastic, anxious, dependent and a rest category 'not otherwise specified personality disorder'. An individual can be diagnosed with more than one personality disorder. DSM uses three clusters to order the personality disorders. Because of the strong overlap between the two systems, the diagnoses according to the ICD-10 were also ordered in those clusters for the purpose of this study. Cluster A contains personality disorders mainly characterised by odd or eccentric behaviour, including paranoid and schizoid personality disorders. Cluster B contains antisocial, impulsive, borderline and histrionic personalities. Dramatic, emotional or impulsive behaviour is typical for people with a disorder from this cluster. 'Fear' and 'anxiety' are typical of personality disorders from cluster C, which concerns avoidant, dependent and anankastic personalities.

The VKP is very sensitive but less specific for the presence of a personality disorder and gives a good indication of the dimensional severity of personality pathology. For this study the dimensional cluster scores are the most important for insight in the effects of personality pathology.

Design

After initial contact, participants were invited to the VALK Foundation in Leiden for assessment. The VALK Foundation is a joint enterprise of the Department of Clinical and Health Psychology at Leiden University, KLM Royal Dutch Airlines and Amsterdam Airport Schiphol. The facility specialises in treating flying phobics. VALK offers a multicomponent treatment programme. (For a detailed description of the treatment programme, see van Gerwen et al. (2002).) During their assessment, the participants completed questionnaires on fear and phobias in general and on fear of flying in particular. In a subsequent semistructured interview, information was gathered on flying behaviour (flying history interview). Then the therapist assessed determinants, phenomenology and severity of fear of flying and a multimodal anamnesis. At the end of this phase, the therapists proposed a treatment plan, based on an individual case conceptualisation. The assessment phase took a total of two to three hours to complete. There were three types of treatment: 1) an individualised therapeutic programme; 2) an individualised preparation phase, followed by a one-day behavioural group training programme (12 hours); and 3) an individualised preparation phase, followed by a two-day cognitive-behavioural group training programme (20 hours). Three months after the in-therapy flight, there was a three-hour follow-up session to monitor maintenance. The first post-treatment data were collected in this phase. Data were collected at pre-treatment and at three, six and 12-month follow-ups. The data derived from the FAS, FAM, VAFAS and VKP were obtained at pre-treatment. At the three-month follow-up, the FAS, FAM, VAFAS and the number of one-way flights taken after treatment were compiled. The VAFAS was used in the two written follow-up evaluations carried out six and 12 months later, and participants were asked to indicate the number of one-way flights they had taken.

Methods of Analysis

This open study used an uncontrolled, pretest/post-test design. Descriptive statistics were used to determine how many people are affected by personality pathology and which personality disorder clusters are involved. Chi-square analyses were performed in order to analyse the association of presence of categorical ICD-10 diagnoses with demographical variables. To determine the correlation between fear of flying and personality pathology statistical calculations were performed on a categorical level with the Mann-Whitney U test and on a dimensional level with Spearman's rho correlations analysis. To establish whether personality pathology affects treatment results in the short and long term repeated measures analysis of variance and multiple regression analyses were performed.

P < 0.05 was considered significant for all statistical calculations. Statistical analyses were performed using SPSS 8.5 for Windows (SPSS Inc., Chicago USA, 1989–99).

Results

Presence of Personality Pathology

The percentage shown of fear of flying participants with personality pathology was 37.9 per cent (N = 349). According to the VKP, 12.9 per cent (N = 119) had two or more personality disorders. There was no significant difference in gender distribution between people with and without diagnosed personality pathology ($Chi^2 = 1.49$, $p = 0.22$).

Moreover, there was an even distribution of personality pathology within age categories; approximately 39 per cent of the people in each age category had a personality disorder ($Chi^2 = 1.51$, $p = 0.82$).

Individuals with a personality disorder are generally found in the lower and secondary vocational education categories. There was a significant difference found in educational level ($Chi^2 = 10.80$, $p = 0.01$). The incidence of personality disorders declines somewhat for people with higher levels of education.

In total, 552 personality disorders were diagnosed. Of the total number of diagnoses, the three from the 'anxious' cluster C, i.e. anankastic, anxious and dependent personality disorders, were the most highly represented, with 22.6 per cent, 17.6 per cent and 12.3 per cent respectively, together with the personality disorder NOS (18.4 per cent). Therefore, most personality pathology was found in cluster C with 52.5 per cent of the total number of diagnoses, while cluster B and in cluster A accounted only for 15.8 per cent and 13.3 per cent respectively of the total. The prevalence of the disorders of the 'bizarre' A cluster was paranoid 8.2 per cent, and schizoid 5.1 per cent. The least common diagnoses were found in the 'dramatic' cluster B, impulsive (8.2 per cent), borderline (4.9 per cent), antisocial (1.6 per cent) and histrionic (1.1 per cent).

Relationship between Personality Pathology and Fear of Flying Severity

A Mann-Whitney U test was used to determine the relationship between presence of personality pathology and degree of fear of flying. Results showed that the average anxiety scores on the fear of flying questionnaires – VAFAS ($p < 0.05$), FAS and FAM ($p < 0.001$) – differed significantly between participants with and without a personality disorder diagnosis (see Table 5.1). On average, participants with personality pathology had higher anxiety scores. However, no significant difference was found on the FAS 'in-flight anxiety' subscale ($p = 0.09$).

A Mann-Whitney U test was performed in order to compare the average of each cluster and the personality disorder NOS category to the average of other individuals who did not receive a diagnosis for the cluster in question (see Table 5.2). Table 5.2 shows that the most significant differences occur in the 'anxious' cluster C, followed by cluster B, NOS and cluster A. Except for the

Table 5.1　Mean flight anxiety scores (M) and standard deviation (SD) of participants with and without a personality disorder (PD) diagnosis at pre-treatment

Assessment instrument	No PD M	SD	PD M	SD	Mann-Whitney U
VAFAS	8.13	1.47	8.40	1.37	90578.00*
FAS					
Anticipatory scale	26.89	12.02	30.27	11.53	83317.00***
In-flight scale	27.69	9.75	28.77	9.41	93298.50
Generalised scale	4.69	4.69	6.67	5.73	79383.50***
Total score	66.58	25.06	73.48	24.50	84006.50***
FAM					
Somatic scale	13.84	9.87	18.58	10.59	72858.50***
Cognitive scale	17.55	7.40	19.68	7.00	82784.00***
Total score	31.39	14.05	38.25	13.71	71256.00***

* p < 0.05, ** p < 0.01, *** p < 0.001

Table 5.2 Mean flight anxiety scores (M) and standard deviation (SD) of participants with a cluster A, B, C or NOS personality disorder diagnosis at pre-treatment

Assessment instrument	Cluster A		Cluster B		Cluster C		NOS	
	M	*SD*	*M*	*SD*	*M*	*SD*	*M*	*SD*
VAFAS	8.51	1.43	8.44	1.53	8.50**	1.39	8.38	1.29
FAS								
Anticipation scale	30.66	11.42	31.21*	11.90	30.56***	11.59	30.15	11.74
In-flight scale	28.49	9.85	28.96	7.95	29.00	9.65	29.38	8.96
Association scale	6.51	5.92	7.57**	6.82	7.08***	6.03	6.20	5.33
Total score	73.24	24.56	75.49	25.50	74.51***	25.45	73.58	23.19
FAM								
Somatic scale	18.89*	11.32	18.91**	10.47	19.54***	11.16	17.44*	10.24
Cognitive scale	19.53	6.86	20.53*	6.25	20.04***	7.12	19.65*	6.74
Total score	38.41**	14.08	39.44***	12.39	39.58***	14.20	37.09**	13.36

* $p < 0.05$, ** $p < 0.01$, *** $p < 0.001$

FAS 'in-flight anxiety' subscale score, all cluster C averages were significantly higher than those for people who did not receive a cluster C diagnosis. On average, people with a personality disorder generally had more fear of flying. This is particularly the case when a cluster C personality disorder is concerned. At the dimensional level, the degree of personality disorder was also studied in relationship to fear of flying.

The Spearman's rho correlation coefficients of the dimensional total score as well as the dimensional cluster scores with measurements of fear of flying are all significant (see Table 5.3), although the magnitude of the associations ranges from small (for the VAFAS and FAS) to medium large on the FAM. As Table 5.3 shows, consistent with the findings on the categorical level, cluster C dimensional score has the most significant and the highest associations with the fear of flying scores, compared to cluster A and B.

Table 5.3   Spearman's rho correlation coefficients

Dimensional score	VAFAS (1)	FAS	FAM
Total	0.11**	0.20**	0.33**
Cluster A	0.08*	0.15**	0.26**
Cluster B	0.08*	0.15**	0.26**
Cluster C	0.13**	0.21**	0.34**
Cluster NOS	0.11**	0.20**	0.33**

* $p < 0.05$, ** $p < 0.01$

A multiple regression analysis was used to determine the effect of the dimensional scores of the clusters (A, B and C) and the personality disorder NOS on the VAFAS, FAS and FAM total scores. The Pearson correlation matrix showed that the dependent (fear of flying) and independent (the clusters and the personality disorder NOS variables had slight to medium strong correlation (ranging from $r = 0.08$ to $r = 0.33$)). The independent variables were mutually correlated to a high degree.

The multiple correlation for the FAS is 0.21 and highly significant ($F[3.918] = 13.62$, $p < 0.0001$). Only the cluster C regression value was found to be significant ($ß = 0.16$, $p < 0.001$). Eleven point one per cent of the variance of the scores for the FAM was determined by the clusters. The multiple correlation is 0.33 and also highly significant ($F[3.918] = 38.22$, $p < 0.0001$). The regression value of cluster C is also significant for the FAM ($ß = 0.26$, p < 0.0001). Consequently, for both fear of flying questionnaires, the higher the cluster C dimensional score is, the higher the anxiety scores.

Predictive Value of Personality Pathology

Of the 922 participants in this study, 10.7 per cent were treated individually, 11.4 per cent took part in a one-day group treatment and 71.5 per cent in a two-day group treatment. Six point four per cent (N = 59) had discontinued treatment after the diagnostic phase and therefore, no follow-up data are available from those 59 participants. Of 41 participants, follow-up data after three months are missing. For the follow-up assessment after six months, there are no VAFAS data for 162 persons. After one year of treatment, for a total of 249 (27.01 per cent) persons, follow-up data on the VAFAS are missing. A Chi^2 calculation was performed to determine whether there was a significant association with respect to availability of follow-up data on the VAFAS, after one year between people with (N = 107) and people without (N = 142) a personality disorder diagnosis. Participants without follow-up data after one year were relatively more diagnosed with a personality disorder (Chi^2 = 3.96, p < 0.05).

Chi^2 calculations were also conducted for the second FAS and FAM assessments, because there were no data for 289 participants on the FAS and FAM. The number of participants for whom data were missing for the second FAS and FAX assessment was randomly distributed among participants with and without a personality disorder (Chi^2 = 0.27, p < 0.05).

The effect of a personality disorder diagnosis on treatment results in the short and long term was studied using an analysis of variance for repeated measures. The VAFAS, FAS and FAM anxiety scores were examined. The VAFAS was administered in four phases, i.e. during the diagnostic phase and three, six and 12 months after treatment. The other two questionnaires were administered during the first two assessment points. The presence or absence of a personality disorder was first examined, then the three clusters and the personality disorder NOS were considered. Table 5.4 gives the average anxiety levels and corresponding standard deviations at the four VAFAS assessments.

The analysis of variance showed a significant main effect for time on the VAFAS ($F[3.669]$ = 2183.01, p = 0.0001). The fear of flying scores significantly decrease over time (see Figure 5.1). No main effect was found for diagnosis and no interaction effect for time versus diagnosis.

There was also a significant main effect for time on the FAS ($F[1,631]$) = 1765.47, p < 0.00 and the FAM $F[1,631]$ = 1762.56, p < 0.00) (see Figures 5.2

Table 5.4   **Mean VAFAS scores (M) and standard deviation (SD) of participants with and without a personality disorder (PD) diagnosis in time**

VAFAS	No PD		PD	
	M	*SD*	*M*	*SD*
1st measure	8.10	1.44	8.49	1.33
2nd measure	2.16	2.00	2.33	2.02
3rd measure	1.91	1.84	2.16	1.87
4th measure	1.82	1.86	1.86	2.08

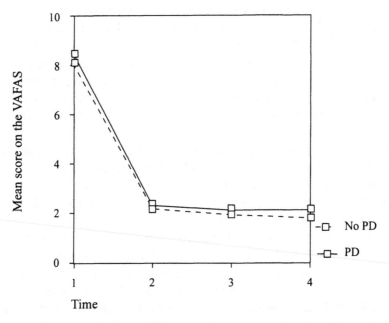

Figure 5.1   **Decrease in flight anxiety measured with the VAFAS for participants with and without a personality disorder (PD) diagnosis at pre-treatment (1), three months (2), six months (3) and 12 months after treatment (4)**

and 5.3). Also no main effect for diagnosis and no interaction effect for time diagnosis on the FAS and FAM was observed. Table 5.5 provides the average anxiety scores and the corresponding standard deviations.

The repeated measures analysis of variance was also performed, with the individual clusters and the personality disorder NOS as between subject. Table

Table 5.5   Mean FAS and FAM scores (M) and standard deviation (SD) of participants with and without a personality disorder (PD) diagnosis in time

	No PD		PD	
Measures	*M*	*SD*	*M*	*SD*
FAS 1st measure	65.81	25.09	73.85	23.47
FAS 2nd measure	18.89	17.46	18.61	17.4
FAM 1st measure	31.45	14.00	38.63	13.00
FAM 2nd measure	7.94	8.64	8.64	8.73

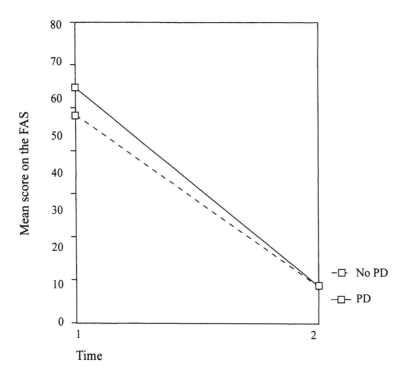

Figure 5.2   Decrease of flight anxiety measured with the FAS for participants with and without a personality disorder (PD) diagnosis

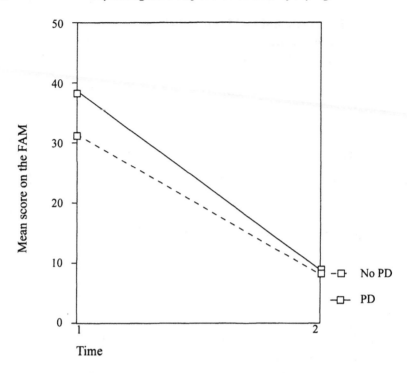

Figure 5.3   Decrease of flight anxiety measured with the FAM for participants with and without a personality disorder (PD) diagnosis

5.6 gives the average scores for the individual clusters and the personality disorder NOS on the three fear of flying questionnaires, assessed at different times.

There was a significant decrease in the anxiety scores for the separate clusters and the personality disorder NOS on each questionnaire (FAVAS: $F[3.662] = 319.37$, $p < 0.00$, FAS: $F[1.624] = 376.91$, $p < 0.00$, FAM: $F[1.624] = 374.29$, $p < 0.00$). Also in these analyses no significant main effect for diagnosis and no interaction effects for time versus diagnoses emerged.

At the dimensional level, treatment results were studied using a multiple regression analysis, where the second fear of flying assessment was used as the dependent variable, and the pre-treatment measurement for fear of flying and the dimensional total score for personality disorders as independent variables.

The regression models for the FAS and FAM were not found to be significant ($p = 0.66$ and $p = 0.63$). There is no linear relationship to be established with a

Table 5.6   Mean anxiety scores for participants with cluster A, B, C or NOS personality disorder diagnoses in time

Assessment method	Mean scores of			
	Cluster A	**Cluster B**	**Cluster C**	**NOS**
VAFAS				
1st measure	8.51	8.44	8.50	8.38
2nd measure	2.57	2.26	2.31	2.54
3rd measure	2.24	2.21	2.11	2.24
4th measure	1.92	2.00	2.00	2.32
FAS				
1st measure	73.27	75.49	74.51	73.58
2nd measure	15.58	14.94	18.19	20.81
FAM				
1st measure	38.41	39.44	39.58	37.10
2nd measure	8.78	7.80	8.73	8.59

multiple regression analysis for these questionnaires between the second fear of flying assessment, on the one hand, and the first fear of flying assessment and the dimensional score on the VKP, on the other.

The VAFAS models at the second and fourth assessments were unreliable. This was apparent from both distribution diagrams of the standardised remainders compared to the standardised predicted Y values. From this, it could be determined that the variance of the remainders is not constant (heteroscedasticity) and that the remainders have not been randomly distributed. In view of the fact that the assumptions for multiple regression are not met, it was decided to study the treatment effect with nonparametric Spearman's rho correlation coefficients. No significant correlation emerged between the dimensional total score on the VKP and the change scores on the VAFAS at 2nd (rho = −0.01) and 4th assessment (rho = −0.02). Accordingly, the degree of fear of flying at the follow-up VAFAS assessments (2nd and 4th assessment) are not associated with personality pathology. The same results were found for the four Clusters (A, B, C and NOS); no significant correlations and rho-scores ranging from 0.00 to 0.05.

Discussion

The main goal of this study was to examine the relation between fear of flying and personality pathology. Thirty-seven point nine per cent of the examined population has at least one personality disorder and 12.9 per cent has two or more personality disorders. The literature shows that it is not unusual for a person to have more than one personality disorder (Hilsenroth, Handler and Blais, 1996). This percentage of personality disorders lies between those that Duijsens, Eurelings-Bontckoe and Diekstra (1996) found with the VKP in their normal population sample (15 per cent) and in a psychiatric outpatient population (63 per cent). In view of the fact that this population consists of relatively healthy people with a well-defined problem, this prevalence is not surprising. There is no significant difference in prevalence of personality disorders for gender and age. This corresponds to the literature for gender, but the prevalence is generally lower in older groups (Girolamo and Reich, 1993). There was a significant difference in prevalence of personality disorder between educational levels. The incidence of personality disorders decreases slightly as educational level increases, which is consistent with the literature (Girolamo and Reich, 1993).

With 52.5 per cent of the total number of personality disorders, cluster C is the most highly represented, whereby anankastic and anxious personality disorders are relatively the most common. Since this population is affected by anxiety symptoms, it is not surprising that cluster C personality disorders are the most frequently occurring. Studies show that a comorbid cluster C disorder is often present in anxiety disorders (including fear of flying) (Arntz, 1999).

Participants with a personality disorder report more fear of flying symptoms at the start of treatment than those without a personality disorder. These outcomes are in keeping with findings from the literature. In general, participants with a personality disorder have more (generalised) symptoms (Dreessen and Arntz, 1998; Arntz, 1999).

There is a positive relationship between the degree of fear of flying (measured with the VAFAS, the FAS and FAM) and dimensional scores for personality pathology especially for cluster C. As the cluster C dimensional score increases, the fear of flying experienced also increases.

These findings can be interpreted in various ways. The cross-sectional design of this study makes it impossible to simply assume that there will be a higher prevalence of personality disorders when more anxiety symptoms are reported. Various studies indicate the effect of state at the time of establishing trait: anxiety symptoms can interfere with 'pure' diagnoses of personality disorders (Dreessen and Arntz, 1998; Griens et al., 2001; Zimmerman, 1994). Self-report questionnaires (such as the VKP) are sensitive to this, which accounts for overestimation in comparison to (semi-)structured interviews. Longitudinal studies are needed to determine these possible contamination effects and to enable a 'purer' estimation of the incidence of personality pathology.

The presence of a personality disorder does not negatively affect treatment results, either in the short or long term. Participants with a personality disorder benefit just as much from treatment as those without. Over time, fear of flying significantly declines, regardless of the presence of personality pathology. At pre-treatment, participants with a personality disorder have significantly more fear of flying symptoms. After treatment, the level of fear of flying does not differ between groups. These findings are not consistent with the majority of review studies on treatment effects (Reich and Green, 1991; Reich and Vasile, 1993; Menning and Heimberg, 2000), but they do correspond to those reported by Dreessen and Arntz (1998). It is apparently possible to overcome complications in the therapeutic process due to personality pathology. One explanation for this could be that the treatment as investigated in the present study is attuned to individual problems. If necessary, additional sessions are offered for more extensive cognitive restructuring at the start of treatment. During the two-day group treatment programme, specific (flight) anxiety is handled in a very direct and structured manner. Personality problems are not a relevant factor in the group treatment.

Another explanation lies in the predominance of the cluster C personality disorders. In other studies, participants with more severe disorders from especially clusters A and B were more prevalent. The prevalence of these clusters may negatively affect treatment results (Dreessen et al., 1994). Since clusters A and B personality disorders were relatively rare in this study, the results may have greater relevance for the treatment of participants with personality disorders in the 'anxiety' C cluster.

The design of this study has several positive methodological points. The sample is large (N = 922), which strengthens the statistical components (Cohen, 1988). Personality pathology (the independent variable) was prospectively assessed, independently of treatment results. The dependent variable, fear of flying, was assessed with specific, symptom-oriented self-report questionnaires (the FAS and FAM). The advantage of these particular assessment instruments is that they are more precise and more sensitive to changes than general anxiety questionnaires. In contrast to many other effect studies, this one used specific and well known assessment instruments with good psychometric properties (Steketee and Chambless, 1992; van Gerwen et al., 1999).

Another positive point is that the dependent variable (treatment outcome) has been dimensionally assessed, instead of dichotomously (successful/ unsuccessful). Moreover, dimensional scores for the independent variables (personality pathology) have been used in addition to categorial scores. The presence of continuous variables made it possible to carry out more powerful parametric tests besides the nonparametric ones. Finally, there are different methods for measuring treatment effects. In this case, a pretest/post-test design was used and change scores were examined. The treatment outcome was assessed with statistical correction for differences in scores at premeasurement. The analysis methods used in this study are preferable to other methods, such as percentage-change scores and rough final scores (Steketee and Chambless, 1992).

The study also has certain shortcomings. Firstly, both dependent and independent variables were identified with self-report questionnaires. The question is whether it can be assumed that people have insight into their own problems and personality and can validly report about them (Arntz, 1999; Verheul et al., 2000).

In addition, self-report questionnaires are known to considerably overestimate problems compared to structured and semistructured interviews (Duijssens et al., 1999). The VKP compensates for this somewhat, since dimensional scores can also be calculated. Accordingly, something can be said about the degree of disorder in the population studied.

Furthermore, follow-up data are unavailable from some participants. After the diagnostic phase, 6.4 per cent (N = 59) discontinued treatment. After three months follow-up, for a relatively small group of 41 participants, data from the VAFAS were unavailable. However, the participants who discontinued treatment together with the participants who did not show up at three months follow-up (N = 100), comprised significantly more participants with a personality disorder. With respect to missing data on the second FAS and FAM assessment (N = 289), no significant association between presence of personality pathology and availability of follow-up assessment was found.

In conclusion, it seems that a personality disorder should not be readily considered an exclusion criterion for cognitive-behavioural treatment of anxiety disorders. At least for a specific, well-defined anxiety, the study reported in this chapter, indicates that personality pathology does not predict a poorer outcome for a short-term, multimodal, standardised cognitive-behavioural fear of flying treatment programme. It is important for therapists to be aware of their own attitudes towards participants with personality disorders. Lack of faith in a positive treatment outcome, might generate a 'self-fulfilling prophecy'. Practitioners should also be careful about ascribing unsuccessful treatment to a comorbid personality disorder.

References

Agras, S., Sylvester, D. and Oliveau, D. (1969), 'The Epidemiology of Common Fears and Phobias', *Comprehensive Psychiatry*, Vol. 2, pp. 151–6.

American Psychiatric Association (1987), *Diagnostic and Statistical Manual of Mental Disorders (DSM-III-R)*, Washington, DC: American Psychiatric Association.

American Psychiatric Association (1994), *Diagnostic and Statistical Manual of Mental Disorders* (4th edn), Washington, DC: American Psychiatric Association.

Arnarson, E.O. (1987), 'The Prevalence of Flight Phobia among Icelanders', paper presented at the First Nordic Meeting, Aviation and Space Medicine, Oslo, Norway.

Arntz, A. (1999), 'Do Personality Disorders Exist? On the Validity of the Concept and its Cognitive-behavioral Formulation and Treatment', *Behaviour Research and Therapy*, Vol. 37, pp. 97–134.

Brink, W. van den (1987), 'Persoonlijkheid: karakter of rolgedrag, validitietsaspecten van de DSM-III-classificatie van persoonlijkheids stoornissen' ['Personality: Character or role behavior, validity aspects of the DSM-III-classification for personality disorders'], *Tijdschrift voor Psychiatrie*, Vol. 29, pp. 296–312.

Cohen, J. (1988), *Statistical Power Analysis for the Behavioral Sciences* (2nd edn), Hillsdale: Lawrence Erlbaum.

Dean, R.D. and Whitaker, K.M. (1982), 'Fear of Flying: Impact on the US air travel industry', *Journal of Travel Research*, Vol. 21, pp. 7–17.

Derksen, J.J.L. (1995), *Personality Disorders: Clinical and social perspectives, assessment and treatment bases on DSM-IV and ICD-10*, Chichester, England: Wiley.

Dreessen, L. and Arntz, A. (1998), 'The Impact of Personality Disorders on Treatment Outcome of Anxiety Disorders: Best-evidence synthesis', *Behaviour Research and Therapy*, Vol. 36, pp. 483–504.

Dreessen, L., Arntz, A., Luttels, C. and Salllaerts, S. (1994), 'Personality Disorders Do not Influence the Results of Cognitive Behavior Therapies for Anxiety Disorders', *Comprehensive Psychiatry*, Vol. 35, pp. 265–74.

Duijsens, I.J., Eurelings-Bontekoe, E.H.M. and Diekstra, R.F.W. (1996), 'The VKP, a Self-report Instrument for DSM-III-R and ICD-10 Personality Disorders: Construction and psychometric properties', *Personality and Individual Differences*, Vol. 20, pp. 171–82.

Ekeberg, Ø. (1991), *Flight Phobia: Prevalence, sympathetic responses and treatment*, Department of Internal Medicine, Ulleval Hospital Oslo, Norway: University of Oslo.

Girolamo, G. de and Reich, J.H. (1993), *Personality Disorders, Epidemiology of Mental Disorders and Psychosocial Problems*, Geneva: World Health Organisation.

Griens, A.M.G.F., Jonker, K., Spinhoven, P. and Blom, M.B.J. (2001), 'The Influence of Depressive State Features on Trait Measurement', *Journal of Affective Disorders*, in press.

Hilsenroth, M.J., Handler, L. and Blais, M.A. (1996), 'Assessment of Narcissistic Personality Disorder: A multi-method review', *Clinical Psychology Review*, Vol. 16, pp. 655–83.

Menning, S.D. and Heimberg, R.G. (2000), 'The Impact of Comorbid Mood and Personality Disorders in the Cognitive-behavioral Treatment of Panic Disorder', *Clinical Psychology Review*, Vol. 20, pp. 339–57.

Millon, T. and Davis, R.D. (1996), *Disorders of Personality: DSM-IV and beyond* (2nd edn), New York: Wiley.

Reich, J.H. and Green, A.I. (1991), 'Effect of Personality Disorders on Outcome of Treatment', *Journal of Nervous and Mental Disease*, Vol. 179, pp. 74–82.

Reich, J.H. and Vasile, R.G. (1993), 'Effect of Personality Disorders on the Treatment Outcome of Axis I Conditions: An update', *Journal of Nervous and Mental Disease*, Vol. 181, pp. 475–84.

Sedere, L.I. and Dickey, B. (1996), *Outcome Assessment in Clinical Practice*, Baltimore: Williams and Wilkins.

Steketee, G. and Chambless, D.L. (1992), 'Methodological Issues in Prediction of Treatment Outcome', *Clinical Psychology Review*, Vol. 12, pp. 387–400.

van Gerwen, L.J., Spinhoven, Ph., Diekstra, R.F.W. and Van Dyck, R. (1997), 'People who Seek Help for Fear of Flying: Typology of flying phobics', *Behavior Therapy*, Vol. 28, pp. 237–45.

van Gerwen, L.J., Spinhoven, Ph., Van Dyck, R. and Diekstra, R.F.W. (1999), 'Construction and Psychometric Characteristics of Two Self-report Questionnaires for the Assessment of Fear of Flying', *Psychological Assessment*, Vol. 11, pp. 146–58.

van Gerwen, L.J. and Diekstra, R.F.W. (2000), 'Fear of Flying Treatment Programs for Passengers: An international review', *Aviation, Space, and Environmental Medicine*, Vol. 71, pp. 430–37.

van Gerwen, L.J., Spinhoven, Ph., Diekstra, R.F.W. and Van Dyck, R. (2002), 'Multi-component Standardized Intervention for Fear of Flying: Description and effectiveness', *Cognitive and Behavioral Practice*, Vol. 9, pp. 138–49.

Verheul, R., Van den Brink, W., Spinhoven, P. and Haringsma, R. (2000), 'Richtlijnen voor klinische diagnostiek van DSM-IV-persoonlijkheidsstoornissen' ['Clinical Diagnostic Guidelines for the DSM-IV Personality Disorders'], *Tijdschrift voor Psychiatrie*, Vol. 6, pp. 409–22.

Wilhelm, F.H. and Roth, W.T. (1997), 'Clinical Characteristics of Flight Phobia', *Journal of Anxiety Disorders*, Vol. 11, pp. 241–61.

World Health Organisation (1992, 1993), *The ICD-10 Classification of Mental and Behavioral Disorders. Clinical Descriptions and Diagnostic Guidelines*, Geneva: World Health Organisation.

Zimmerman, M. (1994), 'Diagnosing Personality Disorders: A review of issues and research methods', *Archives of General Psychiatry*, Vol. 51, pp. 225–45.

Chapter 6

Cognitive Coping and Anxiety among People with Fear of Flying

Vivian Kraaij, Nadia Garnefski and Lucas van Gerwen

Fear of flying among potential passengers is rather common (Agras, Sylvester, and Oliveau, 1969; Dean and Whitaker, 1982; Ekeberg, Seeberg and Ellertsen, 1989; Nordlund, 1983; van Gerwen and Diekstra, 2000). Events such as the terrorist attacks on the Twin Towers and Pentagon by hijacking might even lead to higher numbers of people with flight anxiety. Fear of flying, whether experienced to a mild, moderate or high degree, can affect a person's life in various areas. It can interfere with professional, social and family activities (van Gerwen and Diekstra, 2000). As flying has become an integral part of life in industrialised countries, treatment programmes have been developed to help people with flight anxiety. A review study showed that there are about 50 treatment facilities in the Western world which offer treatment programmes for fear of flying (van Gerwen and Diekstra, 2000; van Gerwen et al., in preparation). These treatment programmes have been proved to reduce fear of flying effectively (Greco, 1989; Howard, Murphy and Clarke, 1983; Roberts, 1989; van Gerwen, Spinhoven, Diekstra and Van Dyck, 2002; Walder et al., 1987). However, little is known about which specific method or elements of treatment programmes works best (van Gerwen and Diekstra, 2000). In order to treat fear of flying most efficiently, it is important to find out what the risk factors for flight anxiety are. Consequently, treatment programmes could pay attention to these risk factors.

Cognitive factors have often been found to be associated with symptoms of anxiety and panic (Acierno, Hersen and Van Hasselt, 1993; Clark and Ehlers, 1993; Girodo and Roehl, 1978; Möller, Nortje and Helders, 1998; Wilhelm and Roth, 1997). In particular, the way people deal cognitively with stressful events may be an important factor in determining well-being. Cognitive coping strategies such as self-blame, catastrophising and rumination have been found to have a positive relationship with maladjustment, while positive reappraisal (thoughts of attaching a positive meaning to the event in terms of personal growth) has been found to have a negative relationship with maladjustment

(Garnefski, Kraaij and Spinhoven, 2001; Garnefski et al., in press; Kraaij, Pruymboom and Garnefski, 2002). It would be of interest to know which specific cognitive coping strategies are related to fear of flying. If certain cognitive coping strategies can be proved to be more or less effective in dealing with stressful flight events, these strategies could be promoted or challenged in treatment programmes for fear of flying. This seems a promising approach as cognitive therapies have been found to be effective in treating anxiety (Clark and Ehlers, 1993; Scogin and McElreath, 1994; Woods, 1993).

In the study described in this chapter we examine the extent to which various cognitive coping strategies in response to a flight were used by airline passengers. Next, the relationship between cognitive coping strategies and symptoms of anxiety are examined.

Method

Respondents and Procedure

Respondents were 261 airline passengers who were all seeking treatment for their flight anxiety at the VALK Foundation located in Leiden, the Netherlands. VALK is a joint enterprise of Leiden University, KLM Royal Dutch Airlines and Schiphol Airport Amsterdam. All 261 persons entered treatment between January 2000 and February 2001 and had made at least one flight during the preceding 10 years. Another 76 persons were not included in the present study because they had either never made a flight (25 persons) or their last flight had been more that 10 years ago (51 persons). The respondents mean age was 38.4 years (SD 10.14, range 18–81) and almost half (45 per cent) were male. The respondents' educational level was relatively high: 47.3 per cent had higher professional or academic training; 21.2 per cent had intermediate vocational education; 4.2 per cent had lower vocational education; 6.9 per cent had pre-university education; 6.9 per cent had higher general secondary education; 10.0 per cent had lower general secondary education; and 3.5 per cent had elementary school education. The majority were either paid employees (68.5 per cent) or self-employed (19.2 per cent). During the assessment phase of the treatment programme, a battery of standardised questionnaires was administered. The present study is based on part of these data.

Measures

Cognitive coping strategies Cognitive coping strategies were measured by the cognitive emotion regulation questionnaire (CERQ) (Garnefski et al., 2001; Garnefski, Kraaij and Spinhoven, 2002). Cognitive coping strategies are defined here as the cognitive way of managing the intake of emotionally arousing information, involving thoughts or cognitions that help to manage or regulate our emotions (see also Thompson, 1991). More specifically, the CERQ assesses what people think after the experience of threatening or stressful life events. The CERQ can be used to measure either a more general coping style, or a more specific response to a specific event. In the present study respondents were asked which cognitive coping strategies they used in response to having made a flight. The CERQ consists of 36 items and nine conceptually different subscales. Each subscale consists of four items. Each of the items has a five point Likert scale ('never' to 'always'). A subscale score can be obtained by adding up the four items (with a range from 0 to 16), indicating the extent to which a certain cognitive coping strategy is used. The CERQ subscales are:

- self-blame, which refers to thoughts of blaming yourself for what you have experienced (e.g., 'I think about the mistakes I have made in this matter');
- acceptance, which refers to thoughts of accepting what you have experienced and resigning yourself to what has happened (e.g., 'I think that I have to accept the situation');
- rumination, which refers to thinking about the feelings and thoughts associated with the negative event (e.g., 'I am preoccupied with what I think and feel about what I have experienced');
- positive refocusing, which refers to thinking about joyful and pleasant issues instead of thinking about the actual event (e.g., 'I think of something nice instead of what has happened');
- refocus on planning, which refers to thinking about what steps to take and how to handle the negative event (e.g., 'I think of what I can do best');
- positive reappraisal, which refers to thoughts of attaching a positive meaning to the event in terms of personal growth (e.g., 'I think I can learn something from the situation');
- putting into perspective, which refers to thoughts of playing down the seriousness of the event or emphasising its relativity when compared to other events (e.g., 'I think that it all could have been much worse');

- catastrophising, which refers to thoughts of explicitly emphasising the terror of an experience (e.g., 'I continually think how horrible the situation has been'); and
- other-blame, which refers to thoughts of putting the blame of what you have experienced on others (e.g., 'I think about the mistakes others have made in this matter').

The psychometric properties of the CERQ (used as a more general coping style) have been proved to be good (Garnefski et al., 2002). In the present study the CERQ measured a more specific response to a specific event, namely a flight situation. The alpha-reliabilities of the subscales in the present study also appeared to be good, with alphas ranging from .67 to .82 (see Table 6.1).

Table 6.1   Reliabilities, means scores and standard deviations of cognitive coping strategies in response to having made a flight

Cognitive coping strategy	Cronbach's alpha	Mean	(SD)
Self-blame	.67	9.15	(3.62)
Acceptance	.71	9.60	(3.48)
Rumination	.77	11.74	(3.74)
Refocus positive	.82	9.28	(3.65)
Refocus planning	.81	12.43	(3.71)
Positive reappraisal	.82	9.44	(3.89)
Putting into perspective	.78	10.71	(3.92)
Catastrophising	.76	7.14	(3.22)
Other-blame	.78	5.01	(1.88)

N = 261.

Anxiety Various kinds of anxiety were measured: generalised anxiety and phobic anxiety were measured by the symptom check list (SCL-90: Derogatis, 1977; Dutch translation by Arrindell and Ettema, 1986); generalised anxiety was measured by the SCL-90 anxiety subscale. This subscale consists of 10 items, measuring various anxiety-symptoms; phobic anxiety was measured by the SCL-90 phobic anxiety subscale. This subscale consists of seven items, measuring anxiety reactions as reflected in the 'agoraphobic' syndrome (e.g., feeling afraid in open spaces or in streets, or feeling afraid to faint in public).

Each of the items has a five point Likert scale ('not at all' to 'very much'). The subscale scores can be obtained by adding up the items belonging to the subscale. Psychometric properties of the SCL-90 have been found to be good (Arrindell and Ettema, 1986).

Anxiety related to flying experienced in different situations was measured by the flight anxiety situations questionnaire (FAS) (van Gerwen, Spinhoven, van Dyck, and Diekstra, 1999). The FAS is a 32-item self-report inventory with a five point Likert-type answering format ('no anxiety' to 'overwhelming anxiety'). The FAS contains three subscales: 1) an anticipatory flight anxiety scale, which consists of 14 items that pertain to anxiety experienced when anticipating an aeroplane flight; 2) an in-flight anxiety scale, consisting of 11 items pertaining to anxiety experienced during a flight; and 3) a generalised flight anxiety scale consisting of seven items referring to anxiety experienced in connection to aeroplanes in general, regardless of personal involvement in a flight situation. The subscale scores can be obtained by adding up the items belonging to the subscale. The psychometric properties of the FAS were proved to be good (van Gerwen et al., 1999).

Symptom modalities in which anxiety in flight situations is expressed was measured by the flight anxiety modality questionnaire (FAM) (van Gerwen et al., 1999). The FAM is an 18-item questionnaire with a five point Likert-type answering format ('not at all' to 'very intensely'). The FAM contains two subscales: 1) the somatic modality, consisting of 11 items pertaining to physical symptoms; and 2) the cognitive modality, consisting of seven items related to the presence of distressing cognitions. The subscale scores can be obtained by adding up the items belonging to the subscale. Psychometric properties of the FAM have been found to be good (van Gerwen et al., 1999).

Results

Use of Cognitive Coping Strategies

To examine the extent to which the various cognitive coping strategies were used in response to a flight, mean scores and standard deviations of the cognitive coping strategies were calculated (see Table 6.1). Respondents reported using the strategies refocus on planning, rumination, and putting into perspective in response to having made a flight to the highest extent. The strategies catastrophising and other-blame in response to having made a flight were reported to be used least often.

Relationship between Cognitive Coping Strategies and Anxiety

To examine the relationship between the cognitive coping strategies and anxiety, Pearson correlations were calculated (see Table 6.2).

First, the cognitive coping strategies were correlated with the more general anxiety measures, generalised anxiety and phobic anxiety. The use of self-blame, acceptance, rumination and catastrophising all had a significant positive relationship with generalised anxiety and phobic anxiety. In addition, other-blame also had a significant positive relationship with phobic anxiety. This means that a higher use of these specific strategies was related to higher levels of anxiety. Refocus positive had a significant negative relationship with generalised anxiety, indicating that a higher use of refocus positive was related to a lower level of generalised anxiety.

Next, the cognitive coping strategies were correlated with anxiety related to flying experienced in different situations. The use of self-blame, acceptance and catastrophising all had a significant positive relationship with anticipatory flight anxiety, in-flight anxiety and generalised-flight anxiety. This means that the use of these specific strategies to a higher extent was related to higher levels of all forms of flight-related anxiety. In addition, rumination had a significant positive relationship with anticipatory flight anxiety and generalised flight anxiety. Other-blame also appeared to have a significant positive relationship with anticipatory flight anxiety. This means that the use of these specific strategies to a higher extent was related to higher levels of these forms of flight-related anxiety.

Finally, the cognitive coping strategies were correlated with symptom modalities in which anxiety in flight situations is expressed. The use of self-blame, acceptance, rumination or catastrophising all had a significant positive relationship with both the somatic and cognitive flight anxiety modality. In addition, refocus planning and other-blame also had a significant positive relationship with the somatic modality. This means that the use of all these specific strategies to a higher extent was related to higher levels of physical symptoms and/or distressing cognitions in flight situations.

Discussion

In line with other studies which measured cognitive coping as a more general coping style (Garnefski et al., 2001; Garnefski et al., in press), respondents reported using refocus on planning, rumination and putting into perspective

Table 6.2   Pearson correlations between cognitive coping strategies and anxiety

	Generalised anxiety	Phobic anxiety	Anticipatory flight anxiety	In-flight anxiety	Generalised flight anxiety	Somatic flight anxiety modality	Cognitive flight anxiety modality
Self-blame	.298***	.191**	.185**	.153*	.166**	.201**	.199**
Acceptance	.193**	.159*	.207**	.169**	.148*	.175**	.226***
Rumination	.273***	.226***	.212**	.046	.269***	.328***	.175**
Refocus positive	−.156*	−.048	.046	−.017	.019	−.046	−.062
Refocus planning	.008	.075	.078	.024	.102	.129*	.007
Positive reappraisal	.052	.109	.077	−.069	−.008	.073	−.119
Putting into perspective	−.025	.003	.083	.025	.049	.064	.049
Catastrophising	.243***	.278***	.323***	.150*	.294***	.359***	.137*
Other-blame	.111	.238***	.130*	.070	.038	.132*	.045

$N = 261$; * $p < .05$; ** $p < .01$; *** $p < .001$.

to the highest extent and catastrophising and other-blame to the lowest extent in response to having made a flight. This suggests that people who are afraid to fly tend to think to a considerable extent about what steps to take and how to handle the stressful flight. They also think about the feelings and thoughts associated with the flight and have thoughts of playing down the seriousness of the event or emphasising its relativity when compared to other events. On the other hand, they seem to have fewer thoughts of explicitly emphasising the terror of the flight and putting the blame of what they experienced on others. When compared to a reference group of adults in the general population (where the cognitive coping strategies were measured as a more general coping style), the respondents with flight anxiety reported using self-blame, rumination and catastrophising to a higher extent. The extent to which rumination was used is even comparable to a reference group of psychiatric patients. Acceptance, positive reappraisal, putting into perspective and other blame were used to a lower extent when compared to the reference group of adults in the general population (Garnefski et al., 2002). These comparisons suggest that especially rumination should receive attention.

The following relationships between the cognitive coping strategies and anxiety symptoms were found: respondents who reported using self-blame, acceptance, rumination and/or catastrophising to a greater extent, also reported significantly higher levels of generalised anxiety, phobic anxiety, anxiety when anticipating an aeroplane flight, anxiety during a flight, anxiety in connection with aeroplanes in general (regardless of personal involvement in a flight situation), physical symptoms as an expression of anxiety in flight situations and distressing cognitions as an expression of anxiety in flight situations. These same relationships with generalised anxiety were found in studies which measured cognitive coping as a more general coping style (Garnefski et al., 2001; Garnefski et al., in press). The findings suggest that thoughts of self-blame for what you have experienced, thoughts of accepting what you have experienced and resigning yourself to what has happened, thinking about the feelings and thoughts associated with the flight, and thoughts of explicitly emphasising the terror of the flight are not an effective way to handle flying experiences and might lead to higher anxiety levels.

The present study suggests that several cognitive coping strategies are related to anxiety. Therefore, treatment programmes could pay attention to these cognitive coping strategies. This could be done by challenging the strategies which are maladaptive, namely self-blame, acceptance, rumination and catastrophising. Rumination, in particular, followed by acceptance and self-blame, should receive attention, since they are used to the highest extent by people with flight anxiety. This approach could be integrated into the well-established cognitive therapies (e.g. Beck, 1976; Ellis, 1962), which focus on changing dysfunctional and irrational cognitions. Many institutions treating flight anxiety include coping training and cognitive restructuring (van Gerwen and Diekstra, 2000; van Gerwen et al., in preparation). The present study gives important clues about which cognitive coping strategies should be challenged in their treatment programmes. To obtain a more comprehensive view, future studies should also focus on other coping strategies, such as behavioural coping strategies and the use of medication or alcohol to cope with flight anxiety.

Some methodological remarks have to be made. A limitation of the study was that cognitive coping strategies and anxiety were both measured by self-report instruments, which may have caused some bias. Future studies should also use other forms of data-collection, such as interviews or experiments. Including physiological measures for anxiety would also strengthen the research findings. Another limitation is that the study had a cross-sectional design and many aspects were measured retrospectively and referred to different points in time. Consequently, it is difficult to draw conclusions regarding the causality or temporal order of these variables. To solve these cause and effect issues, a longitudinal design should be applied. It would be interesting to follow people before, during and after a flight and obtain data on both cognitive coping strategies and anxiety symptoms at several time-points. Another point of concern is the representativeness of the respondents. Whether the findings also apply to people who are afraid to fly but who do not seek help, or to people who do not experience flight anxiety, cannot be told. On the other hand, a strength of the present study is that all people who turned for help for their fear of flying and who actually had made a flight during the last 10 years were included. The findings of the present study can be generalised to people who seek help for fear of flying. Another strength of the present study is that a variety of anxiety measures were used. The overall consistent findings make the results compelling.

Flying is part of life in modern societies. Large numbers of people are afraid to fly. Therefore it is important to find risk factors related to fear of flying. The present study clearly shows that cognitive coping strategies play an important role in relation to a variety of anxiety symptoms in people with flight anxiety. This can be used for the focus and content of treatment programmes for flight-anxiety.

References

Acierno, R.E., Hersen, M. and Van Hasselt, V.B. (1993), 'Interventions for Panic Disorder: A critical review of the literature', *Clinical Psychology Review*, Vol. 13, pp. 561–78.

Agras, S., Sylvester, D. and Oliveau, D. (1969), 'The Epidemiology of Common Fears and Phobias', *Comprehensive Psychiatry*, Vol. 2, pp. 151–6.

Arrindell, W.A. and Ettema, J.H.M. (1986), *SCL-90: Handleiding bij een multidimensionele psychopathologie-indicator* [*SCL-90: Manual for a multidimensional psychopathology indicator*], Lisse, The Netherlands: Swets and Zeitlinger.

Beck, A.T. (1976), *Cognitive Therapy and the Emotional Disorders*, New York: International Universities Press.

Clark, D.M. and Ehlers, A. (1993), 'An Overview of the Cognitive Theory and Treatment of Panic Disorder', *Applied and Preventive Psychology*, Vol. 2, pp. 131–9.

Dean, R.D. and Whitaker, K.M. (1982), 'Fear of Flying: Impact on the US air travel industry', *Journal of Travel Research*, pp. 7–17.

Derogatis, L.R. (1977), *SCL-90: Administation, scoring and procedures manual-I for the r(evised) version*, Baltimore, MD: Johns Hopkins University School of Medicine, Clinical Psychometrics Research Unit.

Ekeberg, Ø., Seeberg, I. and Ellertsen, B.B. (1989), 'The Prevalence of Flight Anxiety in Norwegian Airline Passengers', *Scandinavian Journal of Behaviour Therapy*, Vol. 17, pp. 213–22.

Ellis, A. (1962), *Reason and Emotion in Psychotherapy*, New York: Lyle Stuart.

Garnefski, N., Kraaij, V. and Spinhoven, Ph. (2001), 'Negative Life Events, Cognitive Emotion Regulation and Emotional Problems', *Personality and Individual Differences*, Vol. 30, pp. 1311–27.

Garnefski, N., Kraaij, V. and Spinhoven, Ph. (2002), *CERQ: Manual for the use of the Cognitive Emotion Regulation Questionnaire. A questionnaire for measuring cognitive coping strategies*, Leiderdorp, The Netherlands: DATEC V.O.F.

Garnefski, N., Legerstee, J., Kraaij, V., Van den Kommer, T. and Teerds, J. (in press), 'Cognitive Coping Strategies and Symptoms of Depression and Anxiety: A comparison between adolescents and adults', *Journal of Adolescence*.

Girodo, M. and Roehl, J. (1978), 'Cognitive Preparation and Coping Self-talk: Anxiety management during the stress of flying', *Journal of Consulting and Clinical Psychology*, Vol. 46, pp. 978–89.

Greco, T.S. (1989), 'A Cognitive-behavioral Approach to Fear of Flying: A practitioner's guide', *Phobia Practice and Research Journal*, Vol. 2, pp. 3–15.

Howard, W.A., Murphy, S.M. and Clarke, J.C. (1983), 'The Nature and Treatment of Fear of Flying: A controlled investigation', *Behavior Therapy*, Vol. 14, pp. 557–67.

Kraaij, V., Pruymboom, E. and Garnefski, N. (2002), 'Cognitive Coping and Depressive Symptoms in the Elderly: A longitudinal study', *Aging and Mental Health*, Vol. 6, No. 3, pp. 275–81.

Möller, A.T., Nortje, C. and Helders, S.B. (1998), 'Irrational Cognitions and the Fear of Flying', *Journal of Rational-Emotive and Cognitive-Behavior Therapy*, Vol. 16, pp. 135–48.

Nordlund, C.L. (1983), 'A Questionnaire of Swedes' Fear of Flying', *Scandinavian Journal of Behaviour Therapy*, Vol. 12, pp. 150–68.

Roberts, R.J. (1989), 'Passenger Fear of Flying: Behavioural treatment with extensive in-vivo exposure and group support', *Aviation, Space, and Environmental Medicine*, Vol. 60, pp. 342–8.

Scogin, F. and McElreath, L. (1994), 'Efficacy of Psychosocial Treatments for Geriatric Depression: A quantitative review', *Journal of Consulting and Clinical Psychology*, Vol. 62, pp. 69–74.

Thompson, R.A. (1991), 'Emotional Regulation and Emotional Development', *Educational Psychology Review*, Vol. 3, pp. 269–307.

van Gerwen, L.J. and Diekstra, R.F.W. (2000), 'Fear of Flying Treatment Programs for Passengers: An international review', *Aviation, Space, and Environmental Medicine*, Vol. 71, pp. 430–37.

van Gerwen, L.J., Arondeus, J.M., Diekstra, R.F.W. and Wolfger, R. (in preparation), 'Fear of Flying Treatment Programs for Passengers: An international update'.

van Gerwen, L.J., Spinhoven, Ph., Diekstra, R.F.W. and Van Dyck, R. (2002), 'Multicomponent Standardized Treatment Programs for Fear of Flying: Description and effectiveness', *Cognitive and Behavioral Practice*, Vol. 9, pp. 138–49.

van Gerwen, L.J., Spinhoven, Ph., Van Dyck, R. and Diekstra, R.F.W. (1999), 'Construction and Psychometric Characteristics of Two Self-report Questionnaires for the Assessment of Fear of Flying', *Psychological Assessment*, Vol. 11, pp. 146–58.

Walder, C.P., McCracken, J.S., Herbert, M., James, P.T. and Brewitt, N. (1987), 'Psychological Intervention in Civilian Flying Phobia: Evaluation and a three-year follow-up', *British Journal of Psychiatry*, Vol. 151, pp. 494–8.

Wilhelm, F.H. and Roth, W.T. (1997), 'Clinical Characteristics of Flight Phobia', *Journal of Anxiety Disorders*, Vol. 11, pp. 241–61.

Woods, R.T. (1993), 'Psychosocial Management of Depression', *International Review of Psychiatry*, Vol. 5, pp. 427–36.

Chapter 7

Multi-dimensional Approaches to the Treatment of Passenger Fear of Flying – Practical and Contextual Challenges

Richard J. Roberts

Introduction

Nearly 23 years have passed since the first fear of flying clinic was established in Australia and 13 years since I reported details of the programme and an evaluation of its effectiveness (Roberts, 1989). Since then the prevalence of people affected by a fear of flying appears to have increased and there has been a burgeoning of programmes designed to treat this condition (van Gerwen and Diekstra, 2000). The multidimensional type programme used in the Sydney clinics continues to be replicated. While the efficacy of these types of programmes continues to be reported (Bor, Parker and Papadopoulos, 2000), little headway has been made to determine which particular treatment regimes contribute to the most efficient mode of treatment delivery (Tortella-Feliu and Rivas, 2001; Ost, Brandberg and Alm, 1997; Borrill and Foreman, 1996).

While psycho-social research in this field must give priority to discovering the most efficient and viable means of treating a fear of flying, there are two other factors that require discussion. Firstly, regardless of the scientific merit of the different types of interventions, it is now well established that people affected by a fear of flying can obtain some symptomatic relief through a range of options (Tortella-Feliu and Rivas, 2001; Ost, Brandenberg and Alm, 1997; Bor, Parker and Papadopoulos, 2001; Capafons et al., 1999; Rothbaum and Hodges, 1999; Capafons, Sosa and Avero, 1997; Klein, 1999; Doctor, McVarish and Boone, 1990; Greco, 1989; Muhlberger et al., 2001; Capafons, Sosa and Vina, 1999), including programmes run by professional behavioural therapists of one kind or another as well as lay operators. Such programmes are sometimes sponsored by voluntary organisations or by private entrepreneurs. The responsibility for determining the different components of a programme is not necessarily confined to professionals. This mixture of lay and professional in organising programmes raises challenges in relation to a duty of care to clients and accountability for the services being provided to the public (Jones, 2000).

Secondly, the contemporary context in which these programmes operate includes such realities as decreasing financial and in-kind assistance often provided in the past by major airlines. The decrease in these types of contributions exposes clients to the real costs of such resource intensive programmes. Alternatively, abridging can take place based not upon psychological evidence but dictated by budgetary parameters. Long before 'September 11', major airlines started reassessing the benefits of underwriting many of the 'hidden costs' of programmes including the use of their personnel, facilities and complimentary or highly subsidised seats. Programmes that relied on these donated services must now reassess for practical and financial reasons what should be retained within the programme and how much of these costs could be recovered from increased client fees. Added to these costs are the rapidly increasing insurance premiums related to public liability and professional indemnity insurances.

In the light of these changing social contexts and their associated costs, it is doubtful that resource intensive multi-dimensional type programmes that invoke a wide range of treatment modalities (despite their popularity in the past and in spite of their reported efficacy) can continue in such resource intensive forms.

The purpose of this chapter is to explore a range of practical issues in mounting fear of flying programmes that rely on multi-dimensional approaches including psychological interventions, education, group support and *in vivo* exposure. These practical issues will be discussed within the context of contemporary changes to the airline industry, rising costs and insurance and professional accountability requirements.

In 1989 I reported the main features of the Sydney fear of flying clinic[1] (Roberts, 1989) including the different components of the eight week course, as well as an evaluation of the first 10 years of the clinic's operation. Relying on self-rating scales and semi-structured qualitative feedback, the results demonstrated a significant reduction in fear and discomfort achieved over an eight week period. Follow-up interviews showed the improvements in being able to fly with greater ease and less fear achieved during the clinic were being reported up to five years later.

Four core treatment modalities were provided in this multi-dimensional approach. Firstly, the psychological interventions including progressive muscle relaxation and guided imagery, systematic desensitisation and rational emotive strategies. Secondly, the educational programme, including on-site visits, arranged by the auspicing agency. Thirdly, the use of group work techniques to develop group cohesion and support. This was assisted by the use of volunteers who were present throughout the programme and travelled with the clients on the graduation flights. Finally, the programme used high *in vivo* exposures.

In terms of client feedback, a strong theme emerged of the perceived benefits of the 'hands-on approach' and the mutual support and help clients received from other members of the group, including the volunteers. This presumably referred to the use of extensive *in vivo* exposures as well as the benefits gained from a cohesive group.

The Multi-dimensional Approach

This chapter will now proceed by describing the different components of the programme. Challenges in presenting such a programme will then be discussed. It should be noted that not all components have been present in all clinics as the particular mix depended on the particular mix of personnel taking part in any one clinic. This information complements the details provided in the 1989 article and I make the assumption that the reader is familiar with this material.

1　Psychological Interventions

Progressive muscle relaxation and creative visualisation In a group setting, clients were taught progressive muscle relaxation (PMR) combined with creative visualisation. Clients were given opportunities to practice as a group at the initial meeting, at some sessions throughout the course, on a stationary aircraft and prior to each of the graduation flights. They were instructed to incorporate relaxation practice into their daily schedules and this component was promoted by all clinic personnel as a vital and necessary part of achieving a successful outcome. Each client was provided with a relaxation tape similar to the relaxation protocol used in the clinic. Clear instructions were given to clients about the most conducive settings to practice in, the importance of planning and time management in the use of the tape. An explanation was given of the need to devote greater periods of time in the initial stages of learning to relax with the aim of being able to eventually induce the desired level of relaxation in a shorter period of time and eventually without the assistance of the tape. By the time of the flight it was envisaged that each client would be able to induce a level of relaxation sufficient to control feelings of discomfort or fear. Some clients chose to access the tape using a Walkman and continued using the tape throughout the clinic and a few brought the tape and Walkman with them on the graduation flight.

At each session of the programme, clients would be reminded about their commitment to listening to the tape at least once each day and to practising relaxation exercises. From my observations, it was this component of the programme that was understood best by clients, organisers and the volunteer helpers. Providing a tape was a practical tool about which concrete instructions could be given. The tape was prepared especially by the psychologist taking the sessions and this provided familiarity in terms of both induction mode and voice. Many clients reported gaining benefit from the relaxation exercises not only in terms of the programme's aims but also in other areas of their personal and professional lives.

Systematic desensitisation At the initial class in each clinic some time was devoted to facilitating clients to share their previous flying experiences and especially their particular fear of flying. One reason for this was to enable each participant to compare their situation with others and to highlight the wide variety of factors and contexts that induced feelings of fear or discomfort. Even though these situations were many and varied they usually triggered the same set of reactions and symptoms. While most clients could quickly identify with the reactions to fear and other symptoms, it was usually the case that most were amazed at the wide variety of situations that produced those symptoms. For example, some people reported they flew quite comfortably in large wide-bodied aircraft and their fear was focused on small propeller powered aircraft. For others, the opposite was the case. Some clients found taking off most stressful, for others, it was landing.

In order to assist clients to focus on their own idiosyncratic situations they were instructed how to design a hierarchy of fear relevant to their own situation. This was achieved in part by providing a handout with a detailed example. The example illustrated how many different events associated with flying could be rank ordered from those that produced the most fear or discomfort (for example, 'turbulence') through to those events that produced no feelings of discomfort or maybe even feelings of pleasure and excitement (for example, 'planning an itinerary' or 'buying a ticket'). Each condition or event was written on a separate card and rank ordered to reflect a client's personal hierarchy. Clients were encouraged to think of at least 15 events.

Instruction was then provided as to how these events could be translated into imagery and combined with the relaxation protocol.

This component was introduced in week 4 by which time clients had achieved a degree of success with self-induced relaxation with the aid of the tape.

From my observations, this component of the programme was found useful by about half of the participants in any one clinic. In contrast to following the concrete and simple instructions pertaining to the relaxation exercises, this component required more understanding of the process and more initiative from clients. I suspected that some clients did not even attempt this as an 'add-on' to the basic PMR because it required more planning.

One of the disadvantages of not having the psychologist present at all sessions was that encouragement for the use of the different psychological interventions was left to the lay organisers and volunteers. Whereas all the organisers and volunteers had experienced first hand the benefits of PMR, not all either understood the theory of systematic desensitisation (despite explanations by the psychologist) or had used it themselves and hence encouragement for this aspect of behavioural treatment was spasmodic.

Rational emotive strategies Basic information on cognitive re-structuring including the relationship between emotions and belief systems were explained to clients during the course. Initially clients were requested to draw up lists of their own personal beliefs about flying and the kinds of emotions they had come to associate with these beliefs. As myths of flying were challenged in the education component of the programme, so clients were encouraged to deliberately re-write their lists substituting a more appropriate emotion.

Throughout the programme positive attitudes towards flying as well as the benefits to be achieved in the programme were promoted and reiterated. Clients were discouraged from looking for causes for their dysfunctional behaviours associated with flying and nor were other psychopathologies or family dynamics investigated. The focus was on a patent and rational approach. Any media coverage of incidents or accidents that occurred during a course was openly discussed through group facilitation and wherever possible, appropriate experts brought into the programme to discuss such events rather than relying on media sensationalism.

Clients were challenged to reconsider the feelings they associated with particular events in flying, especially in the light of expert information provided in the education component.

From my observations, attitude change did occur for a high proportion of clients as they were encouraged to develop 'new belief systems' through education and then to attach appropriate feelings and attitudes. As all the volunteers were pilots themselves, they were very useful role models in that they promoted flying as an enjoyable experience. They assisted clients to assimilate new information and thus facilitated the development of new attitudes to the flying experience.

2   Education

Educational presentations provided comprehensive basic and general knowledge about the principles of flight, aircraft design and maintenance, meteorology, air traffic control and safety at all levels. In addition to 'the facts', the presentation was aimed at dispelling common myths and to impart a realistic degree of confidence in the range of systems contributing to the success of a flight.

Experts from the different areas of aviation were brought in to speak to the group. This usually included captains and engineers, senior officers from air traffic control, the bureau of meteorology, air safety and so on. The use of recognised experts lent credibility to the knowledge they espoused.

An important role for the volunteer supporters before and after classes and during tea breaks, was to ensure that clients had understood the basic materials and also to answer questions that clients may not have had an opportunity to ask during formal sessions. This assisted clients to appreciate the relevance of information that had been presented.

From my observations, all clients found the education component fascinating and instructional. Many brought with them myths about flying as well as a poor comprehension of the basic knowledge; for example, principles of flight and the effects of weather conditions were usually not well understood. Sometimes simple explanations (for example, illustrating that 'turbulence' is nothing more than 'rough air') were all it took to help some clients re-craft their belief systems.

3   Group Support and Development of Group Cohesion

The development of a cohesive group was important in providing mutual support and a context in which learning and attitude change could occur. It also provided a 'safe' environment with others who appreciated some of the debilitating effects from the fear. A large proportion of clients revealed that they had been ashamed to admit their fear to others, often including family members and employers. For many clients, the initial meeting was the first occasion they had ever met so many people in a similar situation and who at least appreciated the symptoms they experienced. This provided a cathartic experience for many.

Throughout the programme clients came into regular contact with the volunteers. These were members of a women's aviation association. At some clinics, all clients were initially greeted by a volunteer and accompanied to the classroom. This was particularly important for those clients who had indicated in the initial questionnaire that they had a fear of travelling in elevators, as the clinic was conducted in a multi-storey building at the airport. So from the initial meeting an 'ethos of care' for clients was established.

At each session the same volunteers were present and within the first few weeks mutual associations were formed between volunteers and clients. From my observations, the development of a cohesive group was an important aspect of the success of the programme. Apart from being good role models, volunteers made a particular effort to challenge the dissemination of myths or sensationalism and helped clients refer back to the educational components and to ask questions of the experts when they presented.

4 *Extensive* In Vivo *Exposure*

All components of the clinics were conducted at a large domestic/international airport. This was an important contextual variable in familiarising clients with the noises and smells and other visual aspects associated with a busy airport.

In addition, tours of aircraft maintenance workshops, air traffic control and tower complex, flight simulators and airport facilities were arranged. These tours placed clients in the midst of a real life situation where they had opportunities to see, touch, smell and hear the peculiar aspects of an airport as well as to ask questions directly of employees in many different capacities in the airline industry. Even though classes were held in the early evening, all facilities visited were operational, so clients saw employees at work. This had the effect of 'normalising' the many different support activities associated with flying.

Of particular importance was the tour of a stationary aircraft, usually a 747. Clients were given the opportunity of wandering around, sitting at the controls, viewing the galley, using the galley lift and then being taken through a relaxation session on the aircraft. The opportunity to practise relaxation while actually on-board – and to make associations with the noises (air-conditioning), smells and cabin environment – was an important experience in linking relaxation with the context in which it was to be used.

The so-called 'graduation flights' proved powerful experiences. On each of these clients were paired with volunteers who were able to take the client through the actual flight as well as assist with relaxation and stress management as required. Until the tightening of security introduced in recent years, clients were also able to visit the flight deck during the flight.

A graduation lunch and short bus tour was organised at the flight destination and then clients prepared for the return flight. All clients were presented with certificates and other memorabilia to mark their achievement in completing the course and taking the graduation flight. From my observation, this provided an important real life situation in which clients could 'test' their newly acquired skills and where they could experience an actual flight in a supportive and educational environment.

Challenges

A multi-dimensional behavioural approach for treating a fear of flying in the form of group treatment presents numerous challenges relating to the specific interventions themselves as well as to the organisation of the programme as a whole. These challenges need to be addressed both by clinicians as well as others who seek to auspice such programmes.

Becoming More Efficient

The programme described was an effective form of intervention. Less than 2 per cent of clients failed to take the graduation flights. However, given its resource intensity it could not be described as an efficient treatment. While systematic outcome evaluation of this programme has not been undertaken in recent years, anecdotally, a high success rate has been maintained even with modifications and changes in personnel, auspice, increasing security restrictions and scarcity of resources once donated by the sponsor airline. Furthermore, current research is attempting to establish more efficient forms of treatment, for example (Bor, Parker and Papadopoulos, 2001).

Even though this programme was well established and has been operating since 1979, it remains unknown what particular components of the programme directly contribute to its success. It is assumed that each of the components contributed to the programme's effectiveness as well as working in concert with each other. Anecdotally, a high proportion of clients attributed their success to the relaxation exercises and the support provided by the volunteers and other members of the group. This could be explained because the relaxation exercises were the most easily understood by most clients and all experienced the positive feelings that resulted from high group cohesion. Until more carefully designed research is undertaken, the path to efficiency will remain impeded. However, in terms of an auspicing organisation, its primary concern is the outcome for clients. In the light of a package that has positive outcomes as it stands, there remained reluctance to superimpose a research component that might interfere with that outcome. To this could be added the general ethical issues of introducing research conditions on to a clinical protocol that is known to be effective, if not efficient.

While producing a high rate of success, when evaluated in terms of the percentage of clients who undertook the graduation flights successfully, such a comprehensive programme is not suitable for all clients wishing to reduce their fears of flying. The schedules of many potential clients may not permit attendance at the times the clinics are run given that only a limited number of clinics can be operated in this way each year. The time commitment required by the programme may not suit some potential clients (eight sessions of three hours each). Such a programme is not suitable for those with debilitating symptoms from other emotional conditions and those with English language or conceptual disabilities. Further research is required to address these issues.

Differential Importance of Components

As already mentioned, the programme produced improvements in the management of a fear of flying. However, it is unknown which components contributed to that efficacy and to what degree. This meant that the amount of time devoted to each component was decided on a pragmatic basis – what appeared to have worked in the past and the schedule drawn up for any one clinic influenced the time devoted to particular components as much as any scientific factors. For example, the amount of time spent with the group by the psychologist was partly determined by past arrangements and the effect of this expenditure on the clinic's budget. The psychologist suggested the need for a clinician's presence at more sessions but this was evaluated by the organisers against the budget and other pragmatic considerations that appeared to take precedence over purely clinical issues.

It is thus essential to develop knowledge which will guide the abridging of programmes and enable a more scientific approach to intensive programmes.

Individual versus Group Treatment

From a clinical perspective, the access to personnel and facilities that a group approach enabled provided a treatment environment that had many advantages over the clinician's rooms. Exposure to the real world related to flying facilitated habituation. This is not possible in clinical environments except through the use of fantasy.

In dealing with the group, the clinician was able to utilise standard group work techniques for developing cohesion. Such an experience was reported by clients as a powerful component of the treatment. This context enabled clients to 'normalise' their fear of flying experiences or at least compare them with other clients, be challenged by the debilitating effects reported by other clients and to form 'natural' helper associations in some cases.

The Clinician and the Auspicing Agency

It is important to note that the clinical contribution of the psychologist was seen by organisers as one component in the overall programme. On face value this is an accurate reflection of reality and it must be acknowledged an individual practitioner would find it very difficult to mount such a comprehensive programme. However, the tensions resulting from the interface between clinician and organisation and its volunteers needs acknowledgement.

Where any treatment option involves a multi-disciplinary team approach or a reliance on volunteers (no matter how well they are motivated and committed to the project), management of the tension between the parties will always be necessary. In the programme described above, the auspicing agency was an association of women pilots. From the inception of the programme they were very committed to this project as part of their voluntary service to the community. However, the extent to which they were committed to accepting clinical input in the design and management of the project was often dependent upon the personalities who played a leadership role in the organisation at any one time.

In practical terms there was often conflict in time management with the organisers balancing the different components of the programme. It was sometimes apparent that some organisers and some support volunteers relegated the role of the clinician to a subsidiary rather than a primary role. This was observed in educational or other components being allowed to run into the clinician's time with the group. This was sometimes outside the control of the clinician.

This tension was further illustrated on occasions when applicants for some courses had already been accepted prior to the clinician making an assessment of their suitability from their questionnaire application. The reasons for accepting the client were pragmatic rather than being subjected to any clinical scrutiny. These examples highlight the tension between a purely educational versus a clinical perspective to the programme, as well as a tension between adhering to a packaged formula versus individualisation. It might be these tensions arose from the different underlying theoretical assumptions of the organisers and the clinician.

Use of Volunteers

Despite the tensions referred to above, an undisputed strength of the programme was the advantage of being auspiced by a voluntary organisation. This provided a group of committed volunteers – all pilots – who for altruistic reasons provided individualised support and education to clients as well as facilitating group processes such as formation, cohesion building and termination of the treatment group. The use of volunteers meant that clients received considerable advantages that did not have to be factored into client fees.

On the other hand, while the use of volunteers brought advantages to the clients, the individual appreciation each volunteer had of the different components to the programme posed challenges to organisers and clinician alike. While the clinician conducted familiarisation meetings with the team prior to the commencement of each clinic, from my observations, there were different reactions from volunteers as to their roles and their own 'home spun' formulae about effective help for clients. While the relaxation component was probably the best understood psychological intervention, the understanding of and hence support for other behavioural treatment modes was variable. This was exacerbated as there were often different volunteers taking part in each clinic with only a core group of organisers who remained relatively constant. While this comment is not intended to question the commitment of volunteers – that was beyond doubt – nevertheless, the responsibility for oversight of volunteers' behaviour posed challenges for the clinician.

The presence of the volunteers on the graduation flights was particularly important because each client could be paired with a volunteer whose job it was to assist the client with their relaxation exercises as well as explain the technical aspects of the flight as it proceeded. While initially the clinician was paired with the 'most challenging' client in that particular group, this was later abandoned so that the clinician was free to move about the group in flight or to provide intensive assistance if the need arose. It was also found necessary to ensure that an additional volunteer remained at the base airport in the rare case where the need arose to off-load a client at the last moment.

Current Security Concerns

Since 11 September 2001 all security protocols have been extensively tightened. Prior to this, an important part of the graduation flights was the ability of the client to be taken to the flight deck to meet the flight crew as well as experience the working environment of a flight deck. This also provided an opportunity for the client to walk about the cabin in the company of his or her volunteer. It was often observed that those clients who forewent the opportunity on the forward flight usually took up the opportunity on the return flight as their confidence increased.

Such *in vivo* experiences are no longer possible for security reasons. Whether substitute experiences that can be provided in a flight simulator, for example, will prove as effective remains to be evaluated.

Professional Indemnity Insurance and Public Liability

With the increase in litigation both a clinician and an auspicing agency needs to be aware of the requirements for public liability and professional indemnity insurance coverage. In any intervention regime where there is potential for (unintended) harm, the rights and responsibilities of the parties need to be explicit. The use of volunteers in a treatment programme, no matter how effective, may in the future lead to practical, clinical and legal challenges. This is particularly important in the contemporary context where greater professional accountability is required by professional and registration bodies and where there has been a dramatic rise in public liability insurance premiums as well as professional indemnity insurance requirements. Such circumstances may require greater clinical as well as organisational accountability. This poses particular practical issues for the delineation and prescription of the roles of the professional and the volunteer as well as auspicing organisations. The need to effect these insurance covers will add to the costs to be passed on to clients.

Conclusion

A fear of flying has many irrational elements to it. To this has been added the concerns generated by such events as 'September 11'. A growing number of programmes for the treatment of passenger fear of flying reflects the needs that many people have to manage their fears and dysfunctional symptoms associated with a fear of flying. The multi-dimensional type programme described in this chapter continues to be effective. However, with increased costs and fewer resources, it is now a matter of urgency that further research establishes a more efficient treatment regime. In addition, greater professional accountability means that programmes utilising clinical and educational components will need to open to scrutiny the delineation of responsibility and accountability provided by different members of a treatment team.

Note

1   Since the fear of flying clinic in Sydney was established it has been auspiced by two organisations, firstly the Australian Women Pilots' Association (NSW Branch) and secondly by Fearless Flyers Inc. While there are organisational and political differences between the two agencies, for the purposes of this chapter and its content, I will be treating them as similar. It should be noted that since 1979 both clinical and organisational personnel have changed. These changes have resulted in modifications in the overall programme from time to time. However, for the purposes of this chapter, I will not refer to these periodic changes. It should also be noted that the observations reported here are those of the author relating generally to the period he was actively involved in the clinic as well as other anecdotal material.

References

Bor, R., Parker, J. and Papadopoulos, L. (2000), 'Psychological Treatment of a Fear of Flying', *Counselling Psychology Review*, Vol. 15, No. 2, pp. 13–17.

Bor, R., Parker, J. and Papadopoulos, L. (2001), 'Brief, Solution-focused Initial Treatment Sessions for Clients with a Fear of Flying', *Counselling Psychology Review*, Vol. 16, No. 4, pp. 32–40.

Borrill, J. and Foreman, E. (1996), 'Understanding Cognitive Change: A qualitative study of the impact of cognitive-behavioural therapy on fear of flying', *Clinical Psychology and Psychotherapy*, Vol. 3, No. 1, pp. 62–74.

Capafons, J.I., Avero, P., Sosa, C.D. and Lopez-Curbelo, M. (1999), 'Fear of Flying: Evaluation of an exposure treatment program', *Psicologia Conductual*, Vol. 7, No. 1, pp. 119–35.

Capafons, J.I., Sosa, C.D. and Avero, P. (1997), 'Systematic Desensitization in the Treatment of Fear of Flying', *Psicothema*, Vol. 9, No. 1, pp. 17–25.

Capafons, J.I., Sosa, C.D. and Vina, C.M. (1999), 'A Reattributional Training Program as a Therapeutic Strategy for Fear of Flying', *Journal of Behavior Therapy and Experimental Psychiatry*, Vol. 30, No. 4, pp. 259–72.

Doctor, R.M., McVarish, C. and Boone, R.P. (1990), 'Long Term Behavioral Treatment Effects for the Fear of Flying', *Phobia Practice and Research Journal*, Vol. 3, No. 1, pp. 33–42.

Greco, T.S. (1989), 'A Cognitive-behavioral Approach for Fear of Flying: A practitioner's guide', *Phobia Practice and Research Journal*, Vol. 2, No. 1, pp. 3–15.

Jones, D.R. (2000), 'Fear of Flying – No Longer a Symptom without a Disease', *Aviation, Space and Environmental Medicine*, Vol. 71, No. 4, pp. 438–40.

Klein, R. (1999), 'Treating Fear of Flying with Virtual Reality Exposure Therapy', in VandeCreek, L. and Jackson, T.L. (eds), *Innovations in Clinical Practice: A sourcebook*, Sarasota, FL: Professional Resource Press/Professional Resource Exchange Inc.

Muhlberger, A., Herrmann, M.J., Wiedemann, G., Ellgring, H. and Pauli, P. (2001), 'Repeated Exposure of Flight Phobics to Flights in Virtual Reality', *Behaviour Research and Therapy*, Vol. 39, No. 9, pp. 1033–50.

Ost, L.G., Brandberg, M. and Alm, T. (1997), 'One versus Five Sessions of Exposure in the Treatment of Flying Phobia', *Behaviour Research and Therapy*, Vol. 35, No. 11, pp. 987–96.

Roberts, R.J. (1989), 'Passenger Fear of Flying: Behavioural treatment with extensive in-vivo exposure and group support', *Aviation Space and Environmental Medicine*, Vol. 60, pp. 342–8.

Rothbaum, B.O. and Hodges, L.F. (1999), 'The Use of Virtual Reality Exposure in the Treatment of Anxiety Disorders', *Behavior Modification*, Vol. 23, No. 4, pp. 507–25.

Tortella-Feliu, M. and Rivas, M.A.F. (2001), 'Treatment for the Fear of Flying: A review', *International Journal of Clinical and Health Psychology*, Vol. 1, No. 3, pp. 547–69.

van Gerwen, L.J. and Diekstra, R.F. (2000), 'Fear of Flying Treatment Programs for Passengers: An international review', *Aviation Space and Environmental Medicine*, Vol. 71, No. 4, pp. 438–40.

Chapter 8

Rational Emotive Behaviour Therapy for a Fear of Flying

Kasia Szymanska

Introduction

Thirty years ago Albert Ellis, the founder of rational emotive behaviour therapy (REBT), published a book entitled *How to Master your Fear of Flying* (1977). In this book he described how he overcame his own fear, in particular the 'awfulness of dying' using REBT principles. Since that time, REBT has flourished and it is now practised all over the world. Being an active directive short term therapy which can be used with individuals and groups, it is ideally suited to the treatment of a fear of flying.

Originally developed in 1955, REBT aims to help clients to make long-lasting profound philosophical changes (Dryden et al., 1999). At the time, Ellis, a clinical psychologist, was a practising psychoanalyst. However, he became increasing dissatisfied with psychoanalysis as an effective medium of change for clients. He began to experiment with other forms of more active therapy and take on board the work of psychologists such as Adler and the Stoic philosophers, which emphasised the philosophical underpinnings of psychological disturbance as opposed to childhood experiences. In particular, he was influenced by the work of the Greek philosopher Epictetus who stated that, 'People are disturbed not by things, but by the views which they take of them'.

Prior to 1961, REBT was known as rational therapy. Ellis changed the name to rational emotive therapy to take into account the influence of emotions. In 1993 he changed the name again to rational emotive behaviour therapy to emphasise the role of behaviour in the acquisition of psychological problems. In this chapter I outline how REBT views the acquisition and maintenance of emotional disturbance, the assessment procedure, the techniques used in practice and end with a case study to illustrate the application of REBT to a fear of flying.

REBT Theory

The basic premise of REBT is that human beings have a biological tendency to think both rationally and irrationally. Rationally, individuals have a propensity towards self-preservation, creativity and to combat problems. Irrationally, individuals can be self destructive, superstitious, have a tendency towards procrastination and irrational behaviour. REBT theory maintains that irrational thinking about an event; not the event itself contributes to emotional/ psychological disturbance in individuals. The acquisition of emotional disturbance can be illustrated using the ABCDE model (see Figure 8.1).

A   Activating event/experience/inferences about A
⇓

B   Irrational beliefs, evaluative beliefs about A which tend to be absolutist, rigid and unconditional
⇓

C   Emotional and behavioural consequences, which are unhealthy emotions and self defeating behaviours
⇓

D   Focuses on disputing irrational beliefs to help individuals develop healthy behaviours and emotions
⇓

E   Effective and new outlook

Figure 8.1   The ABCDE model

Rational and Irrational Beliefs

Dryden, Neenan and Yankura (1999) consider rational beliefs to be non-absolute, logical, consistent with reality and preferential in the pursuit of goals. Rational beliefs are expressed in the form of preferences, wishes and wants; e.g., 'I would prefer there to be no turbulence on the flight, however, if there is, it's not the end of the world'. On the other hand, irrational beliefs are absolute, inconsistent with reality, illogical and a hindrance in the attainment of goals. They are expressed in the form of demands such as 'shoulds', 'musts' and 'oughts', e.g., 'I must not feel anxious on this flight'. Furthermore, REBT theory states that adhering to irrational beliefs leads individuals to draw three main conclusions. These are known as derivatives and are evaluative by nature. They are:

- 'awfulising' – believing that a situation is 100 per cent bad or awful;
- low frustration tolerance or 'I can't stand it' – being unable to cope with discomfort; and
- damnation – being extremely critical of oneself and the world.

In accordance with cognitive theory, REBT theory also states that cognitive distortions play a role emotional disturbance. These distortions include all-or-nothing thinking, emotional reasoning, labelling and fortune telling. However, REBT places a greater emphasis on working with shoulds, musts and oughts rather than with cognitive distortions.

Emotions

REBT theory also differentiates between healthy and unhealthy emotions. Healthy emotions include concern, disappointment, sadness and remorse and occur as a result of an individual's rational beliefs. For example, a passenger who thinks that 'I would prefer to have a stress free flight, but if I don't that doesn't mean that I can never fly again' (rational belief) may feel concerned about flying but not overly anxious, while a passenger who perceives that they must be in control on the flight (irrational belief) is more likely to feel stressed and anxious. Other unhealthy emotions include guilt, shame, depression and hurt.

The Differences between REBT and Cognitive Behaviour Therapy (CBT)

Essentially, REBT can be classed as cognitive behavioural approach. However there are a number of key differences between the two theories.

- The first difference lies in REBT's focus on unconditional beliefs and the process of disputing these beliefs. Ellis stated that cognitive behaviour therapists 'ignore discovering and disputing their absolutist shoulds, musts and demands' (Palmer and Dryden, 1993).
- The second difference is REBT's emphasis on, and disputing of, evaluative beliefs such as awfulising, which stem from the client's unconditional rigid beliefs, 'It would be really awful if I lost control on the plane'.
- The third difference is in REBT's greater use of emotive techniques such as shame attacking and rational emotive imagery to achieve emotional change.
- The fourth difference is importance placed on profound philosophical change. REBT aims to help clients to challenge their irrational inflexible,

'absolutist philosophies' and replace them with rational, flexible, 'tolerant philosophies, (Dryden et al., 1999).
• The fifth difference is the distinction in REBT between healthy and unhealthy emotions.

Assessment

Dryden, Neenan and Yankura (1999) state that the goal for therapists is 'to help their clients to minimise the frequency with which they experience emotional disturbance and engage in self-defeating patterns of behaviour' (p. 52). In doing so, rational emotive behaviour therapists conduct a thorough assessment of the client's problem(s) using the ABCDE model, while adopting an active-directive approach with clients within a psychoeducational framework.

In keeping with other cognitive behavioural approaches, rational emotive behaviour therapists advocate the use of questionnaires to collect information about their clients. One such questionnaire is the biographical information form developed at the Albert Ellis Institute for Emotive Behaviour Therapy (Ellis, 1968). This comprehensive 46-question form, in addition to providing biographical information about the client, asks questions about the client's past and present symptoms, their goals, good and bad points and what they would like to change about themselves. Having collected the client's biographical information the first step in assessment is to develop a client problem list (Dryden, 1998). The second step is to assess the client's problem(s) using the ABCDE model described earlier.

This involves a four stage process; firstly, the assessment of the activating event, that triggers B, the client's irrational belief. To elicit the most significant aspect of the activating event, therapists often use the inference chaining at this point. This technique involves asking a series of questions, using, 'Let's say that is true, then what' to identify the critical A. Secondly, rational emotive behaviour therapists assess C, the emotional and behavioural consequences stemming from B, paying particular attention to the verbalised unhealthy emotions. Thirdly, using questioning, rational emotive behaviour therapists assess the B. A 'typical' question used is, 'What were you telling yourself about A to make yourself disturbed at C?' (Ellis et al., 1997). The fourth and final stage is to ascertain the client's goal(s) for therapy. Once the assessment is complete the disputing of irrational belief (D) and the development of an effective and new outlook (E) is focused on. Unlike other cognitive behavioural approaches, REBT does not stipulate the need to make a case formulation, on the basis of which therapeutic strategies are implemented. Rather, REBT stresses the need to teach clients the ABCDE model to help them contextualise their problems (Dryden, 1998).

Practice

The aim of practice in REBT is to promote both intellectual and emotional insight using cognitive behavioural, emotive and imaginal techniques. Therapists initially use disputing to help clients develop rational insight before enhancing emotional insight. Neenan and Dryden (2000) refer to the 'head-gut' split as a way of distinguishing between intellectual and emotional insight. The client may understand intellectually that their beliefs are irrational, however they may not feel this in their stomach.

Cognitive Techniques

From a cognitive perspective, rational emotive behaviour therapists consider disputing as a key process in the development of rational beliefs. The three key forms used are logical, empirical and pragmatic disputing. Logical disputing focuses on helping clients to see that their thinking is not logical. Questions used include: 'Where is the logic?', 'Does it logically follow that because you want a smooth flight therefore you must have it?', 'Can you see any inconsistencies in your thinking?' Empirical disputing helps clients to see that their thinking is not consistent with reality. Questions used include: 'Where is the evidence that you must not feel anxious?', 'What do you mean you can't stand flying, you've been standing it for years?' Pragmatic disputing involves showing the client that sticking to their irrational beliefs is not advantageous. For example the therapist might ask: 'Where does it get you to believe that you must be in control at all times during the flight rather than anxious?' Clients can also write down the advantages and disadvantages of holding onto their beliefs either on a notepad or on a whiteboard.

In addition, rational emotive therapists dispute the three derivatives described earlier in the chapter: awfulising, low frustration tolerance and damnation. Disputing awfulising involves helping clients to view their problems as really bad as opposed to awful, as rational emotive behaviour theory maintains that the word awful stems from the irrational belief meaning, '101 per cent bad, or worse then it absolutely must be' (Dryden, 1987). Therapists often use a 0–100 scale of badness to illustrate to clients that no experience is 100 per awful, despite their original assertion.

Disputing low frustration tolerance involves helping clients to see that despite believing that they 'can't stand it', they do in fact 'stand it', albeit feeling uncomfortable. Disputing damnation involves challenging clients' global evaluations of themselves, such as, 'I'm worthless' or 'I'm useless', as this type of evaluation does not take into account the client's complexity, i.e., their traits, their actions and cognitions.

Behavioural techniques   Rational emotive behaviour therapy argues that behavioural techniques serve to help clients internalise their rational ideas and act on them.

In vivo exposure is one of the most commonly used behavioural strategies. Clients are asked to confront their fear in situ until their level of anxiety reduces. Of course, unless the client has sizeable sums of money to spare it is impossible to ask a client to fly on a regular basis until their anxiety decreases. Instead, the client with a fear of crashing may confront their anxiety by watching films about planes and plane crashes, over and over again until their anxiety levels decrease. *In vivo* exposure can also be used with clients who experience anticipatory anxiety at the airport prior to flying. An *in vivo* exercise for clients with anticipatory anxiety would involve asking clients to go to and stay at the airport until their anxiety decreases. In both cases, clients would be encouraged to cognitively dispute their irrational beliefs while practising the *in vivo* exercises, and not to engage in safety behaviours. This may include having an alcoholic drink at the airport to 'calm their nerves' or closing their eyes when the 'crash sequence' happens on the film (if this is the client's greatest fear).

Learning to recognise behavioural cues that can trigger a downward spiral can also be helpful to some clients. For example, the client who tenses their shoulders as soon as they think about flying would be encouraged to relax their shoulders and then practice challenging their irrational beliefs about flying.

Emotive techniques   Emotive techniques are used to promote emotional insight and are always used in conjunction with cognitive and behavioural techniques, as emotional insight is difficult to achieve on its own.

Shame-attacking exercises, which are specific to REBT, involve encouraging clients to act in a manner which encourages other people to notice them. For example, a client who has a fear of 'going crazy' while on the plane, such as running to the doors and trying to open them and at the same time worrying about what other passengers would think of him, would be encouraged to act in a shameful manner while on 'dry land'. The client may be asked to go into their local pub and shout loudly, 'I'm a flying phobic', with the aim of helping them to see that just because they are acting in a crazy manner, it does not make them a crazy person.

Authentic self-disclosure is a technique developed by Ellis and Knaus (1977) and is used to help clients to verbalise their weaknesses with the aim of helping them to accept themselves despite other people's perceived disapproval. For example, an executive with a flying phobia would tell his colleagues that he has a fear of crashing.·

Emotive verbalisation involves getting clients to dispute their irrational beliefs in a loud and persistent manner. A client, who believes they 'can't bear feeling anxious on the plane' would be asked to forcefully remind themselves in a loud voice, 'I CAN STAND IT even if I don't like it', to strengthen their emotional understanding of their new outlook (E).

Imagery techniques These techniques can be used as an adjunct to the above techniques to challenge irrational beliefs and deepen insight.

Rational emotive imagery (REI) was developed by Maultsby and then adapted by Ellis to use in REBT (1974). Clients are asked to imagine a situation (A) that contributes to their disturbance and feel the accompanying unhealthy emotions (C) and then to dispute the irrational beliefs which contribute to C. Then they are asked to picture themselves changing the unhealthy emotion to a healthy one and to replace the irrational beliefs with rational beliefs. In order to perfect this technique, clients are asked to practise the procedure on a daily basis.

Coping imagery is used to help clients imagine themselves coping with the flight and incorporates them dealing with their perceived negative aspects of the flight, such as their irrational beliefs pertaining to a lack of control and turbulence. Bor et al. (2000) suggest the following five step process to help clients cope:

- step 1: think about your journey;
- step 2: identify what you are most anxious about in relation to the journey;
- step 3: think about how you can overcome your anxiety;
- step 4: visualise yourself coping with the journey, dealing with all the problems;
- step 5: practise this coping imagery on a regular basis.

Clients are then encouraged to practise coping imagery for at least 20 minutes a day.

A key aspect of REBT is the completion of homework assignments. These serve to strengthen the client's rational beliefs through practice. When setting homework assignments it is important that they are set collaboratively and target the client's irrational beliefs (Dryden et al., 1999). Like cognitive behaviour therapists, rational emotive behaviour therapists also encourage clients to use self-help materials to help them gain greater insight into their problems.

A Case Study

This case study is divided into three stages and focuses on Ken, a 35-year-old engineer who experienced severe anxiety while on a long-haul flight. Ken was a seasoned traveller and had not experienced any previous anxiety about flying. Prior to the flight, he had been working long hours for four months and on getting to the airport he sat in the bar to have a couple of drinks and relax before getting on the flight. He first experienced symptoms of anxiety when the plane started to taxi towards the runway. His heart started to race, he felt dizzy and wanted to get out of the plane. He described 'feeling closed in' and noticed that he was sweating profusely. Once the flight was airborne his symptoms 'came and went'. He felt better after having an alcoholic drink but at times felt 'trapped' especially as he was sitting in the window seat. In addition, he felt 'really stupid' and imagined that the passenger next to him probably thought that he was 'mad man', which really worried him, especially in the light of the events on 11 September 2001. He came for therapy because he was planning another long-haul trip and 'couldn't bear going through all that again'.

The Beginning Stage (Sessions 1–3)

Sessions 1–3 involved an assessment of Ken's key problem(s) and goal setting. Ken easily identified his key problem as 'a dread of flying' and his goal was to fly while keeping in control of his feelings. The first step at this stage was to assess the A, secondly to link the A to the C, and thirdly to assess the B. An example of the dialogue pertaining to assessing the critical A went as follows:

Therapist:	When did you first feel anxious about the flight?
Ken:	When the plane started to taxi towards the runway.
Therapist:	OK for the moment, imagine yourself sitting in the 747 by the window, what are you most anxious about?
Ken:	I feel trapped I want to get out.
Therapist:	Okay, what is so anxiety provoking for you about that?
Ken:	I might go and do something stupid like stand up and shout, 'let me out'.
Therapist:	And if you did?
Ken:	They'll all think I'm crazy, mad, how embarrassing!
Therapist:	So Ken, what are you most worried about, feeling trapped, feeling stupid, or the other passengers thinking you are crazy?
Ken:	The other passengers thinking I'm crazy.
Therapist:	So Ken, the bottom line is that you're worried about making a fool of yourself on the plane (the critical A).
Ken:	Of course I am, wouldn't anyone?

Therefore, using inference chaining the client's critical A was discovered and then linked to the C, a feeling of, and symptoms of anxiety. Next Ken's irrational beliefs were assessed, which were:

- It would be the end of the world if I made a fool of myself (awfulising);
- I couldn't stand it if that happened (LFT);
- I'm inadequate if I show myself up (damnation).

Ken's use of alcohol prior to and during the flight was also discussed at this point. The therapist explained to Ken that alcohol was a depressant and only served to make him feel worse and prevented him from getting used to flying. At this stage Ken was also encouraged to use bibliotherapy to learn more about flying phobia. The therapist suggested that he buy *Stress Free Flying* (Bor et al., 2000) to help him understand his fear.

Middle Stage (Sessions 4–6)

The focus of these sessions was on disputing Ken's irrational beliefs, encouraging him to develop rational beliefs and implementing emotive and imagery techniques to facilitate change.

An example of disputing Ken's belief 'I must not make a fool of myself' follows:

Therapist:	Now we are going to dispute the irrational belief, I must not make a fool of myself.
Ken:	Okay.
Therapist:	Do you agree that this belief contributes to you feeling anxious?
Ken:	Yes.
Therapist:	Okay, Ken, can you tell me where is it written that you must not make a fool of yourself?
Ken:	Nowhere, it's in my head.
Therapist:	Does holding onto this belief help you to reach your goal, which is not to feel anxious?
Ken:	No it doesn't, but I don't want to feel like a total fool.
Therapist:	OK, Ken so while you accept logically it doesn't help you to hold onto the irrational belief, you are still worried about making a fool of yourself.
Ken:	Yes.
Therapist:	Ken can I ask you to describe this therapy room in its totality using only four words?
Ken:	I can try, it's square, light, has a window and blue.
Therapist:	That's good but you haven't accounted for the furniture or even us sitting in it.
Ken:	Yes, I know but that would be impossible, I would need to use more then four words.
Therapist:	That's right, it's impossible to describe a room using only four words yet you describe yourself using only one word, 'fool'. Now Ken, what is more complex, you or the room?
Ken:	Me, of course.
Therapist:	In that case do you think it is logical to describe yourself taking into account your complexity using only one word.
Ken:	No, I see what you mean.
Therapist:	Okay, now on the basis of what we have discussed previously about demands vs preferences what can you tell yourself instead?
Ken:	I'd prefer not to make a fool of myself, however if I did it would mean that I was acting in a foolish way but it wouldn't make me a complete fool.
Therapist:	That's right, now can you write that down.

The therapist and Ken continued to dispute his derivatives and write down rational responses. To strengthen his belief in the rational beliefs, Ken wrote down the irrational and rational beliefs on a flashcard and as part of his agreed homework read the list three times a day in a loud voice to deepen his cognitive and emotional understanding. The therapist also taught Ken to relax his shoulders and use the coping imagery technique described earlier for 20 minutes every day.

End Stages (Sessions 7–8)

In the last two sessions, the therapist and Ken went over the techniques discussed in the previous sessions to deepen rational and emotional insight. The possibility of relapse was also discussed and the therapist encouraged Ken not to put himself down if he did relapse but rather to challenge the irrational belief that 'he should not relapse' and continue vigorously to challenge his irrational beliefs. The therapist also suggested that Ken should read 'How to Maintain and Enhance your Rational Emotive Therapy Gain' written by Albert Ellis and available on the Internet at http://www/rebt/org/essays.

Conclusion

While REBT falls within the arena of cognitive behavioural approaches, it has a number of qualities which distinguish it from mainstream cognitive behavioural theories. These include the focus on demands that clients make of themselves, inference chaining, evaluative beliefs and the strategies used to promote rational and emotional insight. Being short term and therefore cost-effective and with an emphasis on teaching clients to be their own therapists also makes it ideally suited to the treatment of flying phobia.

References

Bor, R., Josse, J. and Palmer, S. (2000), *Stress Free Flying*, Dinton: Mark Allen Publishing Ltd.

Dryden, W. (1987), *Counselling Individuals: The rational-emotive approach*, London: Taylor and Francis.

Dryden, W. (1998), 'Understanding Persons in the Context of their Problems: A rational emotive behaviour therapy perspective', in Brunch, M. and Bond, F. (eds), *Beyond Diagnosis: Case formulation approaches in CBT*, London: John Wiley and Sons.

Dryden, W., Neenan, M. and Yankura, J. (1999), *Counselling Individuals: A rational emotive behavioural handbook*, London: Whurr.

Ellis, A. (1968), *Biographical Information Form*, New York: Institute for Rational Emotive Therapy.

Ellis, A. (1977), *How to Master your Fear of Flying*, New York: Curtis.

Ellis, A., Gordon, J., Neenan, M. and Palmer, S. (1997), *Stress Counselling: A rational emotive behaviour approach*, London: Cassell.

Ellis, A. and Knaus, W.J. (1977), *Overcoming Procrastination*, New York: Albert Ellis Institute for Rational Emotive Behavior Therapy.

Mautsby, M.C. Jr and Ellis, A. (1974), *Techniques for Using Rational-emotive Imagery*, New York: Institute for Rational-Emotive Therapy.

Neenan, N. and Dryden, W. (2000), *Essential Rational Emotive Behaviour Therapy*, London: Whurr.

Palmer, S. and Dryden, W. (1993), 'Ellis on REBT: Stephen Palmer and Windy Dryden interview Albert Ellis', *The Rational-Emotive Therapist*, Vol. 1, No. 2, pp. 44–52.

Chapter 9

Cognitive-behavioural Treatment of Fear of Flying – Follow-up at Two Years

Øivind Ekeberg, Johannes Arnesen and Ingerid Seeberg

Introduction

Despite the very low risk associated with scheduled flights, many people are afraid of flying.

Prevalence studies from Norway and Sweden have revealed that 5–10 per cent of the adult population never fly because of flight phobia and that about 50 per cent are apprehensive of flying (Ekeberg, Seeberg and Ellertsen, 1989; Nordlund, 1983). There are, however, rather few controlled studies of the treatment of flight phobia, and some of them suffer from methodological problems. Solyom et al. (1973) found three behaviour techniques, including aversion relief with the use of electric shocks, equally effective, and better than group psychotherapy. The difference, however, was not significant at an 8–24 months follow-up. Denholtz et al. (1975) used an automated audiovisual treatment administered by non-professionals applied to a selected number of patients, 47 per cent of whom had previously been treated for flight phobia. Three different techniques were administered, and those failing in one were later transferred to the treatment considered the best. At a three-and-a-half year follow-up, 60 per cent had flown, 88 per cent of those considered successfully treated (Denholtz et al., 1978). Howard et al. (1983), found four behavioural techniques equally successful in the treatment of a selected number; 23 per cent were previously treated for flight phobia. Girodo et al. (1978), applied cognitive preparation and coping self-talk in a study of undergraduate females. During the post-treatment flight, a planned unexpected missed landing was encountered in order to help differentiating the treatment effect. No differential coping effectiveness was demonstrated throughout the normal course of the flight, whereas during the missed landing, the self statement trained subjects coped better. At a four-and-a-half months follow-up, no measurement of the number of flights post-treatment was made. Haug et al. (1987), in a study of 10 selected patients, found consonant behavioural treatment superior to non-consonant. Nordlund has made two studies, one including a comparison of the number of flights one year before and after treatment (1979), and one with two follow-ups at six months and one year (1984). Both studies, however, lacked control groups. Walder et al. (1987) used three long sessions with information, graded exposure and group support. Ost et al. (1997) compared patients randomly assigned to two treatment conditions: one-session (three hours) of massed treatment, or five sessions (six hours) of gradual exposure and cognitive restructuring. Airline companies offering treatment for fear of flying most often offer treatment in groups of 4–15 (Van Gerwen et al., 2000), but even though an extensive number of participants have been treated, scientific publications are rather few.

There are, thus, a limited number of controlled studies in the field, and they differ considerably regarding methods, outcome criteria and follow-up procedures. Various behavioural methods are used, generally with positive outcome; usually, however, without long-term follow-ups. None of the above studies have investigated whether the treatment would also influence phobic anxiety in other areas.

The aim of the present investigation has been to study:

1) the effect of a cognitive/behavioural treatment programme on flight anxiety in a self-selected sample of flight phobics;
2) whether the treatment effects remained at six months and two years follow-up;
3) whether the treatment might influence other phobic symptoms.

We have previously published data from the first seven groups of anxious fliers treated by us, showing less flight anxiety, more flights undertaken after treatment, less use of alcohol and tranquillisers and fewer other phobic symptoms (Ekeberg, Seeberg and Ellertsen, 1990).

Material and Methods

A small announcement was made in a Norwegian newspaper (*Aftenposten*) during the summer of 1983 advertising the opening of a course aiming at reducing or eliminating fear of flying. No subsequent advertisements have been necessary, as there have always been enough applicants. There have been several reports about the project in journals and newspapers. Some of the participants have applied for treatment after having heard about it from relatives or friends. The model has also been applied in most of the cities that are served by the airline company, Braathens, in Norway.

The study includes 414 participants (270 women, 144 men) who attended the flight phobia treatment programme between 1983 and 1993. They comprise the first 34 groups treated. The mean age for women was 40.4 ± 0.8 (SE) (range 17–67 years), and for men 39.7 ± 0.6 (range 20–66 years) (ns). Seventy-seven per cent were married/cohabiting, 15 per cent were single, 7 per cent divorced and 1 per cent widowed. Eighty-seven per cent were in regular employment, 9 per cent were housewives, 3 per cent students and 1 per cent retired. 'Other nervous problems' were reported by 51 per cent, and 34 per cent had previously been treated by a psychiatrist/psychologist. As shown in Table 9.1, 6 per cent had never flown before, 48 per cent had flown during the previous year and 12 per cent previously, but not during the last 10 years.

The study followed a prospective longitudinal quasi-experimental design. The treatment programme was run once a week for six weeks in groups of 12–15 participants. Three or four groups were treated each year. Applicants were registered on a waiting list and entered treatment accordingly. None was rejected and, thus, the sample was self-selecting. Assessments were performed pre-treatment, post-treatment and at follow-ups after six months and two years.

Table 9.1   Time since last flight before treatment according to gender (%)

	Females	Males
Never flown	7	4
<1 year	46	52
1–2 years	19	13
3–5 years	11	8
6–9 years	8	8
>10 years	10	15
Total	101	100

Treatment Programme

The treatment programme was run once a week for six weeks, four hours each time from 5 pm. On the first day, the group leaders presented themselves and the program. The participants then presented themselves and were encouraged to try to specify their discomfort. They were invited to clarify their thoughts and feelings about flying, and their previous experiences. Many said that they were afraid of flying because they were afraid of dying. They were then encouraged to explain how a flight aroused this feeling of risk, and what specifically they expected to go wrong. It soon becomes evident that lack of knowledge creates great possibilities for negative and catastrophic expectations.

A short film was shown, demonstrating the safety checks and procedures of various components of the aeroplanes. On the following days, 2–3 hour lectures were given by a pilot, an engineer, a cabin attendant and a medical doctor. The technical lecture focused on aspects that make it possible for a plane to fly, and how much strain an aircraft can tolerate. The pilot's lecture focused on how to fly, instruments, safety procedures, back-up systems and aerodynamics. The medical doctor focused on the physical manifestations of anxiety. After each lecture, there was time for questions. On the fifth day, the pilot took the participants on a 15–20 minute flight demonstration in a cockpit simulator, three at a time. On the sixth day, the participants were taken to the control tower and the radar room, where the staff there gave demonstrations. Two other short films were shown, one demonstrating flight procedures as experienced from the cockpit and the control tower and another from the testing of aeroplanes. A psychiatrist (ØE) lead a group session each day, covering topics such as cognitive restructuring, anxiety and how to cope with it, followed by training in breathing and relaxation. There was no focus on psychodynamic reasons for the flight anxiety and deeper psychological problems related to other conflicts were given minimum attention. The approach was cognitive, mainly focusing on negative expectations, trying to correct catastrophic beliefs like 'imagine if ...'. There was also major focus on conditional reflexes and the misinterpretation of several perceptions. An emphasis was put on creating strong group cohesion, and the atmosphere was generally mutually supportive.

Three days after the sixth session, the participants were followed by 3–4 of the teachers on a regular domestic flight to the city of Stavanger, with a flight time of approximately 30 minutes on each leg. Braathens' technical department is in Stavanger, and the participants were shown around aeroplanes undergoing various degrees of service and overhaul. At least one staff member for every four participants joined the flight, both to support and to help interpret various perceptions in more realistic ways.

We do not have a formal follow-up for participants who do not show signs of coping better with their fears. They are, however, invited to make contact, either to get support before eventual flights, or to seek advice for alternative treatment.

Assessments

The treatment effects were measured according to four main criteria:

1) a 19-item flight anxiety scale (FAS) was composed by the first author to measure the degree of flight anxiety. Each item was measured on a 10 cm visual analogue scale (VAS), with the end points verbally anchored (0 = no anxiety, 10 = maximum anxiety). The VAS was used to assess seven other phobic items;

2) the number of flights undertaken during the two years post-treatment compared with the number of flights during the two years before treatment;

3) the use of alcohol and/or tranquillisers during flights was assessed by a five-point ordinal scale;

4) a seven point global flight anxiety (GFA) item (from 0–6) was developed by the first author. The scale has been used to study the prevalence of flight anxiety in Norway, and grade 4–6 is considered equivalent to flight phobia, i.e., including those who are always very afraid, but who do not cancel flights because of it (Ekeberg et al., 1989a).

The questionnaires also contained 11 items covering biographical variables such as gender, age, marital status and occupational state, previous psychiatric treatment and if/when the last flight before treatment had been undertaken. Treatment evaluation covering 12 items was assessed by a 10 cm VAS (0 = no benefit at all, 10 = maximum benefit).

At follow-up after six months and two years, the questionnaires were distributed again with stamped reply envelopes. One reminder was sent to those who did not return the questionnaires.

Analyses

For the statistical analyses, we used the statistical package SPSS-PC+ (SPSS©PC+ Inc., Chicago, Il, USA). Wilcoxon Signed Rank Test, paired and non-paired Student's t-tests were used for comparing measurements at two time points. Measurements at three or more time intervals were compared by analysis of variance. For all statistical calculations, $p < 0.05$ was considered significant.

Results

Figure 9.1 shows the average FAS scores pre- and post-treatment according to gender. The scores were lowered by 54 per cent post-treatment for women ($p < 0.001$) and 55 per cent for men ($p \leq 0.001$). Women scored 10 per cent higher than men. The slightly higher scores at two years follow up compared with six months were not statistically significant for either gender.

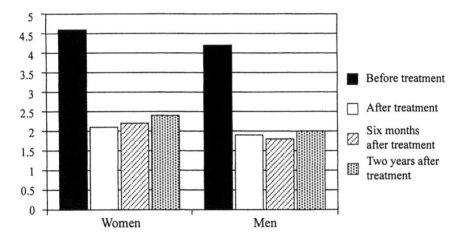

Figure 9.1   Flight phobia before and after treatment according to sex

Figure 9.2a shows the FAS scores for females and Figure 9.2b for males pre-treatment, post-treatment and at two years follow-up for the five items with the highest scores. All items were significantly reduced post-treatment and at follow-up ($p < 0.001$). Both genders were mainly concerned about the same worries. Feeling out of control, however, was clearly the most stressful concern for males, and 25 per cent higher than the next concern.

Table 9.2 shows that both females and males had undertaken more flights during the two years post-treatment than the corresponding pre-treatment period ($p < 0.001$).

Whereas 41 per cent had not taken any flights during two years prior to seeking treatment, this was the case for less than 8 per cent after treatment. Among the females, 22 per cent had taken more than 10 flights during the two years after treatment, compared with 10 per cent before treatment. The corresponding figures for males was 55 per cent after and 23 per cent before.

Among the females, 24 per cent said that they had cancelled flights because of anxiety post-treatment; 10 per cent had cancelled a single flight and 3 per

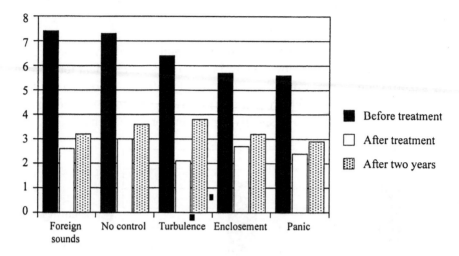

Figure 9.2a   Flight anxiety scores for women

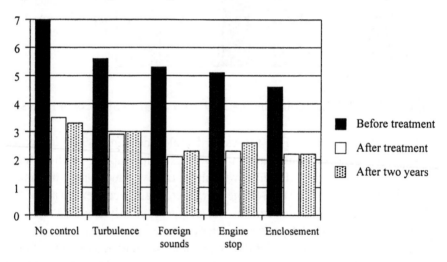

Figure 9.2b   Flight anxiety scores for men

cent more than 10. Among the males, 27 per cent had cancelled flights, 10 per cent a single flight and 6 per cent more than 10.

As shown in Table 9.3, there was significantly less alcohol used two years after treatment compared with before for both genders ($p < 0.001$). After treatment, the majority of both genders did not use alcohol at all. The proportion of females who sometimes drank a lot was reduced from 21 per cent to 3 per cent and for males from 32 per cent to 4 per cent after treatment.

Table 9.2 **Number of flights two years before and two years after treatment according to gender**

	Females		Males	
Number of flights	*Before treatment (%)*	*After treatment (%)*	*Before treatment (%)*	*After treatment (%)*
0	42	9	39	6
1–2	20	18	12	8
3–5	13	23	15	16
6–10	16	29	10	15
11–20	7	16	9	27
21–50	3	4	8	15
>50	0	2	6	13
Total	101	101	99	100

Table 9.3 **Use of alcohol during flights before and two years after treatment according to gender**

	Females		Males	
Use of alcohol	*Before treatment (%)*	*After treatment (%)*	*Before treatment (%)*	*After treatment (%)*
Not at all	35	62	31	56
Sometimes a little	26	26	33	33
Always a little	18	10	4	8
Sometimes a little, sometimes a lot	15	2	27	4
Always a lot	6	1	5	0
Total	100	101	100	101

As seen in Table 9.4, the use of tranquillisers was also less two years after treatment compared with before treatment for both genders ($p < 0.001$). More than 80 per cent did not use tranquillisers at all for their fear of flying after treatment, and 12 per cent of the women used a little after treatment compared with 25 per cent before treatment. The corresponding figures for males were 19 per cent and 8 per cent respectively.

Table 9.5 shows the global flight anxiety. Ninety-one per cent of the women were in grade 4–6 (flight phobia) before treatment and 24 per cent after treatment ($p < 0.001$). The corresponding figures for men were 78 per

Table 9. 4   Use of tranquillisers during flights two years before and two years after treatment

	Females		Males	
Use of tranquillisers	*Before treatment* (%)	*After treatment* (%)	*Before treatment* (%)	*After treatment* (%)
Not at all	51	80	65	84
Sometimes a little	24	8	17	8
Always a little	14	8	5	6
Sometimes a little, sometimes a lot	8	2	8	1
Always a lot	3	2	6	1
Total	100	100	101	100

Table 9.5   Global flight anxiety before treatment and two years after

	Females		Males	
Global flight anxiety	*Before treatment* (%)	*After treatment* (%)	*Before treatment* (%)	*After treatment* (%)
0 Not afraid at all	0	7	0	7
1 Sometimes a little afraid	0	22	0	27
2 Always a little afraid	4	28	9	40
3 Sometimes very afraid	6	19	14	13
4 Always very afraid, but never avoid flying because of it	14	5	17	2
5 Always very afraid, and sometimes avoid flying because of it	49	12	32	7
6 Never fly because of flight anxiety	28	7	29	5
Total	101	100	101	101

cent and 14 per cent. After treatment, 7 per cent of both genders were not afraid at all, and almost one third were only sometimes a little afraid or not afraid at all.

Figures 9.3a and 9.3b show that other phobias for females and males were also significantly reduced after treatment and at follow-up after two years. The average score was 37 per cent lower after treatment for females and 30 per cent lower for males, and the scores were stable at follow-up. The highest scores for both genders were fear of heights followed by fear of elevator and enclosed spaces. The scores for women were approximately 30 per cent higher than for men.

There were no significant differences in the FAS scores for women or men at any time point when comparing those who had flown previously and those who had not. Comparing the number of flights after treatment did not seem appropriate, as participants flying for their work reported more flights both before and after treatment.

Those who had been treated by a psychiatrist or psychologist previously and those who had not were also compared. For women there were no statistically significant differences before treatment (4.6 vs 4.8), or at follow-up after two years (2.6 vs 2.3). Men who had been in treatment had a significantly higher FAS score before treatment (4.9 vs 3.8, $p < 0.01$), but not at two years follow-up (1.9 vs 2.9, ns).

Women with 'other nervous problems' had not significantly higher FAS scores before treatment (4.8 vs 4.5, ns), but at the two years follow-up (2.8 vs 1.9, $p < 0.001$). Men with 'other nervous problems' had significantly higher FAS scores before treatment (4.6 vs 3.8, $p < 0.05$), but not at the follow-up after two years (2.0 vs 1.9).

Table 9.6 shows the participant's mean satisfaction with the treatment programme, with an overall rating of 9.0 for females and 8.2 for males. The females were overall 10 per cent more satisfied than the males ($p < 0.001$). Men were as satisfied as women with items measuring more procedural aspects such as the flight, simulator and the pilot's lecture, whereas women were more satisfied than men with the group and talking activities, the medical lecture and cabin attendant, i.e., items possibly reflecting more feelings and relational aspects.

Discussion

In our large self-selected sample, a fear of flying measured by the FAS, was significantly lowered post-treatment and at follow-up. The number of flights

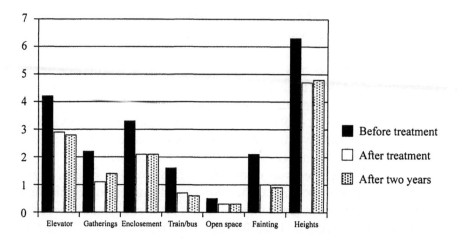

Figure 9.3a   Other phobias, women

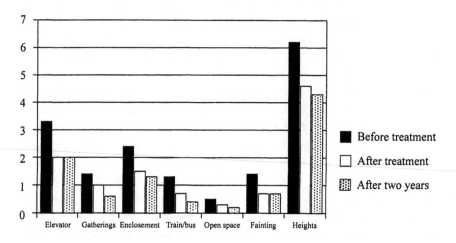

Figure 9.3b   Other phobias, men

undertaken during the two years after treatment was increased compared with the two years before treatment. The use of alcohol and/or tranquillisers during flights to lower anxiety and cope better with flight was reduced at the follow-ups. A significant and stable reduction in other phobic symptoms was found. Finally, the number of subjects with flight phobia was greatly reduced.

Many people with flight phobia avoid some flights. In such cases, a valid measurement of the treatment effect is a comparison between the number of flights in corresponding periods of time before and after treatment. In

Table 9.6   **Evaluation of the treatment programme (mean VAS score, 0–10 scale; 10 = maximum benefit)**

	Females	Males
The whole treatment	9.0	8.2
Films	5.8	4.9
Cabin attendant	6.5	5.1
Pilot lecture	8.2	7.9
Medical lecture	8.2	7.1
Technical lecture	8.0	7.5
Equipment on board	6.6	5.6
Simulator	8.8	8.9
Group talk/relaxation	8.6	8.1
Solidarity/fellowship	8.8	8.0
Control tower	8.1	7.3
Flight	9.0	9.0

Nordlund's study, with an observation period of one year, 12 per cent had taken at least six flights during the first year post-treatment (Nordlund, 1984). Walder et al. after three long sessions, found that 60 per cent had flown at three years follow up (Walder et al., 1987). We made no record after one year, but 51 per cent of the women and 70 per cent of the men had at least six flights at two years follow-up. Denholtz et al. in a three-and-a-half years follow-up found that 60 per cent had flown post-treatment, and that the median number of flights taken by the 26 subjects considered successfully treated, was five (Denholz et al., 1978). The median number of flights was seven in our total sample in the two years follow-up. In the study of Solyom et al., the observation period was 8–24 months (Solyom et al., 1973). The mean number of flights post-treatment in the four treatment groups was 1.7–8, and the maximum number of flights taken by any of the 40 participants was 15. In our study, 22 per cent of the women and 55 per cent of the men had taken more than 10 flights in the two years post-treatment.

In Nordlund's studies (1979, 1984), the subjects were treated in groups. Other studies have offered treatment individually or in groups of 2–3 (Denholtz et al., 1978). Other studies have reported no effect of group psychotherapy, even though Solyom et al. (1973) found it equally good at follow-up with the comment that such an effect would require maturation. Our experience has been that a group size of 12–15 has been appropriate. The opportunity to experience and expose common problems in groups has created a very good group feeling, in accordance with the evaluation of the beneficial effect of 'solidarity/fellowship' and 'talking in groups/relaxation'. It would not be correct to claim that we have practised group psychotherapy in the usual sense, as interpersonal conflicts were never the focus of interest.

For those who do not avoid flights, the anxiety level can be measured by various methods such as self-rating scales, physiological parameters or use of tranquillisers/alcohol during flights. Different selection procedures, treatment methods and criteria for outcome, however, make comparisons between different studies difficult.

The fact that men fly more than women in the follow-up period reflect that they had flown more during the two years before treatment. It has been found that males fly more than females, mainly because they need to fly in relation to their work.

Men and women with other nervous problems differed. Before treatment, men with other nervous problems had higher FAS scores than men without, but at follow-up, there were no significant differences. Women showed a different pattern, as those with other nervous problems had higher FAS than those without at follow-up, but not before treatment. One could expect that those who seek help for flight anxiety have problems with flying regardless of the level of other problems and that other problems might not add substantially more to the specific flight anxiety. The potential for improvement, however, might be greater for those without other problems. This is the pattern found among women. We have no explanation so far for the opposite pattern among men. We have found that males are less inclined to report flight anxiety when asked at home compared with answers given during flight, contrary to that observed among females (Ekeberg et al., 1988).

The gender differences according to previous treatment by psychiatrist or psychologist are almost the same as for those with and without other nervous problems, except that women did not differ according to treatment or not at any time point. Among these variables, we put more emphasis on other nervous problems, as this is a state condition, whereas psychiatric treatment could have taken place many years ago.

The effect of the treatment on other phobias is consistent with the general impression from the treatment where many spontaneously reported to use elevators, drive through tunnels or go by train/bus more easily. In elevators people may get the combined effect of feeling enclosed and at the same time being on an unstable base, experiences that are often reported in flight phobia. We have not studied more specifically how this effect was achieved, but most likely the effect is mediated by the combination of cognitive restructuring and exposure.

We have previously showed that there were no changes in flight anxiety or other phobic symptoms for a control group of subjects on the waiting list (Ekeberg et al., 1990a). There was, however, an increase in the level of anxiety from the entry of the control period to the entry of the treatment programme. Therefore, a moderate anxiety reduction after treatment may be a consequence of relief by completing the treatment, without any substantial change in coping capacity. Accordingly, it is important to also have measures of behaviour such as the number of flights or the use of alcohol or tranquillisers.

Our treatment programme is among the most extensively reported in the literature. Many programmes go for an intensive weekend or fewer weeks. We use a wider range of professionals as well. There are shorter treatments with documented effects. Ost et al. (1997) compared patients randomly assigned to two treatment conditions: one session (three hours) of massed treatment, or five sessions (6 hours) of gradual exposure and cognitive restructuring. At the one-year follow-up, 64 per cent of the patients in both groups took the flight. We have considered making the treatment shorter. The participants, however, have strongly recommended that we do not do so, as they express the need for more time to achieve a more thorough process. Our data on the positive effect after two years makes us reluctant to reduce the quality of the programme. The short version of Ost's programme was one session of three hours of individual treatment. To treat 12 subjects would require 36 hours, compared with the 24 hours for 12 subjects with our programme. We also consider the effect of the group process to be significant. During the later meetings, some of the participants may use what they have learned by helping to correct negative interpretations made by others, which we consider beneficial for both sides. The use of a flight simulator is also a good preparation before the real flight. The participants gain a more realistic view of the control the pilots have, even during severe turbulence, an aborted landing or tire explosion.

We have no screening and diagnosis for participants before treatment, as recommended by van Gerwen et al. (2000). Proper diagnosis is time consuming, and we have so far not given this priority. Even though we consider this important from a scientific point of view, we consider that almost all who participate benefit from the knowledge they get, even though it may not be sufficient to overcome the flight anxiety. We have, however, offered other treatment for several of them, and the impression is that their main problems are other than flight anxiety. Wilhelm et al., found that 27 per cent met the criteria for current panic disorder with agoraphobia, and 17 per cent criteria for that diagnosis in the past (1997a). Accordingly, many flight phobics may need additional treatment that is more appropriately offered by other institutions or services than an airline company.

The overall satisfaction and outcome evaluation was uniformly very high. The lack of variation and the positive correlations make it unlikely to detect evaluation factors that might be associated with a positive outcome. Females were more satisfied with the treatment programme, both overall and with most key aspects. The exceptions were the more procedural aspects of the programme, i.e. the simulator, the flight and the pilot.

We agree with van Gerwen et al. (2000) that a treatment programme should cover at least three areas of change: a) information on aerodynamics and technical aspects; b) coping with anxiety and phobic reactions, including physiological reactions; and c) graded exposure including the test flight. We want the best possible competence within these areas, therefore we use teachers with a range of competences.

We do not use or encourage the use of medications at all in the treatment programme. Firstly, the essential factor in the therapy is the cognitive restructuring and exposure. Secondly, the effects are sufficiently good that we would consider that medication could have untoward effects, as the subjects might attribute their improved coping with the effect of medication and not their own increased coping. In another study, we found only a very moderate effect of selective beta-blocker, but only on the somatic manifestations of anxiety (Ekeberg et al., 1990). This is consistent with Wilhelm et al. (1997b) who found that alprazolam increases physiological activation under acute stress conditions and hinders therapeutic effects of exposure in flying phobia. We have also shown that the sympathetic responses during the test flight are quite similar to those of the regular passengers (Ekeberg et al., 1989). Generally, the sympathetic responses are not that severe, but a heart rate of 80–90 beats per minute is easily interpreted as 150–200 during anxiety.

Results from different studies have to be interpreted with a measure of caution. The participants usually know something about the programmes before they apply. Those who apply for a short weekend programme may be more confident that they will be able to fly after treatment than those who apply for treatment of a longer duration.

Future studies should focus on the degree of other psychiatric problems, in particular other anxiety disorders. If the flight anxiety is the major problem, current treatment programmes should be helpful to most participants. If flight anxiety is only a minor aspect of extensive anxiety disorders, a limited intervention may not suffice. van Gerwen et al. (1997) have described such aspects, and studies showing treatment effects in subgroups are important.

The main conclusion of the study is that treatment as described has significantly reduced flight anxiety. The level of anxiety was lower, an increased number of flights were undertaken post-treatment compared to pre-treatment, the consumption of alcohol/tranquillisers during flights was reduced and the number of participants with flight phobia was lower. The beneficial effects were not significantly altered during the two years follow-up period.

References

Denholtz, M.S. and Mann, E.T. (1975), 'An Automated Audiovisual Treatment of Phobias Administered by Non-professionals', *Journal of Behavior Therapy and Experimental Psychiatry*, Vol. 6, pp. 111–15.

Denholtz, M.S., Hall, L.A. and Mann, E.T. (1978), 'Automated Treatment for Flight Phobia: A 3 1/2 year follow-up', *American Journal of Psychiatry*, Vol. 135, pp. 1340–43.

Ekeberg, Ø., Seeberg, I. and Ellertsen, B.B. (1988), 'The Prevalence of Flight Anxiety in Norwegian Airline Passengers', *Scandinavian Journal of Behaviour Therapy*, Vol. 17, pp. 213–22.

Ekeberg, Ø., Seeberg, I. and Ellertsen, B.B. (1989), 'The Prevalence of Flight Anxiety in Norway', *Nordic Journal of Psychiatry*, Vol. 43, pp. 443–8.

Ekeberg, Ø., Ellertsen, B.B., Seeberg, I. and Kjeldsen, S.E. (1989), 'Plasma Catecholamines in Some Airline Passengers', *Scandinavian Journal of Clinical Laboratory Investigation*, Vol. 49, pp. 183–8.

Ekeberg, Ø., Kjeldsen, S.E., Greenwood, D.T. and Enger, E. (1990), 'Effects of Selective Beta-adrenoceptor Blockade on Anxiety associated with Flight Phobia', *Journal of Psychopharmacology*, Vol. 4, pp. 35–41.

Ekeberg, Ø., Seeberg, I. and Ellertsen, B.B. (1990), 'A Cognitive/behavioral Treatment Program for Flight Phobia, with 6 Months' and 2 Years' Follow-up', *Nordic Journal of Psychiatry*, Vol. 44, pp. 365–74.

Girodo, M. and Roehl, J. (1978), 'Cognitive Preparation and Self-talk: Anxiety management during the stress of flying', *Journal of Consultative Clinicial Psychology*, Vol. 46, pp. 978–89.

Haug, T., Brenne, L., Johnsen, B.H., Berntzen, D., Gotestam, K.G. and Hugdahl, K. (1987), 'A Three-systems Analysis of Fear of Flying: A comparison of a consonant vs a non-consonant treatment method', *Behavior Research and Therapy*, Vol. 25, pp. 187–94.

Howard, W.A., Murphy S.M. and Clarce, J.C. (1983), 'The Nature and Treatment of Fear of Flying: A controlled investigation', *Behavior Therapy*, Vol. 14, pp. 557–67.

Nordlund, C.L. (1979), in Gad, T. and Nordlund, C.L. (eds), *Flygraedd*, Studentlitteratur: Lund, Sweden.

Nordlund, C.L. (1983), 'A Questionnaire of Swedes' Fear of Flying' (English abstract), *Scandinavian Journal of Behavioural Therapy*, Vol. 12, pp. 150–68.

Nordlund, C.L. (1984), 'Treatment of Fear of Flying in Groups' (English abstract), *Scandinavian Journal of Behavioural Therapy*, Vol. 13, pp. 203–16.

Ost, L.G., Brandberg, M. and Alm, T. (1997), 'One versus Five Sessions of Exposure in the Treatment of Flying Phobia', *Behavior Research and Therapy*, Vol. 35, pp. 987–96.

Solyom, L., Shugar, R., Bryntwick, S. and Solyom, C. (1973), 'Treatment of Fear of Flying', *American Journal of Psychiatry*, Vol. 130, pp. 432–7.

van Gerwen, L.J., Sinhoven, P.H., Diekstra, R.F.W. and Van Dyck, K. (1997), 'People who Seek Help for Fear of Flying: Typology of flying phobics', *Behavior Therapy*, Vol. 28, pp. 237–51.

van Gerwen, L.J. and Diekstra, R.F. (2000), 'Fear of Flying Treatment Programs for Passengers: An international review', *Aviation, Space and Environmental Medicine*, Vol. 71, pp. 430–37.

Walder, C.P., McCracken, J.S., Herbert, M., James, P.T. and Brewitt, N. (1987), 'Psychological Intervention in Civilian Flying Phobia. Evaluation and a Three-year Follow-up', *British Journal of Psychiatry*, Vol. 151, pp. 494–8.

Wilhelm, F.H. and Roth, W.T. (1997a), 'Clinical Characteristics of Flight Phobia', *Journal of Anxiety Disorders*, Vol. 11, pp. 241–61.

Wilhelm, F.H. and Roth, W.T. (1997b), 'Acute and Delayed Effects of Alprazolam on Flight Phobics during Exposure', *Behavior Research and Therapy*, Vol. 35, pp. 831–41.

Chapter 10

Multi-component Standardised Cognitive-behavioural Group Treatment Programme for Fear of Flying

Lucas van Gerwen

A recent review showed that there are approximately 50 facilities with comprehensive programmes for treating fear of flying throughout the Western world (van Gerwen and Diekstra, 2000). However, little is known about the effectiveness of these programmes in clinical practice. Available outcome studies have demonstrated that interventions may effectively reduce fear of flying (Greco, 1989; Howard, Murphy and Clarke, 1983; Roberts, 1989; Walder et al., 1987). Most reports on fear of flying interventions are individual case studies (Canton-Dutari, 1974; Deyoub and Epstein, 1977; Diment, 1981; Karoly, 1974; Ladouceur, 1982; Rothbaum et al., 1996; Scrignar, Swanson and Bloom, 1973; Sidley, 1990), although most facilities offer group therapy programmes. Evaluations of group treatment programmes are usually uncontrolled studies involving relatively small groups (Aitken and Benson, 1984; Denholz, Hall and Mann, 1978; Ekeberg, Seeberg and Ellertsen, 1990; Williams, 1982). Furthermore, most of these studies investigate only a specific part of the treatment, like exposure (McCarthy and Craig, 1995; Meldman and Hatch, 1969; Öst, Brandberg and Alm, 1997; Roberts, 1989) or cognitive training (e.g. Borill and Foreman, 1996). There is only one controlled study with a nontreatment group (Howard et al., 1983), which compares systematic desensitisation, flooding, implosion and relaxation. This present study is unique because it is one of the few that examines the effectiveness of a comprehensive group treatment programme for fear of flying in actual clinical practice (Sederer and Dickey, 1996).

Although distinguished by their fear of flying from other types of phobics, flying phobics are a heterogeneous group. Fear of flying can be the manifestation of one or more other phobias, such as claustrophobia or social phobia. It can also be the effect of generalisation of one or more natural environment phobias, such as fear of heights, falling, storms, water, instability, etc. (Wilhelm and Roth, 1997; van Gerwen et al., 1997), as described in DSM-IV (APA, 1994). That is why a multimodal treatment programme seems necessary to help patients who have different mechanisms and backgrounds that underlie their fear of flying.

The present chapter has two objectives. The first is to describe the protocol of a long-standing fear of flying treatment programme developed by the VALK Foundation, located in Leiden, the Netherlands. A joint enterprise of the Department of Clinical and Health Psychology at Leiden University, KLM Royal Dutch Airlines and Amsterdam Airport Schiphol, this facility specialises in treating flying phobics. VALK offers the multi-component programme described below, conceptually based on Bandura's 'belief in self-efficacy' theory (Bandura, 1977). Trainers employed by VALK are all certified clinical psychologists and/or psychotherapists; some are also experienced as airline cabin crew or pilot. After a pilot study of a treatment protocol for fear of flying, involving a limited number of flying phobics, the two protocol versions were standardised in a two-day cognitive-behavioural treatment programme and a one-day behavioural treatment programme. At the first fear of flying conference in Tarrytown, NY, participants concluded that this treatment programme could serve as a model for treating fear of flying (Fodor, 1996).

The second objective of this chapter is to present data on the effectiveness of this flying phobia protocol, as reported by patients who participated in the 1990–99 treatment programme. The effectiveness of two different treatment programmes in actual practice is evaluated: a two-day group behavioural treatment programme with a clear-cut cognitive component and a one-day group behavioural treatment programme without a cognitive training component. The specific aim of this chapter is to demonstrate procedures and clinical outcomes of a long-standing clinical programme, but no attempt is made to compare the relative efficacy of the two treatment versions within the programme empirically.

Programme Protocol

The selection of treatment programme components and the efficiency measures used are based on Bandura's concept of belief in self-efficacy theory. Belief in self-efficacy is defined by Bandura as:

> Belief in one's capability to organise and execute the courses of action required to manage prospective situations. Efficacy beliefs influence how people

think, feel, motivate themselves, and act. Expectations concerning mastery or efficacy are assumed to determine choice of actions, the effort one expends, the persistence in the face of adversity as well as one's emotional or affective experiences (Bandura, 1977, pp. 2 and 3).

Self-efficacy can be enhanced largely through four channels. The first channel is persuasion or formal provision of information. The second is internal self-regulation, which implies developing skills to control inner states, like arousal. The third is modelling or learning by example. The fourth is active attainment, i.e. increasing belief in self-efficacy through active coping with specific tasks or threats. Accordingly, the four components of the fear of flying treatment programme are: 1) provision of information; 2) relaxation and breathing exercises; 3) learning by observing other models in group settings; and 4) mock-up, simulator and test flight exposure. Belief in the self-efficacy concept which underlies the programme is also operationalised in the selection of measures for monitoring chances and assessing the effects of the programme. The programme protocol consists of five phases: 1) assessment; 2) individual preparation; 3) one-day behavioural group treatment or two-day cognitive-behavioural group treatment; 4) follow-up and relapse prevention; and 5) optional refresher group training.

Assessment

After initial contact, usually by telephone, patients were invited for assessment to the VALK Foundation at Leiden University, during which they completed questionnaires on fears and phobias in general and on the fear of flying in particular (see 'Measures' section, below). In a subsequent semistructured interview, information on flying behaviour was gathered (flying history interview), such as the total number of one-way flights made by participants to date, when they last flew, and whether they have received previous treatment for fear of flying. Then the therapist assessed the phenomenology and severity of fear of flying and its determinants. In particular, agoraphobia (often accompanied by panic attacks), claustrophobia and acrophobia were assessed, but also personality traits like perfectionism and a high need for control. Patients were asked in the interview to describe their main phobic complaints and fears underlying their flying phobia. The interview provides a detailed description of flying experiences and fears, and what might have prompted them. Life events (Wilhelm and Roth, 1997) were also assessed, because life events may bring about increased vulnerability at the time of onset of the phobia (Menzies and Clarke, 1995) and the presence of personality disorders. Five clinical psychologists (behaviour therapists) performed the assessments. At the end of this phase, the therapists proposed a treatment plan, based on an individual case conceptualisation. On the basis of this individual case conceptualisation it was determined which complaints precluded participation in the group programme and required preparatory individual treatment. Patients were strongly advised to get treatment for these problems. Moreover, therapists proposed a one or two-day treatment programme. Patients with less severe flying phobia symptoms and those who had never flown were especially advised to take the one-day programme. When patients had a preference for the two-day programme, they were allowed to participate in it. Patients received an information book on fear of flying, which was to be read before the individualised preparation phase (van Gerwen, 1988; van Gerwen and Diekstra, 1996). The assessment phase took a total of two to three hours to complete.

There were two main types of treatment: 1) an individualised preparation phase, followed by a one-day behavioural group training programme (12 hours); and 2) an individualised preparation phase, followed by a two-day cognitive-behavioural group training programme (20 hours). Most patients followed the therapist's advice, but a few chose the programme they wanted. Patients with only a moderate fear of flying were advised to participate in the one-day training programme.

Individualised Preparation Phase

The individualised preparation phase started one or at most two weeks after the assessment phase. The protocol indicated two individual sessions. In this phase, patients learned skills for handling the phobic problems they experience. Information was provided on the training programme and relevant psychological factors involved in fear and anxiety. Moreover, patients were taught relaxation and breathing techniques, and greatly encouraged to practice these exercises at home using a tape. Patients familiar with relaxation exercises and implementing progressive relaxation sometimes received just one session.

Additional individual sessions were offered to patients with a high need to be in control (one extra session), acrophobia (1–2 extra sessions, depending on the severity and type of acrophobia), claustrophobia (1–4 extra sessions, depending on the severity and extent to which patients avoided places like elevators, etc.), traumatic social events (rape, etc.) and traumatic transportation accidents involving cars, trains and buses (2–6 sessions, depending on the nature and severity of the trauma), and traumatic aeroplane accidents (4–12 sessions, depending on the nature and severity of the trauma).

On average there was a two week interval between each individual session. The final individual session involved flight simulation in a stationary aircraft seat. An aircraft cabin wall with 12 aircraft seats was available on VALK premises. A stereo-system provided the sounds of the various flight stages. This simulation was used as a preliminary check of patients' coping skills in a flight situation. Emotions associated with flying are often experienced in this session, providing indications for further treatment. All patients complete this individual phase before entering group treatment.

Group Treatment Phase

Group treatment started one to three weeks after the individual phase. There was a minimum of five and a maximum of eight participants to one or two trainers/therapists. The trainers were experienced clinical psychologists and behaviour therapists with at least five years' experience working with fear of flying patients. Two types of group training were provided, one lasting one day (12 hours) and one lasting two days (20 hours). The two-day programme is described first in this article. After a brief introduction, each training programme started with a two-and-a-half hour presentation by a pilot, covering aerodynamics, moving aircraft parts, procedures and performances as well as air traffic control and meteorological aspects like turbulence. Aircraft maintenance, air traffic control and an explanation of radar and transponder were shown on video (45 minutes). The information component often provided some relief for anxiety resulting from misinformation and unrealistic cognitions. Misinformation about flying is a possible vulnerability factor, since it may lead to catastrophic interpretation of normal flight events. Information might not be necessary for some flight phobics, but it is a proven way of exposing them to stimuli associated with flying. It is also used as an aid in cognitive restructuring techniques that address increased danger expectancies.

Cognitive therapy was then introduced, showing the effects of thoughts on bodily processes (sensations). Patients practised with in-flight cognitions, including all types of anticipatory fear of flying. They were taught how to change thoughts that make them anxious with a rational self-analysis (RSA) form. Rational self-analysis helps to identify the thoughts or judgements that determine emotional reactions to facts or events (Ellis, 1972; Diekstra, Knaus and Ruys, 1982). In addition, information was provided on what the physical effects of anxiety are and what can happen during a panic attack. A cognitive model of panic and anxiety showed how they can result from catastrophic misinterpretation of certain bodily sensations (Clark, 1986; Arntz, 1991).

On the second day, idiosyncratic anxiety-provoking cognitions were identified and discussed. Patients were encouraged to formulate anxiety-reducing cognitions. The rationale was that active coping is needed, without avoiding anxiety completely. Coping skills were ranked in terms of efficacy. Some examples of coping scales were controlled breathing, muscle relaxation, the negative thoughts 'stop' technique and distraction from negative thoughts. Patients were informed of the best possible flight preparation. Next, an imaginary flight was taken, which was tape-recorded. During the various stages of the flight, patients were asked about the coping skills they preferred, while providing correction and training for coping at all stages of the flight. In this way, patients also acquired their own personal 'coping' tape for future flights.

In a hangar at Amsterdam Airport Schiphol, a Boeing 747 was visited and inspected, both inside and out. Patients with claustrophobia were encouraged to visit and lock themselves in the rest rooms. A relaxation exercise was performed in the stationary plane.

Two flights were then taken in a flight simulator, an Airbus A-310 cabin simulator normally used for cabin crew flight safety training. This device accurately simulates a night flight, including sound and motion. During the first flight, patients received an explanation of flight sounds and movements. During the second simulator flight, patients were encouraged to practice coping exercises with other group members. They forced each other to talk during heavy turbulence or to do a breathing exercise.

After successfully completing these two simulated flights, the group headed for the departure hall for a guided flight in Europe, which takes about one hour. During this flight (usually in a Boeing 737), patients were encouraged to practise what they had learned. There was a briefing at the airport of destination, and the return flight provided a second opportunity to practise. The trainers moved among the patients and encouraged them to cope appropriately, giving additional training on board, whenever necessary.

There was a debriefing at Schiphol Airport, and patients received advice based on their in-flight behaviour. If necessary, further treatment was suggested. All patients were encouraged to take another flight on their own within three months.

In the one-day programme, patients received the same information about aviation, but without instructive videos. Cognitive training was not provided.

Coping skills were also ranked with the best possible flight preparation and an imaginary flight tape-recorded. These patients also received their own personal 'coping' tape, mainly with controlled breathing techniques and exercises for releasing muscle tension, but they did not get cognitive instructions. Exposure was exactly the same as in the two-day programme. Table 10.1 shows the differences between the one-day and two-day programmes. In general, the two programmes are the same, with some components omitted from the one-day programme. Except for the tape-recorded imaginary flight, only behavioural coping instructions are given and cognitive instructions are not provided.

Table 10.1 Treatment components of the two treatment group conditions

1-day behavioural training, 12 hours	2-day cognitive-behavioural training, 20 hours
psycho-education – pilot presentation	psycho-education – pilot presentation – video about plane maintenance – video about air traffic control – info on anxiety
instructions on preparation for a flight ranking of coping skills (behavioural) tape recorded imaginary flight	cognitive training RSA instructions on preparation for a flight ranking of coping skills (behavioural and cognitive) tape recorded imaginary flight with cognitive instructions
stationary plane visit in hangar two simulator flights guided return flight	stationary plane visit in hangar two simulator flights guided return flight

Follow-up and Relapse Prevention Phase

Three months after the flight there was a three-hour follow-up session to monitor maintenance and progress and explain a relapse prevention programme, which patients work on themselves. The main strategy of relapse prevention is to make clear to patients that when they fall back into their old habits, they could again experience fear. It was explained to them that stimuli such as strange noises or movements of the plane could reactivate fearful reactions and that continuing to use coping strategies remains important to prevent a relapse.

Patients were able to share their flight experiences after their treatment and ask questions. The first post-treatment data was collected in this phase.

Refresher Group Training

One-day refresher group training with a minimum of eight and a maximum of 20 participants, with two trainers, was optional. It was designed to reinforce learned coping styles and techniques on an additional guided flight. Patients got an opportunity to ask any remaining questions, and this was followed by a guided tour of a hangar or control tower. After completing the tour, the group took a four-hour guided flight in Europe (two hours one way), usually in a Boeing 737. Twenty-five per cent of all patients take refresher group training 6–24 months after treatment.

Method

Participants

The data reported in this study was obtained from 1,026 patients who were assessed and treated by the VALK Foundation from February 1990 to January 1999. The patients were referred from various sources, such as health agencies, health professionals, company health programmes, etc., and some were self-referrals.

After assessment, patients were non-randomly assigned to one of the treatment programmes. A group of 129 patients, 55 men and 74 women with a mean age of 40.6 years (SD = 12.4), participated in the one-day behavioural group programme, while 897 patients, 364 men and 533 women with a mean age of 40.0 years (SD = 10.2), took the two-day cognitive-behavioural group treatment programme.

Measures

The following measures were selected from a more extensive assessment battery that is regularly used to assess patients and measure the efficacy of treatment for the two conditions. The flight anxiety situations (FAS) questionnaire (van Gerwen et al., 1999) is a 32-item self-report inventory with a five point Likert-type answering format, ranging from 1 = 'No anxiety' to 5 = 'Overwhelming anxiety'. The questionnaire assesses characteristics related to anxiety experienced in different flight or flight-related situations and consists of three subscales:

1) an anticipatory flight anxiety scale, containing 14 items that pertain to anxiety experienced when anticipating a flight;
2) an in-flight anxiety scale, containing 11 items pertaining to anxiety experienced during a flight; and
3) a generalised flight anxiety scale, containing seven items referring to anxiety experienced in connection with aeroplanes in general, regardless of personal involvement in a flight situation.

The psychometric properties of the FAS proved to be excellent (van Gerwen et al., 1999). This study showed an empirically divided factor structure, explaining 72 per cent of the variance, an internal consistency of subscales varying between .88 and .97 and test-retest reliability measured with Pearson product moment correlation coefficients with a range of .90–.92.

The flight anxiety modality (FAM) questionnaire (van Gerwen et al., 1999) is an 18-item questionnaire for measuring the symptoms of anxiety or anticipatory anxiety in flight situations. Each symptom is rated on a Likert-type scale with the following categories: 1 = 'Not at all', 2 = 'A little bit', 3 = 'Moderately', 4 = 'Intensely', 5 = 'Very intensely'. The FAM was designed to measure the following modalities in which anxiety in flight situations may be expressed: 1) somatic modality, pertaining to physical symptoms; and 2) cognitive modality, related to the presence of distressing cognitions. The psychometric properties of the FAM proved to be good to excellent (van Gerwen et al., 1999). The study showed an empirically divided factor structure, explaining 56 per cent of the variance, the internal consistencies of subscales was .89 for both subscales and the test-retest reliability was .79 for the somatic modality and .84 for the cognitive modality.

The Dutch version (Arrindell and Ettema, 1986) of the Symptom Check List-90 (SCL-90) (Derogatis, 1977) is a 90-item multi-dimensional self-report questionnaire which measures the level of psychopathology, using a five point scale. Besides yielding a total score for psychoneurotic complaints, the inventory consists of eight subscales: 1) anxiety (10 items); 2) agoraphobia (seven items); 3) depression (16 items); 4) somatic complaints (12 items); 5) insufficiency of thinking and acting (nine items); 6) interpersonal sensitivity (18 items); 7) hostility (six items); 8) sleeping problems (three items).

A visual analogue flight anxiety scale (VAFAS) enabled subjects to indicate the extent to which they were anxious about flying on a one-tailed visual analogue scale. This scale ranges from 0 'No flight anxiety' to 10 'Terrified'. In the follow-up period, this scale was applied three times, at three, six and 12 months.

Two behavioural measures are taken into account. Whether patients participated in the guided test flight and the number of one-way flights taken three, six and 12 months after treatment were assessed.

Design

In this uncontrolled study the effectiveness of the two group treatment programmes offered in regular clinical practice was evaluated. Treatment protocols did not change from 1990–99. Patients were assigned to therapy conditions after assessment according to the therapist's judgement. In both conditions, data collection was identical. Data was collected at pre-treatment and at three, six and 12-month follow-ups. At pre-treatment, the FAS, FAM, SCL-90, and VAFAS were obtained and information gathered on whether the patients had flown before and the number of one-way flights they had taken. At the three-month follow-up, the FAS, FAM, SCL-90, VAFAS and the number of one-way flights taken after treatment were compiled. In the two written follow-up evaluations, carried out six and 12 months afterwards, the VAFAS was used and patients were asked to indicate the number of one-way flights they had taken. When patients did not show up at the three-month post-assessment session or did not return written evaluations, we tried to obtain their VAFAS score and the number of one-way flights they had taken by telephone.

Methods of Analysis

Only patients from the two treatment groups who completed the pre-test and post-test FAS measurements (the main outcome measures) were included in the analyses. For the sake of clarity, we call patients who completed both FAS measurements 'patients with complete follow-up data' in this study. Sixty-seven patients from the one-day training programme and 202 patients from the two-day training programme were not included because of missing data on the FAS questionnaire at the three-month follow-up. They are called 'patients with incomplete follow-up data'. To test the representativeness of the samples, the demographic characteristics and baseline levels on the VAFAS, FAS, FAM and SCL-90a were compared between patients with complete and incomplete follow-up data. Chi-square analyses were used for nominal and paired *t*-tests for ordinal variables.

Patients were non-randomly assigned to the treatment groups. To analyse the comparability of patients with complete follow-up data in the two treatment conditions, the groups were compared with respect to sociodemographic factors and their baseline levels on the questionnaires. Again, chi-square analyses were used for nominal and paired *t*-tests for ordinal variables.

The effectiveness of each of the two flight anxiety training programmes was analysed by separately comparing the pre-measurement and post-measurement levels of the VAFAS, FAS, FAM and SCL-90 scales with paired *t*-tests in both treatment groups. The VAFAS variables measured at four points in time were analysed with a repeated measurement design (MANOVA). Moreover, the VAFAS and the number of one-way flights was completed by 85 per cent of the total group, patients with complete and incomplete follow-up data, until the last measurement. For this reason, a MANOVA for the VAFAS administered at four points in time and the number of one-way flights was performed for the excluded patients as well.

The clinical significance of training effects was analysed by computing Cohen's *d* (Cohen, 1988). Cohen considers $d < 0.20$ to be a slight, $d < 0.50$ to be a moderate, and $d < 0.80$ to be a substantial effect.

The Jacobson and Truax's reliable change index (RCI) was computed to determine the percentages of positive responders (Jacobson and Truax, 1991). This RCI classifies subjects according to whether or not they have improved reliably, independently of the clinical significance of their improvement. For a positive response, the RCI should be > 1.96. In addition to the RCI, clinical significance was determined by computing the percentage of patients who differ in effect by at least the RCI plus one standard deviation (instead of two). The test-retest correlation coefficients required for computing the RCI for the FAS and FAM questionnaires were obtained from a sample of 54 normal people (van Gerwen et al., 1999). For the SCL-90, these coefficients were obtained from a reference group of psychiatric outpatients, reported in the test manual (Arrindell and Ettema, 1987).

$P < 0.05$ was considered significant for all statistical calculations. Statistical analyses were performed using SPSS 8.5 for Windows (SPSS Inc., Chicago USA, 1989–99).

Results

After describing the relevant characteristics of patients who completed the training programme and a comparison of baseline data between the groups, we analysed whether patients changed significantly after treatment for each condition and whether they maintained their treatment gains.

Sociodemographic data on the 1,026 patients (419 men, 40.8 per cent, and 607 women, 59.2 per cent) assessed shows that the subjects' educational level was relatively high. Thirty-eight per cent had received higher education (higher professional or academic training) and 16 per cent a medium-level (professional) education. Forty-six per cent had had elementary school education or lower professional training. Educational level does not significantly differ between gender or age groups, although there is a tendency for younger patients to have a slightly higher educational level.

Fifty-eight point five per cent of the men and 54.4 per cent of the women were paid employees, 32.5 per cent of the men and 18.8 per cent of the women were self-employed, 13.2 per cent were housekeepers (all women), and two smaller groups either did volunteer work or were involved in training or educational programmes.

Only 103 participants (10 per cent) had never flown. Five point two (SD = 7.2) years is the mean number between application for therapy and the last flight for the 923 participants who had flown, with a range of 0 to 58 years. Twenty-two per cent of the patients (202) who had flown before last flew within 12 months of their application for treatment. The majority (78.1 per cent), however, took their last flight more than two years ago. This occurred more than 10 years ago for 19.3 per cent (178). A detailed description of the diagnostic, demographic and clinical characteristics of patients referred to the VALK Foundation are included in a report by van Gerwen et al. (1997).

The group of 129 patients who took the one-day behavioural group programme consisted of 62 patients who had completed follow-up data and 67 who had not. A comparison of those 62 and 67 patients showed no differences with respect to baseline data. Of the 897 patients who followed the two-day cognitive-behavioural group treatment programme, 202 had incomplete follow-up data and 695 had completed all follow-up data. A comparison of the 695 and 202 patients in this treatment condition revealed no differences except on the FAS in-flight scale. Patients with incomplete follow-up data had a somewhat higher mean score on the FAS in-flight scale, 29.92 (SD = 8.20), in comparison to patients with complete follow-up data, 28.33 (SD = 9.47), ($t = 2.34$; $p = .020$).

A comparison of patients with complete follow-up data in the two treatment groups showed only a few significant differences, although patients were non-randomly assigned to one of the two groups (see Table 10.2). There were significantly more patients who had never flown in the one-day condition (21

Table 10.2 Demographic data of the included patients

	1-day training	2-day training	Test-statistic
Number of patients			
– total	62	695	
– men	21 (33.9%)	278 (40.0%)	$\chi 5 = 0.9$; ns
– women	41 (66.1%)	417 (60.0%)	
Age			
– total	41.5 (12.3)	40.7 (10.2)	$t = 0.5$; ns
– men	40.7 (14.8)	40.5 (9.5)	$t = 0.04$; ns
– women	41.9 (11.0)	40.8 (10.7)	$t = 0.6$; ns
Education			$\chi 5 = 5.0$; ns
– basic	8 (12.9%)	78 (11.2%)	
– low	22 (35.5%)	244 (35.1%)	
– medium	15 (24.2%)	105 (15.1%)	
– high	17 (27.4%)	268 (38.6%)	
Employment (men)			$\chi 5 = 3.7$; ns
– self-employment	6 (28.6%)	87 (31.3%)	
– paid employment	11 (52.4%)	171 (61.5%)	
Employment (women)			$\chi 5 = 4.3$; ns
– self-employment	6 (14.6%)	71 (17.0%)	
– paid employment	20 (48.8%)	244 (58.5%)	
– housekeeping	6 (14.6%)	55 (13.2%)	
Flight experience			
– Number of patients:			$\chi 5 = 7.7$; p=.005
– ever flown	49 (79.0%)	628 (90.4%)	
– within previous year	13 (26.5%)	135 (21.5%)	$\chi 5 = 1.4$; ns
– 10 years or more ago	11 (22.4%)	118 (18.8%)	
– years since last flight	5.7 (8.2)	5.2 (6.9)	$t = 0.5$; ns

per cent) than in the two-day programme (9.6 per cent). The therapists who recommended treatment after assessment believed that patients without flying experience would have sufficient benefits from this, and patients accepted the one-day training condition more easily. They also advised patients with high baseline fear levels to follow the two-day training programme.

Participants in the cognitive-behavioural treatment programme also had a significantly higher mean score on the VAFAS at assessment. In addition, patients in the two-day cognitive-behavioural treatment programme had a significantly higher mean score on the FAM somatic subscale. There were four SCL-90 scales, which showed significantly higher baseline scores for participants in the cognitive-behavioural treatment condition: psychoneurotic complaints, agoraphobia, interpersonal sensitivity and hostility. In conclusion, participants in the two-day cognitive-behavioural treatment condition are comparable to those in the one-day behaviour group in terms of demographic data. In terms of baseline data, though, they have relatively higher levels of fear on all measures used, but only six are statistically significant (see Table 10.3).

There is great variability in the number of additional individual sessions that persons participated in and also a difference in additional individual sessions between the two treatment groups. The one-day programme group has a range of 0–7 sessions with a mean of 2.27 (SD = 1.66). The two-day training programme group has a higher range of 0–21 sessions and a mean of 3.48 (SD = 2.29). The difference is significant ($t = 4.06$; df = 755; $p < .000$).

The outcome of the one-day programme shows that treatment is effective for overcoming fear of flying. All participants took the guided test flight. The effectiveness of the one-day training programme is displayed in Table 10.4. Most variables show statistically significant improvement, except for the SCL-90 sub-scales of somatic complaints, hostility and sleeping problems. Changes on the SCL-90 sub-scales of agoraphobia, depression and insufficiency were significant, with a p-value of $< .05$. Cohen's d were considered slight for changes on the SCL-90 sub-scales, except that the change on the anxiety subscale was considered to be moderate. All flying scales and subscales showed considerable performance on Cohen's d. The most important questionnaire, the FAS, showed great improvement with the score that 90.3 per cent of the patients fulfilled the criteria for a reliable change (Jacobson and Truax, 1991) and 75.8 per cent the criteria for a clinically significant effect. The most important sub-scale, the in-flight subscale, showed that 91.9 per cent fulfilled the criteria for a reliable change and 72.6 per cent the criteria for a clinically significant effect. In the one-day condition without cognitive training, 55.9 per cent of the patients showed a clinically significant effect on the FAM cognitive scale.

The effectiveness of the two-day training programme is provided in Table 10.5. All variables show statistically significant improvement. All participants in this programme also took the guided test flight. The flying

Table 10.3 Base line data from the 1-day and 2-day training groups

	1-day training		2-day training		Test statistic
	Mean	(std dev.)	Mean	(std dev.)	
VAFAS	7.60	(1.62)	8.30	(1.37)	$t = 3.3; p < .001$
FAS					
– anticipatory	26.92	(12.29)	28.43	(11.80)	$t = 1.0$; ns
– in-flight	26.87	(7.86)	28.33	(9.47)	$t = 1.2$; ns
– generalise	d5.15	(5.07)	5.42	(4.97)	$t = 0.4$; ns
– total	66.08	(24.02)	69.71	(24.37)	$t = 1.1$; ns
SCL-90	(N = 56)		(N = 694)		
– anxiety	16.88	(5.73)	18.07	(6.90)	$t = 1.3$; ns
– agoraphobia	8.95	(2.93)	10.60	(4.37)	$t = 3.9; p < .000$
– depression	23.64	(6.47)	25.24	(8.56)	$t = 1.7$; ns
– somatic complaints	17.45	(4.99)	18.47	(6.45)	$t = 1.2$; ns
– insufficiency	13.73	(4.62)	14.62	(4.94)	$t = 1.3$; ns
– sensitivity	25.04	(5.60)	26.77	(8.27)	$t = 2.1; p < .05$
– hostility	7.36	(1.65)	7.91	(2.43)	$t = 2.3; p < .05$
– sleeping problems	4.93	(2.31)	5.05	(2.37)	$t = 0.4$; ns
– psychoneuroticism	129.25	(28.82)	139.22	(38.28)	$t = 2.4; p < .05$
FAM	(N = 35)		(N = 584)		
– somatic	11.77	(6.59)	16.03	(10.45)	$t = 3.6; p < .001$
– cognitive	16.29	(6.57)	18.25	(7.39)	$t = 1.5$; ns

Table 10.4 Training effects of the 1-day group treatment

	Premeasurement		3 month follow-up		t-test	Cohen's d	Jacobson and Truax		Clinical effect
	Mean	(std dev.)	Mean	(std dev.)			Mean RCI	Mean % reliable change	
VAFAS (N =62)	7.60	(1.62)	2.18	(1.76)	t = 21.3; p <.000	3.20	—	—	—
FAS (N=62)									
– anticipatory	26.92	(12.29)	8.19	(8.55)	t = 12.5; p <.000	1.77	3.55	67.7%	51.6%
– in-flight	26.87	(7.86)	6.68	(6.01)	t = 18.2; p <.000	2.89	5.52	91.9%	72.6%
– generalised	5.15	(5.07)	1.39	(2.81)	t = 6.5; p <.000	0.92	1.69	35.5%	24.2%
– total	66.08	(24.02)	18.26	(17.40)	t = 15.3; p <.000	2.28	5.34	90.3%	75.8%
SCL-90 (N = 55)									
– anxiety	16.71	(5.64)	13.82	(4.99)	t = 4.1; p <.000	.54	.56	7.3%	10.9%
– agoraphobia	8.85	(2.88)	8.00	(1.75)	t = 2.6; p <.05	.36	.36	7.3%	7.3%
– depression	23.55	(6.49)	21.40	(8.21)	t = 2.1; p <.05	.29	.36	5.5%	10.9%
– somatic	17.11	(4.34)	16.16	(5.28)	t = 1.4; ns	.20	.24	7.3%	10.9%
– insufficiency	13.35	(3.64)	12.27	(3.29)	t = 2.3; p <.05	.31	.29	7.3%	10.9%
– sensitivity	24.80	(5.37)	22.82	(6.25)	t = 3.1; p <.005	.34	.40	3.6%	5.5%
– hostility	7.31	(1.62)	6.89	(1.33)	t = 1.7; ns	.28	.22	5.5%	5.5%
– sleeping problems	4.85	(2.26)	4.47	(2.34)	t = 1.5; ns	.17	.19	7.3%	9.1%
– psychoneuroticism	127.67	(26.53)	116.51	(31.23)	t = 3.1; p <.005	.39	.47	9.1%	9.1%
FAM (N = 34)									
– somatic	11.88	(6.65)	3.68	(4.80)	t = 7.0; p <.000	1.41	1.23	17.6%	35.3%
– cognitive	16.24	(6.66)	4.41	(4.54)	t = 12.2; p <.000	2.08	2.93	73.5%	55.9%

Table 10.5   Training effects of the 2-day group treatment

	Premeasurement	3 month follow-up	t-test	Cohen's d	Jacobson and Truax		
	Mean (std dev.)	Mean (std dev.)			Mean RCI	Mean % reliable change	Clinical effect
VAFAS (N = 695)	8.30 (1.37)	2.58 (2.00)	$t = 74.8$; $p < .000$	3.34	—	—	—
FAS (N = 695)							
– anticipatory	28.43 (11.80)	8.62 (8.37)	$t = 43.9$; $p < .000$	1.94	3.76	77.6%	65.8%
– in-flight	28.33 (9.47)	7.46 (6.89)	$t = 56.6$; $p < .000$	2.52	5.71	90.1%	74.2%
– generalised	5.42 (4.97)	1.33 (2.22)	$t = 23.5$; $p < .000$	1.06	1.84	39.4%	25.8%
– total	69.71 (24.37)	19.44 (17.35)	$t = 53.6$; $p < .000$	2.38	5.61	89.1%	78.7%
SCL-90 (N = 666)							
– anxiety	18.07 (6.95)	13.89 (4.41)	$t = 18.2$; $p < .000$	.72	.81	12.3%	23.0%
– agoraphobia	10.59 (4.37)	8.45 (2.46)	$t = 15.8$; $p < .000$	.60	.90	18.0%	13.7%
– depression	25.16 (8.50)	21.57 (6.82)	$t = 13.0$; $p < .000$	.47	.60	12.0%	15.3%
– somatic	18.44 (6.46)	15.72 (4.26)	$t = 13.3$; $p < .000$	.50	.69	13.8%	13.8%
– insufficiency	14.61 (4.94)	12.73 (4.00)	$t = 12.3$; $p < .000$	.42	.51	6.9%	14.6%
– sensitivity	26.73 (8.22)	23.94 (6.85)	$t = 10.6$; $p < .000$	.37	.56	11.9%	11.9%
– hostility	7.92 (2.46)	7.21 (1.95)	$t = 8.4$; $p < .000$	.32	.37	7.5%	13.4%
– sleeping problems	5.05 (2.39)	4.46 (1.98)	$t = 6.9$; $p < .000$	.27	.30	8.3%	14.6%
– psychoneuroticism	139.05 (38.42)	119.13 (29.18)	$t = 17.1$; $p < .000$	.58	.85	14.7%	18.8%
FAM (N = 577)							
– somatic	16.04 (10.46)	4.29 (5.08)	$t = 29.2$; $p < .000$	1.43	1.76	36.9%	42.6%
– cognitive	18.27 (7.39)	4.09 (4.61)	$t = 46.4$; $p < .000$	2.30	3.51	79.9%	67.9%

scales and subscales showed excellent substantial performance on Cohen's *d*. The effects of the SCL-90 were considered to be moderate to slight, with the best performances on the anxiety subscale. The FAS had a substantial improvement; 89.1 per cent of the patients fulfilled the criteria for a reliable change and 78.7 per cent the criteria for a clinically significant effect. The most important subscale, the in-flight subscale, showed that 90.1 per cent fulfilled the Jacobson and Truax criteria for a reliable change and 74.2 per cent the criteria for a clinically significant effect. In this two-day condition with cognitive training, 79.9 per cent of the patients fulfilled the criteria for a reliable change and 67.9 per cent the criteria for a clinically significant effect on the FAM cognitive scale.

The outcome of this clinical fear of flying programme shows that both treatment programmes are effective for overcoming fear of flying. Table 10.6 shows follow-up data for the VAFAS and the number of one-way flights taken within three, six and 12 months. All participants in the one-day treatment group took a flight on their own in addition to the test flight. The mean number of one-way trips was 11.3 (SD = 15.5). Almost the entire group of patients from the two-day condition (98.6 per cent) flew in the follow-up year (M = 10.2, SD = 10.4). Table 10.6 and Figure 10.1 also show the treatment result of patients with incomplete follow-up data from whom we were able to collect this information. The number of flights made in the one-year follow-up period was equally high among patients with complete follow-up data and patients with incomplete follow-up data. Ninety-four per cent of the patients with incomplete follow-up data in the one-day group had taken 11.2 flights (SD = 13) and 95 per cent of the patients with incomplete follow-up data in the two-day group had taken 8.5 flights (SD = 6.9). As Figure 10.1 shows, all groups maintained their low scores on the VAFAS after three, six and 12 months.

Discussion

This study is one of the few recent investigations on the effectiveness of treatment for fear of flying in clinical practice in a large group of patients. To our knowledge, there are more patients per condition in this study than in any other study dealing with fear of flying treatment programmes to date. What is remarkable in this study is that there is an almost equal number of men and women (41 per cent versus 59 per cent, respectively) who requested treatment, compared to other studies on specific fears and phobias (Fredrikson et al., 1996). Distributions are usually 30 per cent men and 70 per cent women.

Table 10.6 Follow-up flight experiences of patients with complete follow-up data and patients with incomplete follow-up data

| | Patients with complete follow-up data | | | | | Patients with incomplete follow-up data | | | | |
| | 1-day training (N = 62) | | 2-day training (N = 695) | | * | 1-day training (N = 67) | | 2-day training (N=202) | | ** |
	Mean (std dev.)	*N*	*Mean (std dev.)*	*N*		*Mean (std dev.)*	*N*	*Mean (std dev.)*	*N*	
VAFAS										
– premeasurement	7.60 (1.62)	62	8.30 (1.37)	695		7.90 (1.58)	67	8.36 (1.42)	202	
– 3 month follow-up	2.18 (1.76)	62	2.58 (2.00)	695		1.85 (2.50)	59	2.29 (2.12)	172	
– 6 month follow-up	1.71 (1.89)	62	2.20 (1.88)	670		1.51 (1.60)	49	2.11 (2.07)	152	
– 12 month follow-up	1.77 (1.89)	62	2.00 (1.92)	643		1.86 (2.03)	44	1.90 (2.20)	143	
Follow-up at 3 months										
– response	62 (100%)		695 (100%)		$\chi5 = 2.5$; ns	52 (77.6%)		142 (70.3%)		$\chi5 = 0.5$; ns
– did fly	53 (85.5%)		636 (91.5%)		$t = 0.9$; ns	46 (88.5%)		120 (84.5%)		$t = 0.02$; ns
– number of flights	4.6 (6.9)		3.8 (3.3)			4.1 (2.8)		4.1 (3.0)		
Follow-up at 6 months										
– response	62 (100%)		670 (96.4%)		$\chi5 = 0.4$; ns	40 (59.7%)		126 (62.4%)		$\chi5 = 1.8$; ns
– did fly	46 (74.2%)		521 (77.8%)		$t = 0.6$; ns	35 (87.5%)		98 (77.8%)		$t = 1.2$; ns
– number of flights	4.7 (5.9)		4.3 (4.7)			5.5 (5.8)		4.2 (4.0)		
Follow-up at 12 months										
– response	62 (100%)		642 (92.4%)		$\chi5 = 1.7$; ns	37 (55.2%)		105 (52.0%)		$\chi5 = 3.4$; ns
– did fly	53 (85.5%)		504 (78.5%)		$t = 0.3$; ns	24 (64.9%)		84 (80.9%)		$t = 1.1$; ns
– number of flights	4.5 (5.1)		4.7 (4.9)			6.3 (7.4)		4.6 (4.7)		
Total										
– did fly within 12 months	62 (100%)		685 (98.6%)		$\chi5 = 0.9$; ns	49 (94.2%)		147 (95.5%)		$\chi5 = 0.3$; ns
– number of flights within 12 months	11.3 (15.5)		10.2 (10.4)		$t = 0.8$; ns	10.9 (12.5)		8.8 (7.1)		$t = 1.1$; ns

* MANOVA for repeated measurements (N = 705): F-measurement = 788.9; $p < .000$; F-treatment = 5.59; $p < .05$; F-interaction = ns
** MANOVA for repeated measurements (N = 178): F-measurement = 389.2; $p < .000$; F-treatment = 5.64; $p < .05$; F-interaction = 2.94; $p < .05$

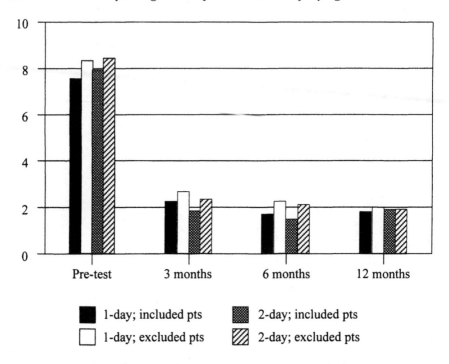

Figure 10.1 The VAFAS flight anxiety scores pre-treatment and after 3, 6 and 12 months follow-up

Two treatment protocols are described. Although the one-day treatment is called pure behavioural treatment, the actual difference between it and the two-day programme is that instructions are not provided in it on how to cope with irrational thoughts (no rational emotive training) and cognitive instructions are not given during the imaginary flight. In this condition, the patients' personal 'coping' tape does not include a correction of irrational thoughts. Of course, the information on flying by a pilot, which is the same for both groups, contains elements of cognitive restructuring. It can be argued that the main difference is the number of hours spent on cognitions in the therapy conditions.

The main outcome of this study is that flying phobics who want to overcome their fear of flying can be adequately helped. All patients in this study took the guided test flight. Using a test flight as the only treatment outcome measure can be misleading, because some phobics do not completely avoid the feared stimulus, and it does not reveal whether patients fly on their own after treatment. The results in this study were measured with different comprehensive measures, which show that the level of anxiety in different air travel situations is reduced. The decrease in anxiety is statistically significant for both groups. Not only are the Cohen's *d*, Jacobson and Truax criteria and clinical effect outcome measures good to excellent for the VAFAS, FAS and FAM scales, but the number of flights made after treatment is also high. FAS generalised flight anxiety was not high for most participants, but only for some patients who have witnessed a flight accident. A possible reason for the lower change in the FAM somatic scale could be that people's cognitions change easily, while they need more time to practice or become habituated. Not all scales in the SCL-90 had substantial results. This was contrary to our expectations and evaluation of patients' verbal messages. We expected better effect scores, especially on the anxiety subscale. It could be concluded that treatment for overcoming fear of flying had an impact mainly on this phobia and did not have a direct generalising effect on other complaints. On the other hand, very dramatic changes were not possible, because most SCL-90 scores were already relatively 'low' at baseline in this sample compared to clinically phobic patients and 'a normal' adolescent population according to Arrindell and Ettema (1986). It could also be concluded that there is relatively little psychopathology present, except for fear of flying and the closely related claustrophobia.

There were a few baseline differences between the two condition groups, a higher score on the VAFAS, FAM somatic scale and some SCL-90 subscales for the two-day condition group. This is understandable because participants were non-randomly assigned to one or two-day group treatment programmes. It was easier to advise patients with fewer complaints and less negative experiences in an aircraft, and accordingly less avoidance (or patients with no flying experience at all) to participate in the one-day group treatment. Moreover, some participants in the two-day condition received significantly more preparatory individual sessions. Baseline measures of coping skills were taken while these patients received extra individual sessions. Some patients referred to the facility were not considered ready to enter the fear of flying programme and had to be prepared for participation and therefore received a number of preparatory sessions. After these sessions, they were allowed to enter the treatment programme. It is possible that this may have built up their coping skills repertoire. This implies that in actual fact the intervention time was, for some patients, greater than described in the protocol for the two treatment versions. The design of the present study was not suitable for making a real comparison between the two treatment modalities in terms of effectiveness. A separate study using a randomised controlled design is required to provide this information. The fact that patients in the two-day condition reported more fear on some scales at baseline compared to the one-day group and that those differences in terms of the main VAFAS and FAS effectiveness measures were no longer present by the time post-treatment scores were taken might be due to giving the right advice to the right person about the programme to be followed. Perhaps randomly assigning participants to a treatment condition would have made a difference. Once again, to answer this question properly, patients would have to be randomly assigned. There are two reasons for the fewer number of participants in the one-day condition and the great amount in the two-day treatment: 1) therapists believed that a two-day training programme would be more effective for patients; and 2) if the therapist showed some hesitation between recommending the one or two-day treatment, patients tended to choose the latter.

In this study, only questionnaires filled out by participants who completed the pre-test and post-test FAS measurements at the three-month follow-up were analysed. One drawback of this study is the high proportion of patients with incomplete follow-up data. Participants lived throughout the Netherlands and were not always able to come to Leiden for the follow-up session. Requests for them to mail the questionnaire were not always successful. For this reason, we might wonder whether our sample was a self-selected group. However, analysis showed no differences in the pre-treatment phase between patients with complete and those with incomplete follow-up data. The only difference was the somewhat higher mean score on the FAS in-flight scale for patients with incomplete follow-up data. Moreover, the available VAFAS post-treatment scores and number of flights taken in the follow-up period failed to show any differences between patients with complete and incomplete follow-up data.

Because of the uncontrolled nature of the study, it remains to be established whether the results in this study are produced by treatment and not due to test-retest or time-related effects. The latter seems unlikely in view of the results of a previous study with a group of comparable fear of flying patients on a waiting list. In this study, in which the same fear of flying questionnaires (FAS and FAM) were used, it was shown that patients on a waiting list did not demonstrate any significant changes (van Gerwen et al., 1999).

Although distinguished by their unique symptoms, flying phobics are not all the same. We believe that the characteristics of flying phobics should reveal which patients can benefit from which treatment in the diagnostic phase. Although the study design precludes a direct comparison of the effectiveness of both programmes, both treatments proved to be effective. Further controlled studies should show whether certain patient characteristics selectively predict outcomes.

We do not know whether the 'right' recommendation to patients is the reason for the effectiveness of both treatment programmes or whether it is due to the fact that both treatments had the most significant components in common. However, both groups reported that the test flight and the flying information were the most useful elements. We believe that patients should be well prepared and motivated by treatment components prior to a test flight. Exposing patients to a flight without preliminary treatment preparation would have posed ethical problems, because most patients in this study had flown before and found it very distressing. In regular clinical practice, it is difficult to investigate all treatment components separately. Moreover, the one-day group condition reported that the second most useful components were information on how to behave during a flight and relaxation training, while the two-day condition group reported cognitive training as the second most important. Accordingly, this study raises a number of interesting questions for further research, such as, what is the minimum number of components, the minimum training time and the best order in which to present components?

References

American Psychiatric Association (1994), *Diagnostic and Statistical Manual of Mental Disorders* (4th edn), Washington, DC: American Psychiatric Association.

Aitken, J.R. and Benson, J.W. (1984), 'The Use of Relaxation/desensitization in Treating Anxiety Associated with Flying', *Aviation, Space and Environmental Medicine*, Vol. 55, No. 3, pp. 196–9.

Arntz, A. (1991), 'Principes en technieken van de cognitieve therapie' ['Principals and techniques from cognitive therapy'], *Directieve therapie*, Vol. 4, No. 11, pp. 252–68.

Arrindell, W.A. and Ettema, J.H.M. (1986), *SCL-90: Handleiding bij een multidimensionele psychopathologie-indicator [SCL-90: Manual for a multidimensional psychopathology indicator]*, Lisse, The Netherlands: Swets and Zeitlinger.

Bandura, A. (1977), 'Self-efficacy: Toward a unifying theory of behavioral change', *Psychological Review*, Vol. 84, pp. 191–215.

Borrill, J. and Foreman, E.I. (1996), 'Understanding Cognitive Change: A qualitative study of the impact of cognitive-behavioural therapy on fear of flying', *Clinical Psychology and Psychotherapy*, Vol. 3, No. 1, pp. 62–74.

Canton-Dutari, A. (1974), 'The Use of Systematic Desensitization in the Treatment of an Airplane Phobia', *Revista latinoamericana de Psicologia*, Vol. 6, No. 2, pp. 151–6.

Clark, D.M. (1986), 'A Cognitive Approach to Panic', *Behaviour Research and Therapy*, Vol. 24, No. 4, pp. 461–70.

Cohen, J. (1988), *Statistical Power Analysis for the Behavioral Sciences* (2nd edn), Hillsdale: Lawrence Erlbaum.

Denholz, M.S., Hall, L.A. and Mann, E. (1978), 'Automated Treatment for Flight Phobia: A 3½-year follow-up', *American Journal of Psychiatry*, Vol. 135, pp. 1340–43.

Derogatis, L.R. (1977), *SCL-90: Administration, scoring and procedures manual – 1*, revised version, Baltimore: Johns Hopkins University School of Medicine, Clinical Psychometrics Research Unit.

Deyoub, P.L. and Epstein, S.J. (1977), 'Short-term Hypnotherapy for the Treatment of Flight Phobia: A case report', *The American Journal of Clinical Hypnosis*, Vol. 19, No. 4, pp. 251–4.

Diekstra, R.F.W., Knaus, W.J. and Ruys, T. (1982), *Rationeel Emotieve Educatie* [*Rational Emotive Education*], Lisse: Swets and Zeitlinger BV.

Diment, A.D. (1981), 'Fear of Flying: Case study of a phobia', *Australian Journal of Clinical and Experimental Hypnosis*, Vol. 9, No. 1, pp. 5–8.

Ekeberg, Ø., Seeberg, I. and Ellertsen, B.B. (1990), 'A Cognitive/behavioral Treatment Program for Flight Phobia, with 6 Months' and 2 Years' Follow-up', *Nordisk Psykiatrisk Tidsskrift*, Vol. 44, pp. 365–74.

Ellis, A. (1972), *How to Master your Fear of Flying*, New York: Institute for Rational Living.

Fredrikson, M., Annas, P., Fischer, H. and Wik, G. (1996), 'Gender and Age Differences in the Prevalence of Specific Fears and Phobias', *Behaviour Research and Therapy*, Vol. 34, pp. 33–9.

Fodor, O. (1996), Minutes of the First Fear of Flying Conference, Tarrytown, New York.

Greco, T.S. (1989), 'A Cognitive-behavioral Approach to Fear of Flying: A practitioner's guide', *Phobia Practice and Research Journal*, Vol. 2, No. 1, pp. 3–15.

Howard, W.A., Murphy, S.M. and Clarke, J.C. (1983), 'The Nature and Treatment of Fear of Flying: A controlled Investigation', *Behavior Therapy*, Vol. 14, pp. 557–67.

Jacobson, N.S. and Truax, P. (1991), 'Clinical Significance: A statistical approach to defining meaningful change in psychotherapy research', *Journal of Consulting and Clinical Psychology*, Vol. 59, No. 1, pp. 12–19.

Karoly, P. (1974), 'Multi-component Behavioral Treatment of Fear of Flying: A case report', *Behavior Therapy*, Vol. 5, pp. 265–70.

Ladouceur, R. (1982), 'In vivo Cognitive Desensitization of Flight Phobia: A case study', *Psychological Reports*, Vol. 50, pp. 459–62.

McCarthy, G.W. and Craig, K.D. (1995), 'Flying Therapy for Flying Phobia', *Aviation, Space, and Environmental Medicine*, Vol. 66, pp. 1179–84.

Meldman, M. and Hatch, B. (1969), 'In vivo Desensitization of an Airplane Phobia with Penthranization', *Behaviour Research and Therapy*, Vol. 7, pp. 213–14.

Menzies, R.G. and Clarke, J.C. (1995), 'The Etiology of Phobias: A nonassociative account', *Clinical Psychology Review*, Vol. 15, pp. 23–48.

Öst, L.-G., Brandberg, M. and Alm, T. (1997), 'One versus Five Sessions of Exposure in the Treatment of Flying Phobia', *Behaviour Research and Therapy*, Vol. 35, pp. 987–96.

Roberts, R.J. (1989), 'Passenger Fear of Flying: Behavioural treatment with extensive *in-vivo* exposure and group support', *Aviation, Space and Environmental Medicine*, Vol. 60, pp. 342–8.

Rothbaum, B.O., Hodges, L., Watson, B.A., Kessler, G.D. and Opdyke, D. (1996), 'Virtual Reality Exposure Therapy in the Treatment of Fear of Flying: A case report', *Behaviour Research and Therapy*, Vol. 34, pp. 477–81.

Scrignar, C.B., Swanson, W.C. and Bloom, W. (1973), 'Case Histories and Shorter Communications. Use of Systematic Desensitization in the Treatment of Airplane Phobic Patients', *Behaviour Research and Therapy*, Vol. 11, pp. 129–31.

Sederer, L.I. and Dickey, B. (1996), *Outcome Assessment in Clinical Practice*, Baltimore: Williams and Wilkins.

Sidley, G.L. (1990), 'Brief Clinical Reports: A multi-component intervention with a lady displaying an intense fear of flying: a case study', *Behavioural Psychotherapy*, Vol. 18, pp. 307–10.

van Gerwen, L.J. (1988), *Vliegangst, oorzaken, gevolgen en remedie [Fear of Flying, Reasons, Effects and Remedy]*, Ambo: Baarn.

van Gerwen, L.J. and Diekstra, R.F.W. (1996), *Help, ik moet vliegen! [Help, I Have to Fly!]*, Utrecht, Holland: Bruna.

van Gerwen, L.J. and Diekstra, R.F.W. (2000), 'Fear of Flying Treatment Programs for Passengers: An international review', *Aviation, Space, and Environmental Medicine*, Vol. 71, pp. 430–37.

van Gerwen, L.J., Spinhoven, Ph., Diekstra, R.F.W. and Van Dyck, R. (1997), 'People who Seek Help for Fear of Flying: Typology of flying phobics (Leiden)', *Behavior Therapy*, 28, pp. 237–45.

van Gerwen, L.J., Spinhoven, Ph., Van Dyck, R. and Diekstra, R.F.W. (1999), 'Construction and Psychometric Characteristics of Two Self-report Questionnaires for the Assessment of Fear of Flying', *Psychological Assessment*, Vol. 11, No. 2, pp. 146–58.

Walder, C.P., McCracken, J.S., Herbert, M., James, P.T. and Brewitt, N. (1987), 'Psychological Intervention in Civilian Flying Phobia. Evaluation and a three-year follow-up', *British Journal of Psychiatry*, Vol. 151, pp. 494–8.

Wilhelm, F.H. and Roth, W.T. (1997), 'Clinical Characteristics of Flight Phobia', *Journal of Anxiety Disorders*, Vol. 11, pp. 241–61.

Williams, M.H. (1982), 'Fear of Flight: Behavior therapy versus a systems approach', *The Journal of Psychology*, Vol. 111, pp. 193–203.

Chapter 11

Brief, Solution-focused Psychological Treatment for Fear of Flying

Robert Bor

How people cope with and adjust to the unique stresses of air travel is of interest to people in the airline industry, psychologists, other health care practitioners and, of course, airline passengers themselves (Bor, 2003). This book focuses specifically on the treatment of fear of flying, while this chapter describes the relevance and application of a brief psychological treatment approach which may be both applicable and effective for a proportion of those who seek psychological treatment for a fear of flying. In the author's clinical experience, approximately 50 per cent of those who seek specialist help do not require the full complement of standard CBT (cognitive behavioural therapy) interventions, including an actual in-therapy flight, over several therapy sessions. A proportion appear to benefit sufficiently from core interventions (e.g., providing information about flight, cognitive restructuring, realistic threat appraisal and coping strategies for dealing with symptoms of anxiety and panic disorder), within a brief therapy framework (Bor et al., 2003). In an era of evidence-based health care (Sackett et al., 1996), coupled with high demand yet finite resources for psychological treatment (Goss and Rose, 2002), it is important for therapists to rapidly assess 'how much' therapy is likely to be required to treat the individual's presenting problem rather than apply the identical treatment package to all problems (Seligman, 1995).

In the preceding chapters, some contributing authors have described standard treatment approaches for fear of flying and highlighted the essential components of the therapy. Encouragingly, the evidence strongly suggests that fears and phobias associated with flying are highly amenable to psychological intervention, particularly where cognitive and behavioural approaches are applied (Taylor, 2000; van Gerwen and Diekstra, 2000). By way of contrast, insight-oriented, explorative and long-term psychological treatment approaches for both individuals and within groups, have a poor record of success (Carr, 1978; Solyom et al., 1973) and are no longer generally regarded as standard treatment options for these problems. Further analysis of a range of one-to-one and group-based CBT treatment approaches commonly applied to treating a fear of flying reveals three main components of these interventions. These include: a) providing information about aerodynamics, principles of flight and safety issues in aviation; b) information about identifying and coping with symptoms of anxiety and phobia, including panic attacks; and c) graded exposure to the actual or simulated experience of flight. Treatment is usually coupled with desensitisation and other interventions designed to improve tolerance and ability to cope with the noxious symptoms that fearful fliers commonly experience (Greco, 1989; Roberts, 1989; Taylor, 2000).

Two assumptions underpin many CBT approaches and programmes described in the literature. The first is that those who seek psychological treatment for their fear all require the same 'package' of interventions, both in terms of the components covered and duration of therapy. The second assumption is that because of the nature of the course of therapy, it is appropriate to confine treatment to specialist settings and to highly qualified and experienced therapists. The first of these assumptions has recently been challenged in the wider psychological literature with regard to emerging evidence on the 'dose effect' in psychotherapy (i.e. how much is necessary or sufficient for different problems) (Kadera, Lambert and Andrews, 1996) as well as the efficacy of brief approaches to treat a range of conditions (Hubble, Duncan and Miller, 2000). The extent to which a broader range of therapists, who may not necessarily be specialists in the treatment of fear of flying, provide professional services for these individuals, has not yet been studied. Furthermore, at the second International Fear of Flying Conference 'Airborne 2000' in Vienna, it became clear that there are still several fear of flying treatment facilities that offer standard treatment programmes without proper diagnostic screening (van Gerwen et al., 2003).

This chapter describes a brief, solution-focused approach to treating people who have a fear of flying. The emphasis here is on the method of approach to treatment and is therefore descriptive rather than a record of systematic and empirical research. The approach used arose from clinical experience gained in treating those who have attended two travel health clinics in London (The Royal Free Hospital Travel Clinic and the Hampstead Group Practice Travel Centre) over a two-year period, between 1999–2000. All clinic attendees would have initially sought expert medical advice and prophylaxis for infections for their intended overseas travel. A leaflet in the waiting area gave information on a psychological treatment service for those who wanted to overcome their fear of flying. It was unclear what proportion of the total number of clinic attendees followed up the contact information provided. However, the psychologist saw a total of 53 individuals in one-to-one therapy over the two-year period. The charge for each treatment session was £100. A group treatment option was not offered. While following standard CBT treatment protocols (e.g., van Gerwen et al., 2002), which may require several sessions of psychological therapy per individual, not including a flight, more than half (32/53; 60 per cent) of the total number of people treated did not require or arrange for follow up beyond the initial one-hour consultation.

The initial concern was that these clinic attendees may have opted out of treatment or the psychologist may have failed to adequately engage these individuals in treatment. Telephone calls to those on the 'attrition list' revealed that the opposite had occurred in 22/32 (69 per cent) of those seen only once. These individuals reported some improvement in coping with their fear of flying. The majority (17/32; 53 per cent) had taken at least one flight within three months of the initial treatment session. This unexpected finding prompted closer examination of the core components of standard initial treatment sessions. The examination highlighted considerable areas of overlap between cognitive behavioural interventions as well as brief, solution-focused approaches. The finding that a proportion of those who sought help to overcome their fear of flying were seen only once could be understood in one of several ways.

1   Treatment paradoxically increased anxiety, thereby exacerbating the problem, and therefore failed. The individual may have elected not to return to therapy.
2   Therapy may have been construed by the individual unhelpful.
3   A single session was all that was warranted or necessary, and treatment might have been effective independently of the theoretical approach used.
4   Treatment was sufficiently effective in a single session and this was due to the brief therapy approach used in the session or
5   The cost of the sessions may have prevented some attendees from continuing with a course of treatment sessions.

Since this was not set up as a clinical trial, but rather a *post hoc* finding within a clinical service, it was not possible to test the relative strength of these possible outcomes empirically, although this is now the focus of a prospective study. The following is a description of the essential features of the initial one-hour, brief therapy treatment session.

Brief Therapy

Emphasis on brief, evidence-based treatment approaches in UK National Health Service, primary care and travel clinic settings, coupled with peoples' lifestyle pressures and expectations of psychological treatment, requires health care professionals to be adept in assessing and treating in the shortest possible time. Brief, solution-focused psychological treatment is not merely 'compressed' long-term therapy; instead, it represents a different approach to conceptualising the onset, maintenance and resolution of psychological problems. It is not within the scope of this chapter to fully describe the theory and practice of time-sensitive therapeutic approaches and therefore readers who are interested in this might wish to consult other contemporary sources (e.g., Bor et al., 2003; Hoyt, 1995; Quick, 1996).

Jay Haley, an eminent psychotherapist, said that if therapy is to end properly, it must begin properly – by negotiating a solvable problem and discovering the social situation making the problem 'necessary' (1978). The initial interview sets the direction and tone of future therapeutic help. Sometimes this is a 'one off' consultation session, and in itself has the potential to be therapeutic and stimulate sufficient change. This is an important point to emphasise, as brief approaches to psychological therapy specifically do not aim to 'cure' in the traditional sense, but rather to pave the way for generating new and creative solutions to problems. This process begins at the point of first contact with the individual (which may be during telephone contact) and aims to inculcate a positive emotional state towards overcoming the problem (Bor et al, 2003; Hoyt, 1995). Development of the unique therapeutic relationship between individual and therapist is dependent on many factors but is specifically linked to the therapist's initial engagement of the individual rather than the theoretical approach used. The context of the first interview (airline treatment programme, university clinic, hospital, general practice, travel health clinic) as well as developmental factors (whether it is a child, adolescent, adult, couple or group) also all have an important bearing on how the person's problem is defined and what the future steps in treatment sessions might be.

Effective therapy in any context also needs clarity of purpose and follows a detailed assessment tailored to and emphasising the individual's unique situation rather than exclusively to the presenting problem (Quick, 1996). The goal and purpose of therapy is defined by the context, issues surrounding the referral and objectives subsequently agreed between therapist and individual. To this end, therapy is collaborative and consultative rather than based on a more hierarchically arranged 'expert-patient' model of interaction. Whatever the context or theoretical stance, basic concepts and steps guide the brief therapy interview. These are based on Weber et al.'s (1986) conceptual approach and described under the sub-headings below.

Practice Guidelines: Four Stages

1   Preparation for the initial contact.
2   Meeting and engaging the person and starting the interview.
3   Definition, clarification and assessment of the problem.
4   Decision making and ending the session.

Within each stage, steps can be clarified which serve as a 'map' to guide the clinical interview. Principles, aims and techniques are interwoven.

Stage 1: Pre-interview considerations Receiving the referral, managing the initial contact, considering practical factors (location, privacy and length of time available) and dealing with issues pertaining to the referring person all require some consideration even before the individual is actually seen. It is important to anticipate the unique issues and problems for each individual. Traditional approaches to therapy define the start of the therapeutic process as the first meeting between health care professional and individual seeking treatment. A brief, solution-focused approach recognises that this process begins when a referral is first considered or discussed (Selvini Palazzoli et al., 1980). The pre-session process clarifies:

*   the referring person's perceptions of the individual's problem;
*   what the referring person is requesting and expecting for the individual (therapy, consultation); and
*   agreement about the subsequent feedback to the referrer following the sessions.

In many cases where a fear of flying is the presenting problem, the individual self-refers, in which case feedback to a third party may not be required. Nonetheless, the therapy session is much enhanced where the therapist has made a preliminary assessment or hypothesis about the nature of the presenting problem. Information that is most relevant to this assessment takes into account the individual's:

*   stage of life (age);

- stage in relation to family (married, single, divorced, caring for elderly parents, living along or away from home);
- reason for referral, and expectations from treatment;
- health background and any previous medical or psychiatric problems,
- social and cultural context or background (ethnic, cultural, religious) and the setting of treatment; and
- experience of flying (e.g., whether any incidents or unpleasant experiences had occurred).

In one case, a 35-year-old married woman was referred by her manager at work who felt that the woman's fear of flying prevented her from more actively pursuing business abroad. A preliminary assessment speculated about whether the fear of flying was a recent or a long-standing one. Causes or triggers might have included changes in family life-cycle (e.g., birth of a child), a recent unpleasant incident when flying (e.g., extensive delays), the psychological state of the woman (e.g., underlying depression or panic attacks, grief from a recent loss), or pressure at work (e.g., to achieve certain targets, for a pending promotion). The intensity of the woman's fear of flying may have been aggravated by the direct involvement of her manager who may have been subjecting her to pressure and exposing her to feelings associated with a fear of failure.

An hypothesis is not necessarily 'true'. It allows speculation about the problem, the possible cause(s) or trigger(s), the likely impact and why it may present now. The initial contact provides opportunity to explore and revise the hypothesis.

Stage 2: Meeting and engaging the individual A brief approach to treatment requires the therapist to quickly build a rapport with the individual. This is an important and basic tenet of brief therapy (Quick, 1996). The rationale for abbreviating this part of the session is to rapidly, though positively, connect with the individual in the course of their describing his or her problem(s). This conveys that therapy does not 'build up' steam over time, but is focused and intense from the outset. In other words, the individual feels that every moment counts in brief therapy. The implied message is that the therapist is skilled and confident in addressing sensitive issues and is also aware of time considerations.

A useful opening remark, after initial pleasantries is 'what most would you like to discuss today and what would you like to achieve from this meeting?'

The aim of this is to establish a relationship in which there is freedom to discuss any problem and recognise and avoid the assumption that fear of flying might not be the uppermost problem on the person's mind. Furthermore, an agenda for the session is solicited early and the setting of goals is implied. The individual is actively engaged from the outset. Two further 'problem-defining' or 'problem-clarifying' questions are relevant and may follow this opening question.

'Which problem would you most like to deal with today/now?' This is especially relevant where the person lists a series of problems. Prioritising his or her problems is a psychotherapeutic intervention designed to reduce anxiety to manageable proportions, identify main concerns and specific concerns and work on setting achievable goals. Unrealistic goals or expectations can also be addressed, setting the stage for a collaborative relationship. The therapist needs to understand the specific nature of the fear of flying and its context rather than assume that this is similar for everyone. The next appropriate question that follows might be: 'What is it specifically about flying that troubles you the most?' and 'When do you have to fly again?'

This recognises that the problem of a fear of flying is experienced in different ways ranging from claustrophobia, agoraphobia, and a fear of a loss of control, to separation anxiety and general worries about aviation safety (Taylor, 2000; van Gerwen et al., 2000; Wilhelm and Roth, 1997). The therapist should discuss this and seek clarification where needed. The questions to be addressed in the therapist's mind are:

- what is the main problem for the individual;
- how does it affect him or her;
- what might trigger/maintain the problem;
- what might be done to solve it?

Stage 3: Gathering information; making an assessment It is wrong to assume that a fear associated with flying is due solely to adverse fears or anticipatory fears associated with air travel. For a proportion of those who seek treatment, lack of accurate information about flight might be a primary source of worry. In addition, some people develop a secondary fear of having a phobia and worry that this might signal the onset of a more serious and pervasive psychological problem. This may give rise to feelings of shame associated with having a psychological problem. It is for these reasons that a full and detailed assessment of the individual must first be made before treatment commences. Failure to carry out even a brief general mental health assessment could result in the underlying problem being overlooked, with obvious consequences for the efficacy and duration of psychological treatment.

The essentials of the initial assessment include finding out:

1   when the problem first started and what might have triggered it. Careful attention should be paid to life-stage transitions (e.g., shortly after the birth of a child, or following a bereavement) (Menzies and Clarke, 1995) and distressing experiences associated with previous experiences of air travel (e.g., exceptional turbulence, or 'bumpy' landings etc.);

2   how the individual has coped with or reacted to air travel in the past. It is essential to hear the person's unique story about the development of their problem (White and Epston, 1990). A fear of flying may have been preceded by many years of stress-free air travel. This foundation might serve as a building block from which to better understand the nature of the person's fear and from which to build up their coping skills and confidence;

3   how the problem affects the individual's life and routine, as well as their relationships and career (Taylor, 2000);

4   the extent to which co-factors relating to their psychological state (e.g., depression, relationship problems, career difficulties etc.) may have triggered, exacerbated or caused the fear of flying. It may be necessary to first treat this problem before turning one's attention to the fear of flying (Menzies and Clarke, 1995);

5   what specific reactions they have had generally, and in terms of their anxiety specifically, to different stages of preparing for and experiencing air travel. For example, buying an air ticket; packing for the trip; the journey to their airport; check-in formalities; boarding the aeroplane; the safety demonstration etc. Each of these stages should be measured on a Likert-type scale (see Bor, Josse and Palmer, 2000 for a more detailed account of this or van Gerwen et al., 1999, for a standardised psychometric instrument);

6   whether anyone else in the family has a fear of flying or suffers from other fears and phobias. A positive family history of these problems is common. It is also helpful to discover how that relative learned to cope with or overcome their problem (Menzies and Clarke, 1995);

7   what steps the individual has already taken to cope with or to overcome their fear of flying. Some solutions (e.g., self-medication, over-reliance on alcohol or avoidance) may serve to maintain or even exacerbate the problem. In brief therapy, problems are sometimes viewed as failed

solutions to difficulties and occur when the individual either repeats the same solution ('more-of-the-same' response) or has no new ideas about how to solve the problem (de Shazer, 1985; Watzlawick, Weakland and Fisch, 1974) This understanding paves the way for suggesting alternate solutions (White and Epston, 1990);

8   the extent or severity of the fear of flying. For example, an individual who is totally phobic and refuses to even board an aircraft will presumably require more intensive and focused desensitisation and other cognitive and behavioural interventions than an individual who is not wholly incapacitated by their fear and does not avoid flying altogether;

9   the extent of the motivation to overcome the problem. Merely seeking treatment may signal some motivation but it is necessary to determine whether this is sufficient. Motivation is directly related to treatment efficacy and outcome;

10   what might become of the person in different areas of their life if psychological treatment proved unsuccessful? It is always necessary to speculate about the implications or possible consequences of failure, as this is a real possibility for a small proportion of those who undergo treatment for a fear of flying;

11   if there is already a flight planned and for what reason (dealing with the anticipation).

The above can be assessed and explored through a number of small and practical steps. For example:

Defining the problem and origin through different questions: 'Can you say something about how you see the problem?' 'How does it affect you?' 'When did the problem start?'

- Helping the person to be *specific* and exemplify how the fear of flying *impacts upon life and lifestyle.* Identify any *critical events or changes* that might have precipitated the fear of flying. Answers given offer clues about possible life events that may have coincided with the onset of the problem. They also prompt enquiry about the person's underlying reason for seeking treatment. For example: 'What made you decide to seek help right *now*?'

- Determine what *maintains the fear of flying.* This might include an exploration of coping behaviours (e.g., avoidance of flying; or not seeking treatment) or *attempted solutions* to the problem. It is important to frame this enquiry in a positive tone. For example: 'What steps have you taken to help cope with your fear of flying? What has been most effective and helpful to you?'

• *Map the 'lifecycle' of the fear* of flying. Encourage description of when the fear begins, intensifies and abates. It is necessary to attend to specific details including cognitive and behavioural cues that the person identifies. In brief therapy, exceptions and unanticipated positive experiences are solicited and explored. The themes of 'coping' and 'competence' are introduced and amplified (Gill, 1999). For example:

> 'When you board the aircraft and you feel most vulnerable and distressed, you said that you often think about running off the aeroplane while it is still at the gate. You said that this ranks 9/10 on your scale of stress. Has there been time when it did not feel as high as that? What happened on that occasion? How did that lead you to feel about having this problem and your ability to overcome it?'; and
> 'What stops you from getting off the aeroplane when this does happen?'

This acknowledges that the person can sometimes cope reasonably well with the problem and that they are not always overwhelmed by their fears.

• Ask: '*What would need to be different* to make that situation just a bit more tolerable for you?' This may serve to dispel the wish for complete eradication of the fear of flying, which is unlikely in the short-term. It also begins to introduce the concept of gradual though incremental change and improvement.

• Consider the *impact of the problem on relationships*, by describing how the problem presents and what specifically the person experiences that they have come to construct or label the problem as a 'fear of flying'. It is also helpful to explore what impact the problem has on people around him/her. It is important to determine whether their reactions contribute to the problem or could be useful in the treatment of the fear.

In the course of brief therapy, every utterance, question, statement or interpretation is designed to facilitate understanding *and* change. A single session consultation may include an abbreviated discussion about the following topics that are covered in standard fear of flying treatment sessions: a) understanding flight; b) coping with anxiety and panic; and c) coping with psychological problems and adversity more generally (Bor, Josse and Palmer, 2000).

a) Understanding flight It is important to listen to the person's specific concerns about flying and to address these and correct misunderstandings. Let them set the agenda and list their concerns. Fears about safety and recent specific incidents and accidents are often raised. While many people who seek treatment are knowledgeable about safety records within the airline industry, they are nonetheless not convinced, or highlight exceptions to general rules. Attempting to 'outmanoeuvre' the person with further justifications is seldom effective and may require exploration or understanding of why objective data is not convincing. Avoid arguing about airline safety statistics and specific cases. Extensive discussion eventually creates a futile and combative dynamic in the session. It is preferable to explore why the person is not easily reassured or is so easily disbelieving. This accommodating response can also be achieved by examining a parallel problem (such as rail safety records, incidents of birth defects in the general population, which for some reason the person may have more trust in). In taking a meta-position to the person's preoccupation with exceptions, it may be helpful to ask 'In coming here today (or fetching your child from school), how much did you think about and weigh up the chances of having an accident? What swayed or convinced you to come along anyway? How is this similar or different to your experience of flying?' or 'What has lead you to believe that you don't have the power or strength to overcome these ideas/fears?' Referring the person to popular self-help books on overcoming a fear of flying is a useful adjunct to this part of the face-to-face therapy.

b) Coping with stress and anxiety Present a condensed account of how the body reacts to stress. It may be helpful to the therapeutic process to aim to reduce the complex material in this subject to no more than around ten to twenty sentences. Simple illustrative diagrams may accompany the description. Standard interventions in CBT can then be described for controlling specific symptoms (e.g., breathing, distraction, and non-avoidance of flying, thought insertion and relaxation technique). This should include responding to actual exposure as well as to help manage their anticipatory anxiety to reduce the intensity of the symptoms they experience on aircraft. Skills and techniques should be broken down into manageable steps and rehearsed in the session. Medication as an adjunct can also be considered although not during an accompanied in-therapy flight or during any form of in-therapy exposure.

c) Coping with problems and adversity more generally The solution-focused approach to therapy offers additional interventions that address both the self-beliefs and the emotional state of the individual. 'Miracle questions' (Quick, 1996) are extensively used as a means of mentally projecting the person into a problem-free or problem-manageable future. This can help to disrupt a pattern of predictable and catastrophising thoughts. An example of a miracle question is: 'If you were to wake up and not have this fear, what might be enjoyable about flying?' Further questions designed to overcome resistance and negative attributions include:

1   what are some possible advantages of not feeling in control;
2   could you think of a time in your life where you felt anxious or panicky and tell me how you coped? What skills did you learn then that you might be able to apply to flying;
3   think of someone you know who copes well with flying. How does he or she cope with flying and what hints or techniques could you adopt;
4   what would you notice about yourself if you actually got on a aeroplane and found the experience less distressing than usual? What might somebody who knows you well notice about you?

It is always necessary to explore the person's ultimate fear, or negative core belief (Beck, 1995). Often, this exploration reveals a hierarchy of linked fears, which may have their origins in the person's fear of shaming themself. For example:

Therapist: What is your main fear about getting on a aeroplane?
John: That I will feel trapped and can't escape.
Therapist: OK, and what is your fear about feeling trapped in a situation from which you can't escape?
John: That I'll panic and go crazy!
Therapist: What is your *main fear* about panicking and worrying that you might go crazy?
John: That's a tricky one. Maybe that I'll scream, froth at the mouth and vomit ... or become aggressive and angry ...
Therapist: And if that were to happen?
John: I'd feel ashamed and in the spotlight.
Therapist: It may be helpful for us to talk about your fear of losing control and shaming yourself.

In this case, John's fear of being trapped prevented him from boarding an aeroplane. When this was explored in more depth, a core belief emerged, that he would react in a way that would lead to his shaming himself. In this case, the fear of flying could be broken into constituent or core beliefs and coping skills were then considered to challenge this.

Brief therapy also works with narratives or stories about a fear of flying with a view to helping people alter these. Many people who have an intense fear of flying, live by a story of *non-flying*. For example: 'I avoid trips ... I go by car ... I hate holidays ... I won't fly because it's too much stress for me and the family ....' Therapy can help to generate a narrative of the *possibility of flying* and encourage talk about how life might be different if the person could better manage their associated fears.

Decision-making and Ending the Session

The end is important for any therapy session. Knowing when to stop in brief therapy requires skills and expertise, both of which develop over time with practice and increasing confidence. It is important to convey hope and optimism, asserting that every small change can help in relation to conquering their fear of flying. This stage of therapy may provide an opportunity to lower expectations, which may be unrealistic or indicative of all-or-nothing thinking. Toward the end of the initial session, the therapist should solicit feedback from the individual in a way that helps to better understand what has been most helpful. This is always framed positively. For example:

- 'what ideas will you most be taking away from this meeting?';
- 'if we had some more time, what would you want to do more of?'

The therapist then summarises the session, emphasising the concerns of the person as well as his or her strengths and competencies. Emphasis is placed on what can be realistically achieved through therapy and what the individual can *do* to cope with and manage their fear. It includes a summary of what decisions have been reached regarding the next steps in overcoming the problem. These may include reading about flying, visiting an airport, taking a short flight, or practising relaxation methods. A list of self-help books that people can use to help overcome their fear of flying outside of therapy sessions is contained at the end of this chapter.

Conclusion

Fear of flying can be treated by CBT, through a protracted course of treatment or, in some cases, within a single session. It is increasingly recognised among therapists that the treatment orientation should fit with the unique problems and circumstances of the individual rather than be addressed through a standard and possibly inflexible treatment schedule. The approach described in this chapter is a synthesis of CBT combined with brief, solution-focused therapy. It has a clear structure but errs on the side of possibility that a single or a few sessions may suffice. Further research is clearly required to help identify the 'active' ingredients of psychological treatment of fear of flying, as well as which individuals are most likely to benefit from which therapeutic approaches.

References

Beck, J. (1995), *Cognitive Therapy: Basics and Beyond*, New York: Guildford Press.

Bor, R. (Ed.) (2003), *Passenger Behaviour*, Aldershot: Ashgate.

Bor, R., Josse, J. and Palmer, S. (2000), *Stress Free Flying*, Quay Books: Wiltshire, UK.

Bor, R., Miller, R., Gill, S. and Parrott, C. (2003), *Doing Therapy Briefly; A post-modern approach*, London: Macmillan.

Carr, J. (1978), 'Behaviour Therapy and the Treatment of Flight Phobia', *Aviation, Space and Environmental Medicine*, Vol. 49, pp. 1115–19.

De Shazer, S. (1985), *Key to Solutions in Brief Therapy*, New York: W.W. Norton.

Gill, S. (1999), 'The Competent Patient', in Bor, R. and McCann, D. (eds), *The Practice of Counselling in Primary Care*, London: Sage, pp. 172–83.

Goss, S. and Rose, S. (2002), 'Evidence-based Practice: A guide for counsellors and psychotherapists', *Counselling and Psychotherapy Journal*, Vol. 2, pp. 147–51.

Greco, T. (1989), 'A Cognitive-behavioural Approach to Fear of Flying: A practitioner's guide', *Phobia Practice and Research Journal*, Vol. 2, pp. 3–15.

Hubble, M., Duncan, B. and Miller, S. (eds) (2000), *The Heart and Soul of Change*, Washington DC: American Psychological Society Press.

Kadera, S., Lambert, M. and Andrews, A. (1996), 'How much Therapy is Really Enough?', *Journal of Psychotherapy Practice and Research*, Vol. 5, pp. 132–51.

Menzies, R. and Clarke, J. (1995), 'The Etiology of Phobias: A non-associative account', *Clinical Psychology Review*, Vol. 15, pp. 23–48.

Quick, E. (1996), *Doing What Works in Brief Therapy*, San Diego: Academic Press.

Roberts, R. (1989), 'A Cognitive-Behavioural Approach to Fear of Flying: Behavioural treatment with extensive *in-vivo* exposure and group support', *Aviation, Space and Environmental Medicine*, Vol. 60, pp. 342–8.

Sackett, D., Rosenberg, W., Gray, J., Haynes, R. and Richardson, W. (1996), 'Evidence-based Medicine: What it is and what it is not', *British Medical Journal*, Vol. 312, pp. 71–2.

Seligman, M. (1995), *What you Can Change ... and What you Can't*, New York: Fawcett Columbine.

Selvini Palazzoli, M., Boscolo, L., Cecchin, G. and Prata, G. (1980), 'The Problem of the Referring Person', *Journal of Marital and Family Therapy*, Vol. 6, pp. 3–9.

Solyom, L., Shugar, R., Bryntwick, S. and Solyom, C. (1973), 'Treatment of Fear of Flying', *American Journal of Psychiatry*, Vol. 130, pp. 423–7.

Taylor, S. (2000), *Understanding and Treating Panic Disorder*, Chichester: John Wiley.

van Gerwen, L., Aronders, J., Diekstra, R. and Wolfger, R. (2003), 'Update of Fear of Flying Treatment Programs for Passengers: An international review', *Aviation, Space and Environmental Medicine*, in press.

van Gerwen, L. and Diekstra, R. (2000), 'Fear of Flying Treatment Programs for Passengers: An international review', *Aviation, Space and Environmental Medicine*, Vol. 71, pp. 430–37.

van Gerwen, L., Spinhoven, P., Diekstra, R. and Van Dyck, R. (2002), 'Multicomponent Standardized Treatment Programs for Fear of Flying: Description and effectiveness', *Cognitive and Behavioural Practice*, Vol. 9, pp. 138–49.

van Gerwen, L., Spinhoven, P., Van Dyck, R. and Diekstra, R. (1999), 'Construction and Psychometric Characteristics of Two Self-report Questionaires for the Assessment of Fear of Flying', *Psychological Assessment*, Vol. 11, pp. 146–58.

Watzlawick, P., Weakland, J. and Fisch, R. (1974), *Change: Principles of problem formation and problem resolution*, New York: W.W. Norton.

Weber, T., McKeever, J. and McDaniel, S. (1986), 'A Beginner's Guide to the Problem-orientated First Family Interview', *Family Process*, Vol. 24, pp. 257–64.

White, D. and Epston, D. (1990), *Narrative Means to Therapeutic Ends*, New York: W.W. Norton.

Wilhelm, F. and Roth, W. (1997), 'Clinical Characteristics of Flight Phobia', *Journal of Anxiety Disorders*, Vol. 11, pp. 241–61.

Appendix

Below is a list of self-help books for passengers from a range of countries and perspectives.

Angel-Levy, P. and Levy, G. (1982), *The Complete Book of Fearless Flying*, Minneapolis: Wetherall Publishing Co.

Aronson, J.L. (1973), *How to Overcome your Fear of Flying*, New York: Warner.

Bayaz, A., and Krefting, R. (1993), *Vliegangst overwinnen* [*Conquering Fear of Flying*], Amsterdam: De Driehoek.

Bertoli, V.F. (2001), *Vuele sin temor. Orientacion e informacion para resolver el miedo a volar* [*Flying without Fear. Orientation and Information for Relaxed Flying*], Buenos Aires, editorial Salerno.

Bond, D.D. (1952), *The Love and Fear of Flying*, New York: International Universities Press.

Bor, R., Josse. J. and Palmer, S. (2000) *Stress-free Flying*, Salisbury: Mark Allen Publishing Ltd.

Braunburg, R. (1989), *Fliegen ohne Flugangst* [*Flying without Fear of Flying*], Stuttgart: Motorbuch Verlag.

Braunburg, R. and Pieritz, R.J. (1979), *Keine Angst vor Fliegen* [*No Fear of Flying*], Niederhausen: Falken Verlag.

Brown, D. (1996), *Flying without Fear*, Oakland, CA: New Harbinger Publications.

Brown, G.A. (1989), *The Airline Passenger's Guerilla Handbook. Strategies and tactics for beating the air travel system*, Washington, DC: The Blakes Publishing Group.

Burke, B. and van Gerwen, L.J. (2003), *Let your Fear Fly. Control your Fear of Flying*, Aldershot: Ashgate.

Burns, D.D. (1981), *Feeling Good*, New York: William Morrow Co.

Byrne Crangle, M. (2001), *Conquering Your Fear of Flying*, Dublin: Newleaf.

Byrne Crangle, M. (2002), *Vliegangst overwinnen* [*Conquering your Fear of Flying*], Belgie-Nederland: Deltas.

Cummings, T.W. (1981), *Help for the Fearful Flyer. Answers to 75 questions about flight and about fear*, Coral Gables, FL.

Cummings, T.W. (1989), 'Flying Phobia', in Lindeman, C. (ed.), *Handbook of Phobia Therapy: Rapid symptom relief in anxiety disorders*, Nortvale, NJ: Jason Aronson, Inc.

Cummings, T.W. and White, R. (1987), *Freedom from Fear of Flying*, New York: Pocket Books.

Cummings, T.W. and White, R. (1988), *Freedom from Fear of Flying*, New York: Grafton Books.

Cummings, T.W. and White, R. (1989), 'Freedom from Fear of Flying', in Lindeman, C. (ed.), *Handbook of Phobia Therapy: Rapid symptom relief in anxiety disorders*, Nortvale, NJ: Jason Aronson, Inc.

Doctor, R.M. and Kahn, A.P. (1989), *The Encyclopedia of Phobias, Fears and Anxieties*, New York: Facts on File, Inc.

Dentan, M. (2001), *Comment ne plus avoir peur en avion. Apprivoisir l'avion* [*How to be Fearless while Flying*], Paris: Le cherche midi editeur.

Ehret, C.F. and Waller Scanlon, L. (1983), *Zo voorkomt u jet lag* [*Overcoming Jet Lag*], Amsterdam: Sijthoff.

Ellis, A. (1972), *How to Master your Fear of Flying*, New York: Institute for Rational Living.

Fairechild, D. (1992), *Jet Lag? Jet Smart*, Maui, Hawaii: Flyana Rhyme, Inc.

Forgione, A.G. (1988), Flying Program, *Fearless Flying*, 4 cassette series.

Forgione, A.G. and Bauer, F.M. (1980), *Fearless Flying. The Complete Program for Relaxed Air Travel*, Boston: Houghton Mifflin Company.

Grande, E. (1990), *Flying can be Fun. A Guide for the White-knuckled Flyer*, Middleton, MA: Dyenamiks, Inc.

Greist, J.H. and Greist, G.L. (1981), *Fearless Flying. A Passenger Guide to Modern Airline Travel*, Chicago: Nelson-Hall.

Grizzard, L. (1989), *Lewis Grizzard on Fear of Flying*, Marietta, GA: Longstreet Press Inc.

Gunn, W.H. (1987), *The Joy of Flying. Overcoming the Fear*, Mission, KS: Wings Publications.

Hartman, C. and Huffaker, J.S. (1995), *The Fearless Flyer. How to Fly in Comfort and without Trepidation*, Oregon, The Eighth Mountain Press.

Heinemans, J. (1989), *Vliegen met plezier – zonder angst* [*Flying with Pleasure – without Fear*], Utrecht: Bruna.

Hodge, M. and Byskal, J. (1991), *Ready for Take-off. The Complete Passengers Guide to Safer, Smarter Air Travel*, New York: Signet.

Hoyt, M. (1995), *Brief Therapy and Managed Care*, San Francisco: Jossey Bass.

Hutchins, K. (1990), *Learning to Fly without Fear*, New York: Berkley Books.

Institute for Psychology of Air Travel Inc. (1978), *Active Stress Coping*, Boston: Institute for Psychology of Air Travel Inc.

Institute for Psychology of Air Travel Inc. (1980), *A Flight Captain Answers Questions*, Boston: Institute for Psychology of Air Travel Inc.

Institute for Psychology of Air Travel Inc. (1980), *Guided Flight to Portland*, Boston: Institute for Psychology of Air Travel Inc.

Kowet, D. (1983), *The Jet Lag Book. The Foolproof Way to Lose your Fear of Flying*, New York: Crown Publishers.

Lafferty, P. (1980), *How to Lose your Fear of Flying*, Los Angeles: Price/Stern/Sloan.

Mayes, K. (1991), *Beat Jet Lag. Arrive Alert and Stay Alert*, London: Thorsons.

Nance, J.J. (1986), *Blind Trust*, New York: Quill.

Ridley, L. (1987), *White Knuckles. Getting over the Fear of Flying*, New York: Doubleday.

Seaman, D. (1998), *The Fearless Flier's Handbook: The internationally recognized method for overcoming the fear of flying*, Berkeley, Ten Speed Press.

Seaman, D. (1998), *The Fearless Flier's Handbook: Learning to beat the fear of flying with the experts from the Qantas Clinic*, Berkeley, Ten Speed Press.

Smith, M.J. (1978), *Kicking the Fear Habit*, New York: Bantam Books.

Stauffer, C.L. and Petee, F. (1988), *Fly without Fear*, New York: Dodd, Mead and Company.

Sternstein, E. and Gold, T. (1991), *From Take Off To Landing. Everything you Wanted to Know about Airplanes but had no one to ask*, New York: Pocket Books.

Ten Have-De Labije, J. (1988), *De Lucht in. Over vliegen zonder angst* [*Going into the Air. About Flying without Fear*], Amsterdam: Boom.

Tomaro, M. (1995) *Flying in the Comfort Zone. Therapeutic Learning for Flyers*, Milwaukee, WN: The Institute for Human Factors Inc.

van Gerwen, L.J. (1988), *Vliegangst. Verschijnselen, oorzaken en remedie* [*Fear of Flying. Symptoms, Reasons and Remedy*], Baarn: Ambo.

van Gerwen, L.J. and Diekstra, R.F.W. (1996), *Help, ik moet vliegen!* [*Help, I Have to Fly!*], Utrecht: Bruna.

van Gerwen, L.J. (2000), *Help, I Have to Fly!*, Leiden: The VALK Foundation.

Yaffé, M. (1987), *Taking the Fear out of Flying*, Devon: David and Charles Publishers.

Ziegler, V.W. (1983), *Freude am Fliegen. So bekämpfen Sie Ihre Flugangst* [*Joy when Flying. How to Fight your Fear of Flying*], Vienna: Orac/Pietsch.

Ziegler, V.W. (2000) *Freude am Fliegen. Aviaphobie. So bekämpfen Sie Ihre Flugangst* [*Joy when Flying. Aviaphobia. How to Fight your Fear of Flying*], Vienna: Ibera Verlag.

Chapter 12

Virtual Reality Exposure Therapy in the Treatment of Fear of Flying

Page L. Anderson, Barbara Olasov Rothbaum and Larry F. Hodges

More research has been conducted examining the use of virtual reality exposure therapy (VRE) for the fear of flying than any other phobia, and results from a randomised clinical trial show that it is equally effective as *in vivo* exposure (Rothbaum et al., 2000) with treatment gains maintained at 12 month follow-up (Rothbaum et al., 2002). As the September 11 terrorist attacks have increased fear of flying among the North American public while at the same time restricted access for traditional *in vivo* exposure therapy, VRE is a viable alternative to help the many that are suffering. This chapter describes virtual reality, the theoretical rationale and empirical evidence for its use in the treatment of fear of flying, clinical guidelines, and examples of its use in a private practice setting.

What is Virtual Reality?

Virtual reality (VR) allows individuals to become active participants within a computer-generated three-dimensional world. To become a part of the virtual world, individuals wear a head-mounted display (HMD), which consists of display screens for each eye, earphones and a head-tracking device. The HMD provides the participant multi-sensory cues in the virtual world (Hoffman, 1998) and allows the virtual world to change in a natural way with head and body motion. For example, a person in a virtual aeroplane who suddenly hears thunder may turn to look out of the window at the bad weather. These multi-sensory cues and natural motion serve to 'immerse' the individual into the computer-generated environment and create a sense of 'presence' within the environment. The more immersed one becomes, the more one feels like a part of the world (Wiederhold, Davis and Wiederhold, 1998).

How can Virtual Reality Assist in the Treatment of Fear of Flying?

In order to overcome a fear, one must face the fear. However, simply facing the fear is not enough. In fact, there are many fearful fliers who fly regularly, yet the fear does not diminish. Emotional processing theory (Foa and Kozak, 1986; Foa, Steketee and Rothbaum, 1989) provides a framework for understanding the conditions under which facing a fear helps attenuate anxiety using exposure therapy. The theory suggests that fear memories can be construed as structures that contain information regarding stimuli (e.g., turbulence), responses (e.g., racing heart), and meaning (e.g., 'We're going to crash'). In order to cope with a fear, two conditions must be met. First, the fear structure must be activated. If the fear is inaccessible, then it will not be able to be modified (Lang, 1977). Second, while the fear structure is activated, information must be provided which includes elements 'incompatible with some of those that exist in the fear structure, so that a new memory can be formed. This new information, which is at once cognitive and affective, has to be integrated into the evoked information structure for an emotional change to occur' (Foa and Kozak, 1986, p. 22). Exposure therapy is believed to facilitate emotional processing by activating the fear structure and allowing the individual to stay in the situation long enough to process information inconsistent with the feared stimulus. Any method capable of activating the fear structure and modifying it would be predicted to improve symptoms of anxiety. Thus, VR is a potential tool for exposure therapy in the treatment of flying phobia.

Evidence that VR is a Useful Tool for Exposure in the Treatment of Anxiety

A body of literature is accumulating from case studies and controlled clinical trials supporting the notion that VR is an effective tool for conducting exposure therapy in the treatment of anxiety disorders. Case studies have shown that VR is useful in the treatment of specific phobia, including fear of heights (Rothbaum et al., 1995), fear of flying (North, North and Coble, 1997; Rothbaum et al., 1996; Smith, Rothbaum and Hodges, 1999), fear of spiders (Carlin, Hoffman and Weghorst, 1997), and claustrophobia (Botella, Banos, Perpina, Villa, Alcaniz and Rey, 1998). A case study (Rothbaum et al., 1999) and an open clinical trial (Rothbaum et al., 2001) have also documented the utility of using VR in the treatment of post-traumatic stress disorder among Vietnam veterans. Most recently, case studies have supported the use of VR in treating public speaking anxiety (Anderson, Rothbaum and Hodges, in press).

The first published controlled study using VR in the treatment of a psychiatric disorder compared VRE to a waiting list control in the treatment of acrophobia, or fear of heights (Rothbaum et al., 1995). Results indicated significant decreases in anxiety, avoidance, and distress for the VRE group but not for the control group. Interestingly, 70 per cent of the treatment completers spontaneously exposed themselves to real-life height situations by the end of treatment without being instructed to do so. This study provided the first evidence that treating fears in the virtual world could generalise to improvement in the real world. Recently, a randomised controlled clinical trial comparing VRE to *in vivo* exposure in the treatment of fear of heights found the two treatments to be equally effective (Emmelkamp et al., 2002).

Virtual Reality in the Treatment of Fear of Flying: Evidence from Controlled Studies

Based on these encouraging results, the investigators chose to develop a virtual aeroplane to test its efficacy in treating the fear of flying (FOF) for several reasons. First, FOF is a significant problem, affecting an estimated 10–25 per cent of the population (Dean and Whitaker, 1980). Also, standard exposure therapy for FOF is inconvenient and cumbersome for therapists. Furthermore, there are many uncontrollable elements in standard exposure for FOF (e.g., weather, only one take-off and landing per flight) that could be controlled in a virtual environment.

The relative efficacy of VRE versus standard exposure (SE) as compared to a waiting list (WL) control group was tested (Rothbaum et al., 2000). Random assignment of participants, standardised treatment delivery, homogeneous DSM inclusion criteria, blind independent assessment, and a commercial flight behavioural avoidance test assured a methodologically rigorous study. Forty-nine participants who met DSM-IV criteria for either panic disorder with agoraphobia in which flying was the primary feared situation or a specific phobia of flying were randomly assigned to one of the three conditions. Forty-five participants, or 15 per group, completed the study.

Treatment consisted of eight individual therapy sessions conducted over a six-week study period. The first four sessions consisted of training in anxiety management skills, including breathing retraining, cognitive restructuring for irrational beliefs, thought stopping, and hyperventilation exposure. Anxiety management sessions were followed by exposure to a virtual aeroplane (VRE) or exposure to an actual aeroplane at the airport (SE). VRE sessions were conducted twice weekly in the therapist's office according to a treatment manual (Rothbaum et al., 1999b). These sessions included such stimuli as sitting in the virtual aeroplane, taxiing, taking off, landing, and flying in both calm and turbulent weather. During VRE sessions, an HMD provided visual and audio cues, and a chair with a woofer under the seat provided tactile cues (i.e., vibrations). The therapist communicated with the patient via a microphone.

For SE sessions, *in vivo* exposure was conducted at the airport by exposing patients to pre-flight stimuli (e.g., ticketing, waiting area) and by spending time on a stationary aeroplane habituating to aeroplane stimuli and conducting imaginal exposure (e.g., takeoffs, landings). Immediately following the treatment or waiting list period, all patients were asked to participate in a behavioural avoidance test consisting of an actual commercial round-trip flight. The therapist accompanied participants in a group on a flight that lasted about one-and-a-half hours each way.

The results indicated that both VRE and SE were superior to the WL condition, with no differences between VRE and SE on any outcome measure. For WL participants, no significant differences were found between pre- and post-treatment self-report measures of anxiety and avoidance, and only one of the 15 waiting list participants completed the graduation flight. Compared with WL, participants in VRE and SE reported significantly fewer symptoms of anxiety and avoidance on all self-report measures and rated themselves on average as 'much improved'. Furthermore, participants receiving SE or VRE were approximately three and one-half times more likely to take the commercial flight than the waiting list control group. Follow-up data gathered at one year post-treatment indicated that participants maintained their treatment gains (Rothbaum et al., 2002). At the 12-month follow-up, 93 per cent of the VRE and SE participants had flown since completing treatment and reporting continued improvement in anxiety. These data represent the first controlled study to compare the use of VRE in the treatment of a specific phobia to the current standard of care, *in vivo* exposure therapy as well as the first 12-month follow-up of VRE treatment. The findings suggest that VRE is as efficacious as SE on every outcome measure used. This controlled study lends support to the assertion that VRE can successfully treat FOF within the confines of a therapist's office. With the same comparison groups in a larger sample, the above results were replicated.

One uncontrolled report from an independent laboratory also found that VR was effective in treating FOF, with 68 per cent of the treated participants flying after VRE treatment (Kahan et al., 2000). This study also found no group differences in treatment response among fearful fliers diagnosed with specific phobia, panic disorder, claustrophobia, or fear of heights. Although this study provides some preliminary support for the efficacy of this technology for FOF as tested by a different research group, the results must be interpreted cautiously, as the researchers did not utilise random assignment or a control group (Cook and Campbell, 1979).

Thus, data from case studies, uncontrolled studies, and a randomised clinical trial unequivocally support the use of VRE in the treatment of fear of flying. However, treating fear of flying in the context of a research study is different than in clinical practice. Research studies utilise strict inclusion/exclusion procedures and conduct therapy according to a standard protocol. As any therapist knows, clinical practice tends to be more 'messy' and 'unusual' circumstances are commonplace. Below are some guidelines that we have developed from both our research studies and clinical practice for conducting VRE, including strategies to help make the VRE seem more 'real'. Next, examples of patients from the clinical practice of the first author are presented to highlight some issues that arise when using VRE within a comprehensive treatment programme for the fear of flying.

Guidelines for Virtual Reality Exposure Therapy for the Fear of Flying

Patients should remain in the exposure situation long enough for their anxiety to decrease By remaining in the situation until their anxiety decreases, they are learning two important lessons: a) whatever they have been scared of does not occur; and b) their anxiety can decrease and they can feel more comfortable in the presence of their feared situation. Do not begin a new level of exposure (e.g., take-off) unless there is sufficient time remaining in the session to allow the patient ample time to habituate.

Patients should progress at their own pace Individuals differ in their speed of habituation to anxiety-provoking situations. Some patients fly in turbulent weather on the first VR exposure session, while others may need the first session to habituate to the engine noises. We track habituation using a self-report subjective units of distress (SUDs) scale. SUDs may ranges from 0–100, in which 0 represents no anxiety or discomfort and 100 represents panic-levels of anxiety or discomfort.

Patients should be praised for exposures completed and encouraged to push themselves further Therapists need to keep in mind that what the patient is doing is difficult for him or her and requires courage. We define courage as 'acting in the face of fear; being scared and doing it anyway'. Fearful fliers know that their fear is irrational, so it is especially important to validate how frightened they feel and to sincerely praise them for facing it.

The use of subtle avoidance and distraction interfere with therapy The therapist should inquire about and challenge subtle forms of avoidance. Examples with fearful fliers include only flying certain airlines, refusing to fly in less-than-perfect weather, keeping good luck charms, listening to music in order to drown out engine noises, and not looking out of the window. These should be described as avoidance strategies that will interfere with habituation and extinction and keep the phobia alive.

Expectations for Therapy

Just as with any type of exposure therapy, it is important for therapists to provide a clear rationale and realistic expectations for treatment. Patients who believe that VR is the magic bullet and patients who are overly sceptical should be assisted in moderating their beliefs.

Guidelines for Assisting Patients in Achieving Immersion in Virtual Reality Exposure

Ease into the VR The therapist should ask the patient to sit in the HMD with her eyes closed while the software is loading. This is an excellent opportunity to transition the patient from the real world to the virtual world. The therapist should describe the events leading up to the exposure and give the exposure a context (e.g., the patient describes standing in line to check in baggage).

Patients can talk about a previous traumatic event related to their fear Many (but not all) patients with flying anxiety have had a difficult flight. Ask the person to describe the situation in detail, focusing on their thoughts, feelings, and bodily sensations while in the virtual aeroplane.

Pay attention to the patient's narrative During VRE, patients will sometimes report how they would feel 'if this was real life'. Try to redirect the patient to speak and act as if this is real life. One way to accomplish this goal is to have the person speak in the first person and in the present tense.

Use interoceptive exposure During VRE patients may use one of any number of interoceptive exposure exercises to generate the physical sensations they typically feel when highly anxious, such as increased heart rate, sweating, dry mouth, and dizziness (Craske and Barlow, 1993). Activities to generate such sensations include overbreathing (breathing heavily through the mouth for two minutes, breathing through a straw (two minutes) and body tensing (one minute).

Capitalise on anticipatory anxiety The therapist can build the patient's anticipatory anxiety by referring to past experiences or upcoming events that need to be faced. The therapist should try to use the patient's own words to describe the experience.

From the Laboratory to the Clinic: Case Examples of VRE in the Treatment of FOF

Case 1: Intensive Three-day Treatment of Specific Phobia

Many people contact our clinic in metro-Atlanta, Georgia, from across the country for treatment of fear of flying. We provide services for people from out-of-town, particularly if there is no behaviour therapist locally, although we always tell people that we believe it is best to be treated locally and that the efficacy of intensive treatment for fear of flying has not been tested systematically. For people who remain interested, we conduct an in-depth phone screen to rule out people who are actively using substances, psychotic, or have a serious psychiatric problem that would benefit from ongoing treatment (e.g., severely depressed, high levels of agoraphobia). We emphasise that intensive treatment is indeed intense, usually nine sessions over three days, and highly encourage the person to rent a car to drive to our clinic and plan to fly back home.

'Ken'[1] is a 45 year-old Caucasian, married, college-educated male living in Colorado who contacted our clinic for treatment after locating us on the internet. He is an example of a good candidate for intensive treatment: he reported no other psychiatric symptoms; he did not have a history of psychiatric treatment; he had read about cognitive-behavioural therapy and the rationale made sense to him; and he was highly motivated for treatment. Ken drove from Colorado with his family to our clinic in Atlanta, Georgia for treatment.

Ken received eight sessions of individual therapy over the course of three days. The first session was dedicated to assessment. Sessions 2 and 3 were spent in anxiety management skills training. Sessions 4–6 focused on using virtual reality exposure therapy. The therapist met the patient at an airport for *in vivo* exposure and consolidation of treatment for the final sessions (7 and 8).

The assessment phase consisted of a brief psychosocial interview, with most of the time dedicated to understanding the patient's fear of flying. Ken reported that he was apprehensive of his first flight, at age 10, but that he eventually grew to enjoy flying to the extent that he took flying lessons and actually piloted two flights. He became increasingly apprehensive over the past 3–4 years, began cancelling flights based on weather conditions and had not flown in one-and-a-half years at the time he presented for treatment. He believed that the thing that contributed most to his fear of flying was his 'creative mind' (e.g., envisioning something loose on the plane). His primary method for coping was to try to 'get my mind off it' with books or music. He wanted to overcome his fear for work-related reasons: as the president of a consulting practice, air travel was required to grow his business.

Day 1 (Sessions 1–3) consisted of assessment, presentation of the rationale for treatment, teaching of breathing relaxation, and introduction to cognitive restructuring. The patient was also given some written materials that included information about the process of flight to use to counter scary thoughts. For homework, the patient was instructed to practice breathing, read the written materials, and complete a thought record regarding flying.

On Day 2, the sessions (4–6) focused on VR exposure therapy and on review of homework. The patient was oriented to the VR equipment and engaged in exposure to take-off, calm flight, turbulence and landing. The feeling of the adjustment of the engine after take-off was his most anxiety-provoking situation and was repeated several times. The patient reported relatively low levels of anxiety throughout – with the highest being 30 on a scale from 0–100 during the adjustment of the engine. By the end of the session, the patient was reporting an anxiety level of 0.

On the final day of treatment, the therapist met the patient at Hartsfield International Airport, in Atlanta, Georgia for *in vivo* exposure. The therapist was able to arrange to go with the patient to an elevated, restricted-access ground communication tower due to a long-standing relationship with an airline. The tower is situated between two runways and provides a 360° close-up view of planes taking off and landing. The tower is also filled with knowledgeable airport personnel, including mechanics, ground traffic control, and pilots. It is a wonderful opportunity to ask questions of extremely knowledgeable and experienced airline staff. The patient reported very low levels of anxiety throughout the *in vivo* exposure (five at most).

The therapist and patient spent the remainder of the time at the airport, reviewing anxiety management skills and consolidating treatment gains. After Day 1 of therapy, the patient scheduled a flight for the following week. The patient reported that he felt well-prepared for the approaching flight. The therapist, however, was somewhat sceptical that the patient had not experienced high enough levels of anxiety during either the VR or the *in vivo* exposure to allow the processes of habituation and extinction to take place. Luckily, the patient was on target. He phoned the therapist after returning from his flight to report that the flight had gone very well. He rated his highest level of anxiety during the outgoing flight as a 20 and the return flight as a 5.

Case 2: Adjunctive Treatment for Severe Panic with Agoraphobia

Our clinic also has been contacted by local therapists who want to use VR exposure therapy as an adjunct to ongoing treatment. In the following case example, 'Sheila' was being treated by a behavioural therapist for severe panic disorder with agoraphobia. The referring therapist contacted the first author to discuss VRE as an adjunct to prepare the patient for an upcoming international flight. The referring therapist was focusing on behavioural treatment for panic, including progressive muscle relaxation and interoceptive exposure.

Sheila is a 47-year-old, married, African-American woman with an advanced degree, living in Atlanta, Georgia. She was initially treated for panic disorder in her early 20s and had responded quite well to behavioural therapy. However, over the past few years, agoraphobia had crept back. At the time she contacted her former therapist, she avoided crowds, malls, open spaces, enclosed places, and any situations that would make it difficult for her to escape. Her avoidance was having a significant impact on her functioning, as she was unable to participate in many family activities. She was having panic attacks on almost a daily basis. Her symptoms included shortness of breath, racing heart, chest pain, sweating, nausea, derealisation, numbness, and the fear that she would lose control. Her primary panic symptom was a 'tightening' feeling that she would get across her forehead.

The patient also reported significant depressive symptoms, including sad mood, difficulty sleeping and feelings of worthlessness. However, her depressive symptoms appeared secondary to the panic disorder and did not prevent her from engaging in therapy. She denied other symptoms of mania, anxiety, psychosis, or substance use.

Sheila received seven therapy sessions over the course of a month. Although the patient was very optimistic about the effectiveness of exposure therapy in the long run, she was sceptical that she would be able to travel to Paris in less than one month. However, she was quite motivated, as her children wanted her to participate in the family vacation. The first session included assessment, presentation of the rationale, and teaching of a breathing relaxation exercise. Session 2 focused on teaching the patient cognitive restructuring, as the referring therapist was focusing primarily on behavioural techniques. The next 5 sessions alternated between VR exposure therapy (Sessions 3, 5, and 7) and *in vivo* exposure at the airport (Sessions 4 and 6). Her highest and lowest anxiety ratings during situations that provoked the most anxiety during the VR and *in vivo* exposure are presented below:

Table 12.1 Highest and lowest anxiety ratings

Session	Exposure type	Situation	Highest anxiety	Lowest anxiety
3	VR	Anticipating take-off	30	10
4	SE	Stationary plane w/ interoceptive exposure	30	10
5	VR	Take-off w/ interoceptive exposure	45	20
6	SE	Coordination tower	30	10
7	VR	Take-off	10	10

The above table indicates the patient's decreasing level of anxiety over the course of the therapy. Although the anxiety ratings were low, the patient appeared to benefit from both the VR and *in vivo* exposure. The VR exposure was particularly effective in accessing negative thoughts (e.g., 'I cannot be confined in one place for 10 hours') and talking back to the thoughts while experiencing the sights and sounds of flight (e.g., 'I have been in a car for eight hours without stopping'). The *in vivo* exposure was helpful because the patient had not been in the airport in several years and it prepared her for what to expect. Between sessions, the patient was instructed to practise interoceptive exposure (breathing through a thin straw) and to engage in other *in vivo* exposures (e.g., parking miles away from her seat at a sporting event, sitting in a dim room alone for an hour). Between Sessions 6 and 7, the patient took a 'practice' one-hour flight to Florida in preparation for the international flight, which went beautifully, with no panic attacks the entire time.

As shown above, we often combine VR and *in vivo* exposure in our clinical practice, whereas in research studies we compare the treatments to each other. There is no research to date that has compared the single treatments to their combination for any of the anxiety disorders, including FOF. Since September 11, we have no longer been able to conduct *in vivo* exposure at the airport, due to increased security. Both case examples reported relatively low levels of SUDs, yet both were treatment successes. Further research is needed to help quantify the relation between levels of anxiety, immersion, and treatment outcome.

Conclusion

Outcome research conducted to date suggests that VR is a powerful tool in the treatment of fear of flying and its efficacy is equal to the current standard of care, *in vivo* exposure. In the current context of the war on terrorism with heightened security and restricted access to airport stimuli and planes, VR is a viable alternative to *in vivo* exposure at a time when more people than ever are afraid to fly.

Advantages for the use of VR in treatment of FOF include greater control of situations (choosing the weather conditions), greater convenience (patient and therapist can conduct exposure in the therapist's office), and improved patient confidentiality. There are disadvantages of VR exposure therapy, as well. At times, the virtual environment may not match the idiosyncratic fear of the patient and for some patients the VR simply does not feel real enough to elicit any anxiety. Also, in the past, VR has been prohibitively expensive to use outside of research institutions. However, the cost has declined dramatically. The first VR fear of heights study was conducted on a $150,000 Unix platform that required a graduate student in computer science to operate. The most recent fear of flying study utilised a virtual reality system that was run from a PC by a relatively computer-illiterate therapist. The head-mounted display represents the bulk of the hardware cost ($2,000–$5,000). As costs have declined, research institutions, medical centres, and private practitioners from the USA, Canada, Israel and Australia use VR in the research and treatment of anxiety (www.virtuallybetter.com).

Perhaps the most compelling advantage of VR beyond its efficacy is its potential to reach the general public. One unexpected by-product of the research described in this chapter is the media attention it has engendered. The clinical research described here has been shown on CNN, *The Today Show*, Discovery Channel, MSNBC, *Dateline NBC*, National Public Radio, *USA Today*, the *New York Times* and the *Atlanta Journal Constitution*, to name a few. This type of media exposure has tremendous potential to educate the public about help for anxiety. In addition to media appeal, VR seems to have general public appeal as well. People who might never be interested in traditional therapy are accustomed to computers helping them in everyday life. In fact, there is some evidence that patients prefer VR to *in vivo* exposure. During the first clinical trial, when given the choice, WL participants overwhelmingly chose VR therapy over *in vivo* therapy for FOF (Rothbaum et al., 2000), suggesting that it may be easier for people to take the first step to confront their fear of flying when they can do it in a virtual world.

Note

1   Patients' names and details have been changed to protect anonymity.

References

Anderson, P., Rothbaum, B.O. and Hodges, L.F. (in press), 'Virtual Reality in the Treatment of Social Anxiety: Two case reports', *Cognitive and Behavioral Practice*.

Botella, C., Banos, R.M., Perpina, C., Villa, H., Alcaniz, M. and Rey, A. (1998), 'Virtual Reality Treatment of Claustrophobia: A case report', *Behaviour Research and Therapy*, Vol. 36, pp. 239–46.

Carlin, A.S., Hoffman, H.G. and Weghorst, S. (1997), 'Virtual Reality and Tactile Augmentation in the Treatment of Spider Phobia: A case report', *Behavior Research and Therapy*, Vol. 35, pp. 153–8.

Cook, T.D. and Campbell, D.T. (1979), *Quasi-experimentation: Design and analysis issues for field settings*, Chicago: Rand McNally.

Craske, M.G. and Barlow, D.H. (1993), 'Panic Disorder and Agoraphobia', in Barlow, D.H. (ed.), *Clinical Handbook of Psychological Disorders*, 2nd edn, New York: Guilford, pp. 1–47.

Dean, R. and Whitaker, K. (1980), *Fear of Flying: Impact on the US air travel industry*, Boeing Company Document #BCS-00009-RO/OM.

Emmelkamp, P.M.G., Krijn, M., Hulsbosch, L., de Vries, S., Schuemie, M.J. and van der Mast, C.A.P.G. (2002), 'Virtual Reality Treatment versus Exposure in Vivo: A comparative evaluation in acrophobia', *Behaviour Research and Therapy*, Vol. 40, No. 5, pp. 509–16.

Foa, E.B. and Kozak, M.J. (1986), 'Emotional Processing of Fear: Exposure to corrective information', *Psychological Bulletin*, Vol. 99, pp. 20–35.

Foa, E.B., Steketee, G. and Rothbaum, B. (1989), 'Behavioral/cognitive Conceptualizations of Post-traumatic Stress Disorder', *Behavior Therapy*, Vol. 20, pp. 155–76.

Hoffman, H. (1998), 'Virtual Reality: A new tool for interdisciplinary psychology research', *CyberPsychology and Behavior*, Vol. 1, No. 1, pp. 195–200.

Kahan, M., Tanzer, J., Darvin, D. and Borer, F. (2000), 'Virtual Reality-assisted Cognitive-behavioral Treatment for Fear of Flying: Acute treatment and follow-up', *Cyberpsychology and Behavior*, Vol. 3, No. 3, pp. 387–92.

Lang, P.J. (1977), 'Imagery in Therapy: an Informational-processing Analysis of Fear', *Behavior Therapy*, Vol. 8, pp. 862–86.

North, M.M., North, S.M. and Coble, J.R. (1997), 'Virtual Reality Therapy for Fear of Flying', American Journal of Psychiatry, Vol. 154, No. 1, p. 130.

Rothbaum, B.O., Hodges, L., Alarcon, R., Ready, D., Shahar, F., Graap, K., Pair, J., Herber, P., Gotz, D., Wills, B. and Baltzell, D. (1999), 'Virtual Reality Exposure Therapy for Vietnam Veterans with Posttraumatic Stress Disorder', *Journal of Traumatic Stress*, Vol. 12, pp. 263–71.

Rothbaum, B.O., Hodges, L.F., Anderson, P., Price, L. and Smith, S. (2002), '12-month Follow-up of Virtual Reality and Standard Exposure Therapies for the Fear of Flying', *Journal of Consulting and Clinical Psychology*, Vol. 70, pp. 428–32.

Rothbaum, B.O., Hodges, L.F., Kooper, R., Opdyke, D., Williford, J. and North, M.M. (1995), 'Effectiveness of Virtual Reality Graded Exposure in the Treatment of Acrophobia', *American Journal of Psychiatry*, Vol. 152, pp. 626–8.

Rothbaum, B.O., Hodges, L., Ready, D., Graap, K. and Alarcon, R.D. (2001), 'Virtual Reality Exposure Therapy for Vietnam Veterans with Posttraumatic Stress Disorder', *Journal of Clinical Psychiatry*, Vol. 62, pp. 617–22.

Rothbaum, B.O., Hodges, L. and Smith, S. (1999b), 'Virtual Reality Exposure Therapy Abbreviated Treatment Manual: Fear of flying application', *Cognitive and Behavioral Practice*, Vol. 6, No. 3, pp. 234–44.

Rothbaum, B.O., Hodges, L.F., Smith, S., Lee, J. H. and Price, L. (2000), 'A Controlled Study of Virtual Reality Exposure Therapy for the Fear of Flying', *Journal of Consulting and Clinical Psychology*, Vol. 68, pp. 1020–26.

Rothbaum, B.O., Hodges, L., Watson, B.A., Kessler, G.D. and Opdyke, D. (1996), 'Virtual Reality Exposure Therapy in the Treatment of Fear of Flying: A case report', *Behaviour Research and Therapy*, Vol. 34, pp. 477–81.

Smith, S.G., Rothbaum, B.O. and Hodges, L. (1999), 'Treatment of Fear of Flying using Virtual Reality Exposure Therapy: A single case study', *The Behavior Therapist*, pp. 154–8.

Wiederhold, B.K., Davis, R. and Wiederhold, M.D. (1998), 'The Effects of Immersiveness on Physiology', in Riva, G. and Wiederhold, B.K. (eds), *Virtual Environments in Clinical Psychology and Neuroscience: Methods and techniques in advanced patient-therapist interaction. Studies in health technology and informatics*, Vol. 58, Amsterdam, Netherlands Antilles: IOS Press, pp. 52–60.

Chapter 13

Computer-assisted Therapy for Flight Phobia

Xavier Bornas, Miquel Tortella-Feliu and Jordi Llabrés

In this chapter we describe the computer-assisted therapy for flight phobia. Since it is an exposure therapy, we start with a brief explanation about the theoretical foundations of the exposure techniques. Then we present the different exposure procedures that have been used to treat flight phobia (*in vivo*, using slide projectors, virtual reality, and computer-assisted), and we make a detailed description of the computer-assisted fear of flying treatment (CAFFT) developed by Bornas and his colleagues. To the best of our knowledge, this is the only computer-assisted exposure therapy for fear of flying. In the next section we summarise the research testing process on the CAFFT: efficacy, clinical usefulness, and appropriateness depending on the client's fear profile. The last section of the chapter is devoted to some concluding remarks. We underline the advantages of the CAFFT but also the limitations, and we suggest some future lines of research.

Exposure: Why does it Work?

Since the early 1980s exposure therapy has been extensively used for the treatment of anxiety disorders (Barlow and Wolfe, 1981). Traditionally, exposure techniques have been based on the extinction of conditioned responses. When a conditioned stimulus (CS) is repeatedly presented without being followed by the unconditioned stimulus (US), the conditioned response (CR) extinguishes.

We can think of fear of flying as a set of conditioned responses (e.g., heart beating, sweating, trembling, etc.) which are elicited by different conditioned stimuli related to flying (e.g., the taking-off sounds, the plane seats, the crew messages, and so on). The USs may not always be the same (e.g., crashing), but none of them actually follows the CS (fortunately!).

One reason that people maintain phobic behaviour for years is that they learn to avoid the CS diligently, and the CR never has a chance to undergo extinction. Fearful flyers usually avoid not only taking trips on planes but also going to airports, watching TV news reporting aeroplane crashes, etc. Indeed, there are also some more subtle avoidance strategies. For example, having some alcoholic beverages before flying may prevent people coping effectively with the CSs because of the alteration of the normal biological responses to them. It should be expected that the fear conditioned responses would extinguish if phobic people keep coping with the CSs instead of avoiding them (the CSs not being followed by any US).

Exposure procedures involve setting up a situation in which: a) phobic people are given the chance to cope with the CSs; and b) the CS no longer predicts the US. It is well known that fear can be extinguished by doing so, but it should be realised that the extinction process may not be the only explanation for the success of the exposure therapy. Extinction is a rather mechanistic explanation which has been complemented by a more cognitive view. From this perspective, phobic people learn to think different along the exposure sessions since they become aware that they actually can cope with the CSs. Some kind of cognitive restructuring seems to take place through the exposure process. They become more self-confident, and they do not look at the CSs as threatening or dangerous stimuli. We probably require both explanations (the mechanistic one, in terms of biological habituation, and the cognitive one), and psychologists are still searching for a comprehensive theory about how fear responses are actually reduced. Exposure therapy is effective and can be applied irrespective of the specific exposure type or modality used (*in vivo*, imaginal or simulated), as we will see in the next section.

Exposure: How is it being used Today?

Currently, *in vivo* exposure is the treatment of choice for specific phobias. Despite the large body of research that demonstrates the efficacy of this kind of exposure, only one random trial evaluated the efficacy of *in vivo* exposure for flight phobia (Öst, Brandberg and Alm, 1997). Unlike other phobias, the difficulty and expense of *in vivo* flight exposure have daunted many researchers and therapists (Rothbaum et al., 1996). Others have attempted to simulate flight situations that cause fear in a way that is both realistic and vivid. Simulated exposures were first tried in the 1970s, using slide projectors, with promising results (Denholtz and Mann, 1975; Solyom et al., 1973). Denholtz and Mann (1975), for example, found systematic desensitisation to flight pictures to be more effective that either relaxation alone or exposure to flight film without relaxation. However, practical problems such as difficulties in integrating sound and image, therapist control of stimuli, recording of patients' self-assessed anxiety, and so on, may have limited the application of this exposure strategy over the next 20 years.

The rapid development of new technologies that can easily overcome these limitations has again led researchers to develop new simulated-exposure treatments, with other possible benefits beyond their efficacy: reducing therapist contact time, standardisation of treatment, and widespread low-cost use (Newman, Consoli and Taylor, 1997). In addition, simulated exposure might be more useful for those patients who are reluctant to experience directly *in vivo* exposure therapy (an actual flight). As Selmi et al. (1990) and Newman et al. (1997) found, cognitive-behavioural procedures, such as exposure, are particularly well suited to interactive computer programmes because they are highly structured with well-delineated procedures, target specific symptoms, and it proceeds in a systematic fashion. This is valid for both virtual reality and computer-assisted exposure therapies.

The newest technology used to simulate fear stimuli is virtual reality (VR) (Glantz et al., 1996; North, North and Coble, 1998). Rothbaum et al. (1996) presented the first case study in which VR was successfully used as a key component in the treatment of a flight phobic patient, and Rothbaum et al. (2000) conducted the first controlled study on VR for the treatment of fear of flying. VR exposure was as effective as standard exposure. Mühlberger et al. (2001) also have demonstrated that one-session VR exposure effectively reduced flight phobia to a greater extent than relaxation training. VR exposure treatment for a fear of flying is discussed by Rothbaum and her colleagues in Chapter 12 of this book.

The use of computer programmes is an alternative to VR for fear stimuli simulation. Computer-assisted programmes are specific types of software aimed to confront patients, in a hierarchically structured way, with real images and sounds related to the fear stimuli presented on the screen of a personal computer. Although the first application of this procedure was unsuccessful in the treatment of spider phobia in two children (Nelissen, Muris and Merckelbach, 1995), Coldwell et al. (1998) described a computerised exposure-based therapy programme for the fear of dental injections that was effective in reducing this fear in a small sample. Computer-assisted exposure has been recently used to reduce fear of flying with promising results (Bornas et al., 2001c).

The computer-assisted fear of flying treatment (CAFFT) is a computerised exposure treatment that requires little therapist involvement and may be completed within about four hours of actual exposure. The rationale for CAFFT is as follows: air travel can be conceptualised as a series of chronological events with critical moments. CAFFT divides air travel into five sequential stages: 1) preparation for travel; 2) preflight activities the day of the flight; 3) boarding the plane and take off; 4) in-flight conditions; and 5) the descent of the plane and landing. Although most people with flight phobia experience anxiety during most stages of air travel, the majority of patients experience idiosyncratic patterns of anxiety intensity throughout the flight experience. That is, they fear certain critical moments more than others.

CAFFT configures automatically the patient's fear hierarchy based on his or her answers on the fear of flying questionnaire-II (FFQ-II; Bornas et al., 1999), integrated into the programme. Each item is associated with one of the exposure sequences. The CAFFT calculates the mean score for each stage of flight and then orders the presentation of stages from the one with the lowest score to the one with the highest score. Each stage of flight consists of a chronological series of photographs (at home, at the airport, walking onto the plane, etc.) shown on the screen of a personal computer with paired sounds taken in real settings. For example, the flight preparation sequence starts with three pictures of windows of three different travel agencies and appropriate street noise. The next picture was taken inside one of these travel agency shops and the patient hears typical office sounds. This sequence continues with pictures showing an open suitcase on a bed, the suitcase closed and ready near the door and ends with a picture of the airport bus in the street. In addition to these five sequences, the CAFFT also includes a sixth sequence of pictures and matching audio stimuli related to aircraft accidents. This sixth sequence was included in the CAFFT because anxious apprehension about the possibility of the aeroplane crashing is hypothesised to be a key component to many flight phobics' fear (Howard, Murphy and Clarke, 1983; Van Gerwen et al., 1997; Wilhelm and Roth, 1997). Exposure to this sequence does not seek to eliminate the instinctual and adaptive fear response to an actual plane crash, but to reduce the extreme anxiety that some flight phobic patients experience when they just think of the possibility of crashing or when they see a plane crash on television. The sequences include about 15 pictures and last between 3–4 minutes each.

After being presented with all the photos-sounds in a sequence, the patient rates his or her anxiety on a 1–9 point Likert scale. The programme repeats the sequence until the patient rates his/her anxiety as a 1 or a 2. Once the patient has habituated, the programme advances to the next sequence in the patient's fear hierarchy. The patient completes therapy after he/she has habituated to all stages of flight. At this point the patient can choose to receive additional exposure to any of the six sequences prior to taking an actual flight (overexposure phase). At pre-treatment assessment, just after FFQ-II has been completed, the patient is asked to mark if flying at night and/or with bad weather conditions is associated with more fear. In this case, overexposure is carried out with pictures and sounds reproducing these special conditions.

Computer-assisted Exposure for Flight Phobia: Does it Work?

The first study of the usefulness of CAFFT comprised a single case study (Bornas et al., 2001a). A 34-year-old man with severe fear and avoidance of flying received six 50-minute CAFFT sessions and two 20-minute booster sessions. He met DSM-IV (APA, 1994) criteria for a specific phobia (flying) and he had cancelled four previously booked flights in the last five months. The first day the patient was given a brief rationale for the treatment and some instructions about the functioning of the programme. Once started, the exposure treatment was automatically administered by the computer programme as described previously, the only difference being that the images were enlarged by means of an LCD projector. The results of this study showed a dramatic reduction on the patient's self-reported anxiety following CAFFT treatment: from 251 to 59 in FFQ-II total score (the maximum score on the FFQ-II questionnaire is 270). In addition, the patient's anxiety decreased to 43 following an actual flight taken a few days after completing treatment. At six months post treatment, the patient reported that he had flown three more times without anxiety.

Despite these encouraging results the study had some limitations. Firstly, although interventions by the therapist were minimal, the therapeutic effect of the therapist's presence remained unknown. Secondly, from the cost-effectiveness point of view, the CAFFT should be compared with other fear of flying treatments (e.g., relaxation training). Thirdly, in order to increase the portability of the treatment it should be presented on a standard desktop computer instead of an LCD projector. Finally, it could be shorter (in this study the patient requested the booster sessions to make sure he was ready for his *in vivo* flight).

Therefore, the next step in the process of testing the CAFFT had to be a controlled study (Bornas et al., 2001c). In order to be included in this study, each subject had to meet criteria for specific situational phobia (APA, 1994), or agoraphobia or a panic disorder with agoraphobia, with fear of flying as the most clinically relevant behaviour pattern. Thirty-seven women and 13 men participated in the study. The subjects were randomly assigned to one of three groups: two treatment groups (one receiving computer assisted exposure (CAE) and one receiving also aeronautical information and relaxation training before exposure (IRCAE) and one waiting list control group (WLC). Four male therapists participated in the study. All four therapists had at least two years of clinical experience in cognitive-behaviour therapy and had been trained to use the treatment software for three months prior to the study beginning. Direct intervention by the therapists was limited to the minimum advice necessary during exposure treatment.

The results of this study demonstrated that both methods of treatment were significantly more successful than being in the waiting list control group, and the CAE method of treatment led to a greater reduction in subjects' fear of flying than the IRCAE treatment did. In other words, 14 subjects in the CAE group took an actual flight after the simulated exposure (93.4 per cent), while only nine (50 per cent) in the IRCAE group took it. In the waiting list control group, two out of 17 subjects (11.8 per cent) took a flight during the same period. The mean improvement scores from the FFQ-II assessment of subjective fear of flying, before and after treatment (before flying) were 53.28 (SD = 49.98) for the IRCAE group, 92.43 (SD = 42.18) for the CAE group and 0.68 (SD = 24.63) for the waiting list control group.

No significant differences were observed between the pre-treatment scores and those taken after subjects were provided with aeronautical data and relaxation training (all subjects refused to take a real flight at this point). Therefore, this treatment component did not contribute significantly to reducing fear of flying. Furthermore, once subjects' self-assessed fear of flying is clearly reduced after CAE treatment (up to 100 points of reduction in FFQ-II), no significant additional decreases in FFQ-II ratings occur at the post-flight assessment stage (up to 30 points) or after taking flights during the follow-up period (up to six points). The CAE group's mean score for the FFQ-II after treatment (M = 56.11, SD = 13.25) was below the mean value in nonphobic samples (M = 65.24, SD = 30.8) (Tortella-Feliu and Fullana, 2000), and the group's reduction in fear was therefore highly significant ($t(12) = 6.61$, $p < .0001$). On the other hand, the IRCAE group's mean score at the post-treatment stage (M = 82.71, SD = 42.4) was still slightly higher than the mean observed in non-phobic samples, although the improvement observed after the pre-treatment assessment was statistically significant ($t(8) = 3.9$, $p < .01$).

Finally, the results of this study suggest that CAE therapy alone is a better clinical choice than CAE combined with information and relaxation training. During both methods of treatment, the main reduction in fear was obtained after CAE. The post-treatment real flight did not contribute significantly to reducing self-assessed levels of flight phobia. Thus CAE could be effective in itself in the treatment of flight-phobic patients, instead of being used in the training stages or previous skill acquisition phase prior to the *in vivo* exposure represented by the actual flight. To sum up, the efficacy of the CAFFT was corroborated by this study, although further research is needed to overcome some limitations (see Bornas et al., 2001c).

The next question refers to the clinical usefulness of the CAFFT: would the CAFFT be effective when applied by non-expert therapists? What results would it get in clinical settings? To answer these questions (Bornas et al., 2001b) conducted two studies. The first one (S1, N = 12) consisted of the application of the CAFFT at the clinical Fear of Flying Unit located at the Palma (Mallorca) airport. The second study (S2, N = 8) was conducted by German researchers, who did not participate in the development of the CAFFT, at the University Clinic of Psychiatry and Psychotherapy in Tübingen. Computer-assisted exposure therapy was conducted in both studies by young female therapists with less than one year of clinical experience. They received a brief but intensive training on the use of the software. Exposure was automatically administered as described above, but the size of the computer screen was 21 inches in S1 instead of the larger one used in previous studies and in S2.

Results of S1 showed that all 12 patients who started treatment completed it as well as the actual flights. The mean time of exposure (meaning the time the patient remained seated in front of the computer) was somewhat more than three hours (189.92 minutes; SD = 64.02; range 91–303 minutes). Treatment caused significant decreases in fear of flying as reflected in three measures: FFQ-II ($F = 40.39$, $p < .0001$), Fear of Flying Scale (FFS; Haug et al., 1987) ($F = 23.11$, $p < .0001$) and General Discomfort 1 to 9 scale ($F = 21.06$, $p < .0001$). *Post hoc* contrasts revealed significant differences between pre-treatment and post-CAFFT assessments and between pre-treatment and post-flight assessments for all three measures. According to Jacobson's categories (Jacobson and Truax, 1991), one patient did not change (8.3 per cent), two patients improved (16.7 per cent), and nine patients recovered (75 per cent).

Seven out of eight subjects in study 2 completed the treatment as well as the actual flights. The mean time of exposure was 192.5 minutes (SD = 49.24; range 118–267 minutes).Treatment caused significant decreases in fear of flying as reflected in the FFQ-II ($F = 17.99$, $p < .0001$), FFS ($F = 10.78$, $p < .01$) and general discomfort 1–9 Likert-type question ($F = 21.03$, $p < .0001$). *Post hoc* contrasts yielded significant differences between pre-treatment and post-CAFFT assessment as well as between pre-treatment and post-flight assessment for all three measures. Differences between post-CAFFT and post-flight assessments were only significant for the general discomfort question, but not for the FFQ or the FFS. One patient (12.5 per cent) did not change, four patients improved (50 per cent) and three recovered (37.5 per cent).

Treatment conditions, as reflected in actual CAFFT exposure time, were quite similar in both studies. Similar exposure times and reduction of fear were also found in previous studies when the CAFFT was applied by experienced clinicians. Despite a higher percentage of recovered patients in Study 1 (75 per cent) compared to Study 2 (37.5 per cent), this difference did not reach significance. Overall, it seems that CAFFT may be effectively used by most clinical psychologists regardless of their clinical experience and even their knowledge about fear of flying.

Another interesting question regarding CAFFT usefulness refers to the prediction of outcomes based on the specific fears of fearful flyers. It is widely recognised that fear of flying is not a unitary fear. It has been argued that it could be the expression of several underlying components including a fear of crashing, fear of heights, fear of confinement, etc. Howard et al. (1983) set out six basic components of flight phobia, with fear of crashing being the most prevalent one, although other fears also played an important role. More recently, other studies have shown similar results but new components have been taken into account (i.e., van Gerwen et al., 1997). Furthermore, while flight phobia is considered a situational specific phobia in the DSM-IV, some authors have pointed out that it can be better conceptualised as the expression of other non-situational phobias or as a part of panic-agoraphobia disorders. Some differences have been found among fearful flyers depending on these diagnoses (McNally and Louro, 1992; Wilhelm and Roth, 1997).

Some research has been conducted on the clinical features of people who seek treatment for fear of flying in order to analyse their contribution to the CAFFT treatment outcome (Fullana and Tortella-Feliu, 2001; Tortella-Feliu, Fullana and Bornas, 2001). In the study by Fullana and Tortella-Feliu (2001), focusing on outcome predictors of CAFFT treatment, only two variables from the initial assessment were related to post-treatment fear of flying severity: the more the fear of instability and fear of heights the worse the results. A multiple regression analysis showed that only fear of instability could predict post-treatment severity, explaining up to 40 per cent of the variance. Demographic variables, the other clinical characteristics of fear of flying (including pre-treatment fear severity), diagnostic status and other psychopathological variables (depressive and anxiety symptomatology) were unrelated to outcome.

At one year follow-up, post-treatment self-reported fear of flying severity was the only predictor of the scores on fear measures. Related to this, a negative correlation was found between one of the FFQ-II subscales at initial assessment (fear related with previous flight situations: packing at home, travelling to the airport, etc.) and fear of flying severity at follow-up. The greater the fear in previous flight situations at initial assessment the less the fear severity at follow-up. The treatment programme deals specifically with this kind of situation and perhaps the intervention is more useful for those who are specially fearful in these conditions than for people who are just scared while flying. It could be also argued that subjects with high anticipatory fear are more 'pure' phobics (more concerned with negative consequences of flying – crashing – than with the flight *per se*) and profit more from this kind of intervention. This question needs to be investigated in the future. Moreover, at one year follow-up, none of the pre-treatment variables could predict outcome, not even fear components associated with a worse result at the end of treatment. We also studied which variables could be related to flying or not flying during the follow-up period by means of logistic regression analysis. No predictors were found, and this is probably due to the fact that only three subjects did not take any flights during this year.

Computer-assisted Exposure: What about the Future?

Although we do not know exactly why exposure therapy works, we do at least know that it works very well with fear of flying. New technologies provide powerful tools to develop structured exposure treatments for flight phobia,[1] and the CAFFT presented here is a good example. The CAFFT was firstly planned because of the specific difficulties involved in using *in vivo* exposure, but also because of the need to provide effective, low-cost treatment for thousands of people who neither take a flight nor have a chance to attend any standard treatment (e.g. because of geographical reasons).

The process of software development was long and hard, and probably this is the reason why one can only find a few computer-assisted therapeutic programmes (not only for fear of flying but also for other specific phobias). Psychologists rarely have the skills and the resources necessary to build up such programmes, but they can collaborate with other researchers from the computer science areas. On the other hand, several script languages are currently available in plain English (such as Metatalk or Openscript), and this may facilitate the development of software for and by psychologists.

Once the software was ready, the third step was to test the CAFFT. The case study was encouraging: the CAFFT seemed to work effectively. The controlled study confirmed that fear of flying can be reduced without relaxation training: exposure alone was enough. Nevertheless, this had been demonstrated in a highly controlled research setting. What about using the CAFFT in other clinical conditions? Researchers from another country, who had not participated in the software development process, used the CAFFT; and it was also found to be effective (Bornas et al., 2001b). Young inexperienced clinicians used the CAFFT at an airport with regular clients; and it worked again. The next question was: who can benefit most from the CAFFT? From our data we believe that most fearful flyers can benefit. The specific fear of the client does not matter (crashing, heights, enclosed spaces, etc.) nor does the severity of his or her fear of flying. However, our data are not conclusive. Furthermore, a small percentage of clients do not benefit from the CAFFT and we are not yet in a position to offer a clear reason; further research is needed.

There is still one last question that guides our recent research. As mentioned above, one of our main goals was to make available a low-cost and effective treatment for flight phobia. Until now, the therapist was always with the clients during CAFFT sessions, thus increasing the cost of the therapy. Even when the therapist's actions were reduced to the minimum (i.e. in the controlled study), he/she had to give some directions, answer some questions, and so on. We observed that most of these actions could be provided by the computer. Clients looked at the therapist or asked questions to him/her because he/she 'was there' and the computer had no answers. A further question is: would the CAFFT be effective if we removed the therapist and programmed a computer to answer the client's questions? In other words, can the CAFFT be self-administered at home? Can it be truly computer-driven (instead of computer-assisted)? If so, the main goal of the research and development process will have been achieved. At present the self-administered version of the CAFFT is ready and we are currently seeking to answer some of these questions.

Note

1   Both virtual reality and computer-assisted therapies are examples of technology-based treatments, and they have shown their efficacy in controlled studies. However, VR is much more expensive today, so that computer-assisted treatment is preferable to VR in terms of cost-effectiveness.

References

American Psychiatric Association (1994), *Diagnostic and Statistical Manual of Mental Disorders*, 4th edn, Washington, DC: American Psychiatric Association.

Barlow, D.H. and Wolfe, B.E. (1981), 'Behavioral Approaches to Anxiety Disorders: A report on the NIMH-SUNY, Albany, research conference', *Journal of Consulting and Clinical Psychology*, Vol. 49, pp. 448–54.

Bornas, X., Fullana, M.A., Tortella-Feliu, M., Llabrés, J. and García de la Banda, G. (2001a), 'Computer-assisted Therapy in the Treatment of Flight Phobia: A case report', *Cognitive and Behavioral Practice*, Vol. 8, No. 3, pp. 234–40.

Bornas, X., Tortella-Feliu, M., García de la Banda, G., Fullana, M.A. and Llabrés, J. (1999), 'Validación factorial del Cuestionario de Miedo a Volar' ['The Factor Validity of the Fear of Flying Questionnaire'], *Análisis y Modificación de Conducta*, Vol. 25, No. 104, pp. 885–907.

Bornas, X., Tortella-Feliu, M., Llabrés, J., Barceló, F., Pauli, P. and Mülhberger, A. (2001b), 'Clinical Usefulness of a Simulated Exposure Treatment for Fear of Flying', *Revista Internacional de Psicología Clínica y de la Salud (International Journal of Clinical and Health Psychology*, Vol. 2, No. 2, pp. 247–62.

Bornas, X., Tortella-Feliu, M., Llabrés, J. and Fullana, M.A. (2001c), 'Computer-assisted Exposure Treatment for Flight Phobia: A controlled study', *Psychotherapy Research*, Vol. 11, No. 3, pp. 259–73.

Coldwell, S.E., Getz, T., Milgrom, P., Prall, C.W., Spadafora, A. and Ramsay, D. (1998), 'CARL: A LabVIEW 3 computer program for conducting exposure therapy for the treatment of dental injection fear', *Behaviour Research and Therapy*, Vol. 36, pp. 429–41.

Denholtz, M.S. and Mann, E.T. (1975), 'An Automated Audiovisual Treatment of Phobias Administered by Non-professional', *Journal of Behavior Therapy and Experimental Psychiatry*, Vol. 6, pp. 111–15.

Fullana, M.A. and Tortella-Feliu, M. (2001), 'Predictores de resultado terapéutico en el miedo a volar en avión' ['Outcome Predictors in the Treatment of Fear of Flying'], *Psicothema*, Vol. 13, No. 4, pp. 617–21.

Glantz, K., Durlach, N.I., Barnett, R.C. and Aviles, W.A. (1996), 'Virtual Reality for Psychotherapy: From the physical to the social environment', *Psychotherapy*, Vol. 33, pp. 464–73.

Haug, T., Brenne, L., Johnsen, D.H., Brentzen, D., Götestam, K.G. and Hughdal, K. (1987), 'A Three Systems Analysis of Fear of Flying: A comparison of a consonant versus a non-consonant treatment method', *Behaviour Research and Therapy*, Vol. 25, pp. 187–94.

Howard, W.A., Murphy, S.M. and Clarke, J.C. (1983), 'The Nature and Treatment of Fear of Flying: A controlled investigation', *Behavior Therapy*, Vol. 14, pp. 567–87.

Jacobson, N.S. and Truax, P. (1991), 'Clinical Significance: A statistical approach to defining meaningful change in psychotherapy research', *Journal of Consulting and Clinical Psychology*, Vol. 59, pp. 12–19.

McNally, R.J. and Louro, C.E. (1992), 'Fear of Flying in Agoraphobia and Simple Phobia: Distinguishing features', *Journal of Anxiety Disorders*, Vol. 6, pp. 319–24.

Mühlberger, A., Herrmann, M., Wiedemann, G. and Pauli, P. (2001), 'Treatment of Fear of Flying with Exposure Therapy in Virtual Reality', *Behaviour Research and Therapy*, Vol. 39, pp. 1033–50.

Nelissen, I., Muris, P. and Merckelbach, H. (1995), 'Computerized Exposure and *in vivo* Exposure Treatments of Spider Fear in Children: Two case reports', *Journal of Behaviour Therapy and Experimental Psychiatry*, Vol. 26, No. 2, pp. 153–6.

Newman, M.G., Consoli, A. and Taylor, C.B. (1997), 'Computers in the Assessment and Cognitive Behavior Treatment of Clinical Disorders: Anxiety as the case in point', *Behavior Therapy*, Vol. 28, pp. 211–35.

North, M., North, S. and Coble, J.R. (1998), 'Virtual Reality Therapy: An effective treatment for phobias', in Riva, G., Widerhold, B.K. and Molinari, E. (eds), *Virtual Environments in Clinical Pscyhology and Neuroscience*, Amsterdam: IOS, pp. 112–19.

Öst, L.-G., Brandberg, M. and Alm, T. (1997), 'One versus Five Sessions of Exposure in the Treatment of Flying Phobia', *Behaviour Research and Therapy*, Vol. 35, No. 11, pp. 987–96.

Rothbaum, B.O., Hodges, L., Smith, S., Lee, J.H. and Price, L. (2000), 'A Controlled Study of Virtual Reality Exposure Therapy for the Fear of Flying', *Journal of Consulting and Clinical Psychology*, Vol. 68, No. 6, pp. 1020–26.

Rothbaum, B.O., Hodges, L., Watson, B.A., Kessler, G.D. and Opdyke, D. (1996), 'Virtual Reality Exposure Therapy in the Treatment of Fear of Flying: A case report', *Behaviour Research and Therapy*, Vol. 34, pp. 477–81.

Selmi, P.M., Klein, M.H., Greist, J.H., Sorrell, S.P. and Erdman, P. (1990), 'Computer-administered Cognitive-behavioral Therapy for Depression', *American Journal of Psychiatry*, Vol. 147, pp. 51–6.

Solyom, L., Shugar, R., Bryntwick, S. and Solyom, C. (1973), 'Treatment of Fear of Flying', *American Journal of Psychiatry*, Vol. 130, pp. 423–7.

Tortella-Feliu, M. and Fullana, M.A. (2000), 'Prevalencia, dimensiones y vías de adquisición en el miedo a volar en avión' ['Prevalence, Dimensions and Acquisition Pathways of Fear of Flying'], *Revista de Psicopatología y Psicología Clínica*, Vol. 5, No. 1, pp. 13–26.

Tortella-Feliu, M., Fullana, M.A. and Bornas, X. (2001), 'Características clínicas del miedo fóbico a volar en avión' ['Clinical Characteristics of Fear of Flying'], *Psicología Conductual*, Vol. 9, No. 1, pp. 63–78.

van Gerwen, L.J., Spinhoven, P., Diekstra, R.F. and Van Dyck, R. (1997), 'People who seek help for fear of flying: typology of flying phobics', *Behavior Therapy*, Vol. 28, pp. 237–51.

Wilhelm, F.H. and Roth, W.T. (1997), 'Clinical Characteristics of Flight Phobia', *Journal of Anxiety Disorders*, Vol. 11, pp. 241–61.

Chapter 14

Flight Crew Involvement in the Fear of Flying

Michael P. Tomaro

A Growing Problem Aloft

The skies are becoming more crowded, not only with more airplanes, but also with more passengers. Long term, this is a very happy circumstance for the aviation industry – more passengers, more work, more money! Short term, however, the news is both good and bad. The good is: more passengers, more work, more money. The bad is more passengers, more work, more problems! (Wells, 1991).

Among these problems is the emotion of fear – that nasty emotion that makes believers in all of us. The fear of flying is widely reported as being consistently among the top ten of all fears or phobias in the population (Anxiety Disorders Association of America, 2002). For the airline industry, fear becomes a factor in two ways. First, it tends to keep otherwise capable passengers away from aeroplanes (Dean and Whitaker, 1983). Secondly, for those brave souls who decide to try to put their fear aside and fly anyway, the flight crews' interpersonal skills are challenged when a passenger decides at the last minute, or after take-off, that he or she really didn't want to fly after all and asks to be deplaned – NOW! While such a circumstance is often the butt of numerous jokes, it is quite safe to say that when it happens anywhere but the cartoon strip, it is indeed no laughing matter (Hawkins, 1987, p. 208).

A passenger in the grips of an acute fear reaction is not only suffering tragically, he or she can also represent a significant threat to the safety and comfort of the flight. If flight crew members could simply say to such a person, 'Stay seated, behave yourself and talk to your therapist about this when you get home', there would be no need for a chapter such as this. Since frightened souls tend to respond poorly to verbal command (some verbal commands even increase fear/anxiety levels in some passengers), it behoves the airlines industry to provide its flight crews with the interpersonal skills necessary to help identify, to prevent and diffuse fear or anxiety as soon as is practically possible. Included in these interpersonal skills should also be a keen awareness of those communications which might inadvertently cause a mildly frightened individual to 'cycle up' to an even higher level of fear/anxiety.

The purpose of this chapter is to offer aircrew and airline industry administrators guidelines for coping with the frightened passenger during all phases of the flight. The goals of these recommendations are not to help the airline industry cure the fear of flying, but rather to cope in such a way as to minimise the consequences of the emotion to the frightened passenger as well as to other passengers, the flight crews and the airline itself.

Integrating Guidelines with Procedures

The complex nature of moving large numbers of passengers requires that the airline industry depend heavily upon organised procedures – at check-in, passenger boarding, before take-off, taxi, departure, take-off, cruise, descent and landing, and deplaning. All policies and procedures are aimed at moving individuals safely, but as a group – not as a group of individuals. Individual needs of any kind tend to erode the efficiency of the procedures, creating 'exceptions' which are time-consuming and expensive. Most passengers recognise this fact and are able to defer their individual needs in the interest of efficiency and safety. Fearful flyers with more than a mild level of anxiety are less capable of deferring their individual needs and consequently represent an intrusion to efficiency and safety from check-in to deplaning (Tomaro, 2000, p. 153). Policies and skills for dealing with the fearful flyer must therefore be developed that integrate with general procedures as efficiently as possible. Can compassionate individual attention be given to the frightened passenger with minimal disruption to the flight and its schedule? Consideration of where the individual needs of the fearful flyer juxtapose themselves with the airlines' conduct of a flight should reveal what type of help, and how much is possible at each phase of the flight. This understanding will allow for the development of training procedures for airline personnel involved with the fearful flyer at each phase.

The reader will notice a paradox in the system being offered. That is, when the airline has the maximum ability to offer services to the fearful flyer, the fearful flyer feels the least need for service – and vice versa – when the airline has the least ability to offer service, the fearful flyer has the greatest need for personal attention. Some of the recommendations, therefore, will be based upon this paradox.

Pre-flight – Fearful Flyer's Needs and Airline Abilities

Clinical observation suggests that disequilibrium in the fearful flyer begins at the point of booking the flight reservation. This act represents the fearful flyer's first commitment to fly – significantly elevating anxiety. Fearful flyers' awareness of airlines and aeroplanes heightens at the point of sale. Newspapers (and websites) are scanned for accident reports and safety data. Weather reports are watched with greater frequency. Stress symptomatology (e.g., sleep loss, muscle tension, nightmares, impatience, distractibility) increases significantly and family and interpersonal relations are strained. From the point of sale to the completion of the trip (or the cancellation of it) the fearful flyer's life is misery in motion. It is also 'maladaptive action in motion' in that few fearful flyers who enter this emotional tunnel have any good ideas about what type of adaptive activity could help stop, or reduce their misery. As a consequence, fearful flyers' anxiety continues to rise as flight time grows nearer (see Selye, 1980).

Since no airline has any procedures for dealing with passengers until the check in process begins (see Hawkins, 1987 p. 299), it can be said that airline companies have the maximal ability to respond to the fearful flyer at and after the point of sale until the beginning of the check in process. Since this chapter is not about what airlines *are* doing for fearful flyers at the point of sale, no policy review will be made. The subject to be explored is what airlines *can* do within the confines of necessary procedural boundaries that might provide the fearful flyer with some effective and necessary coping skills.

Hospitals prepare patients for surgery, the military prepares soldiers for combat, airlines can prepare passengers for flight – well in advance of the pre-takeoff safety briefing provided by the aircrew. Since the airline does not know the identities of any of the anxious passengers for any given scheduled flight, participation in a 'preparation for flight' programme would be completely voluntary. Presented and marketed properly, such a programme would attract numerous fearful flyers who feel the need for substantive information about their reactions to the flight environment, the dynamics of flight, and the industry that sells it.

Essential Elements of a 'Preparation for Flight' Programme

From the point of view of the airline, a preparation for flight programme must be considered both preventive and promotive. It is preventive in the sense that anything that can be done to convey positive coping abilities to fearful flyers reduces the chances of a disruptive episode of anxiety after push-back from the boarding gate. It is promotive because the more the airline can do to win the confidence of its most frightened consumers, the more consumers of all types will utilise that airline (Tomaro, 2000, p. 231). Accomplishing the goal of prevention will automatically ensure the goal of promotion.

Clinical observation and research suggest that there are elements that could be easily addressed in a 'preparation for flight' programme: providing aircraft knowledge (Tomaro, 2000); providing knowledge of anxiety control through muscle relaxation and controlled breathing (Tomaro, 2000); positive modelling of coping with the flight environment both by demonstration as well as by example (Bandura, 1977). For those fearful flyers with deeper clinical problems, a community-based referral network of competent professionals could be easily assembled and distributed.

The importance of aircraft knowledge is introduced to fearful flyers by Tomaro (2000) with Figure 14.1. Providing aircraft knowledge with an accompanying therapeutic benefit requires that: 1) a misperception be identified; and 2) a corrective perception be made. Tomaro (2000) has identified eight misperceptions of the aviation environment that, when corrected, have a positive effect upon flight anxiety. These are: 1) the aircraft is balanced upon its centre line; 2) the wings could break off the fuselage (especially during turbulence); 3) the aircraft could tail-slide shortly after takeoff; 4) the aircraft could easily roll upside down in a turn; 5) the engines lift the aircraft off the ground; 6) there is air-less space in the atmosphere (the 'air pocket' myth of turbulence); 7) the aircraft slows down and could fall when the captain reduces power; and 8) the aircraft is in a free fall during descent. These misperceptions are easy to identify and correct by any capable airline employee that would participate in a 'preparation for flight' programme.

In similar fashion, the rationale for and the methods used in systematic muscle relaxation and controlled breathing are easily taught (Benson, 2000). These are powerful fear/anxiety control techniques. As with the misperceptions of the aircraft, it is not enough to just tell the fearful flyer 'what' to do, it is also important to explain 'why' from the perspective of the task to be accomplished by the fearful flyer when trying to control unwanted anxiety.

The teacher of a 'preparation for flight' programme will find that most individuals are unaware of the effects of their muscle tension levels on their anxiety – despite the fact that these same individuals report muscle tension as the first cousin to their anxiety. They follow the unspoken formula that 'my muscles will relax if or when my anxiety goes away' rather than 'my anxiety

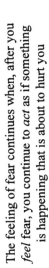

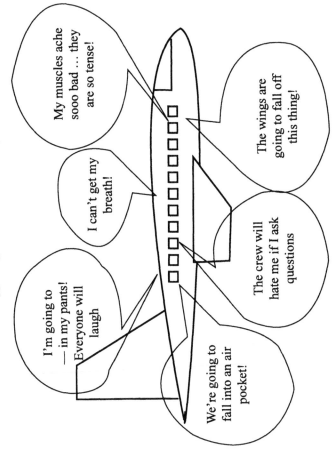

Figure 14.1 Importance of flight knowledge for the fearful flyer

Source: Tomaro, 2000.

will go away after I relax my muscles'. Figure 14.2 provides Tomaro's graphic portrayal of the effects of muscle relaxation.

Bandura (1977) has demonstrated that anxiety can be reduced when the anxious individual observes a positive model coping effectively with an anxiety provoking object. Positive modelling of the flight environment can be accomplished in two ways. First, the professionalism of the marketing and implementation of a preparation for flight programme will cast the airline in a positive light throughout the consuming community. To paraphrase a popular financial firm, the message will be conveyed to the community that the airline cares for its clients 'one passenger at time' – conveying an intense interest on the part of the air carrier in the individual well-being of all on board the aircraft. Secondly, either during the conduct of specific flight preparation sessions, or as part of a larger general marketing campaign, air carriers can use individuals to model effective anxiety blocking behaviour in a variety of preflight and in-flight situations (e.g., long check-in lines, flight delays, turbulence, aircraft turns, etc.). Such a strategy allows the airline to construct an anti-anxiety atmosphere while at the same time attending to its needs to attract and retain passengers.

The final element of an effective 'preparation for flight' programme involves the development of a referral system for the more clinically anxious flyers who require services beyond that which an air carrier can provide. The air carrier is in a unique position to ensure that effective community treatment resources and proper expertise be brought to the service of their fearful flyers. Since Captain Cummings' (Cummings and White, 1987) pioneering work with fearful flyers, a considerable therapeutic literature has evolved. The Airborne Conference (2000) in Vienna was the first to develop a series of treatment guidelines for the fear of flying. Community resources world wide could be developed that had both the capacity and expertise to implement such guidelines. Additionally, with a little logistical work, fear of flying therapists could be helped by the air carrier when the time came for therapeutic 'graduation flights'.

Effects of a 'Preparation for Flight' Programme

Some data currently available can be used to suggest the benefits of a programme such as that recommended above (Tomaro, 2000). First and foremost, the goal of the above activity will be to prevent more serious episodes with fearful passengers when they arrive at the check-in gate to do what they have been dreading for weeks or even months, since their purchase of a ticket. It is expected that an effective pre-flight programme would drastically reduce

By the end of this book, you will see how the chemistry of muscle relaxation combined with self-knowledge and knowledge of the aviation environment are potent fear fighting tools

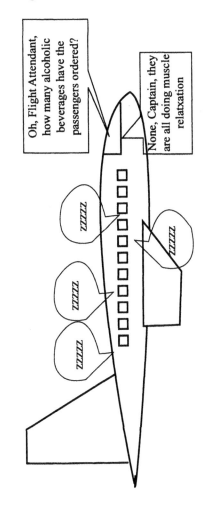

Figure 14.2   Importance of muscle relaxation for the fearful flyer

Source: Tomaro, 2000.

the consumption of alcohol as well as reduce the number of short-tempered passengers who express their fear through angry complaints triggered by some of the inevitable frustration associated with airline travel (e.g., weather delays, mechanical problems, baggage problems, missed connections, etc.).

A second benefit to the airline will be the increased numbers of passengers who have reduced fear levels. One study (Tomaro, 2000) established that individuals with reduced fear levels flew three times more two years after taking a fearful flyers' class than two years before the class. In dollar amounts, that amounted to a return of $5 for every $1 invested in teaching methods proven to reduce the fear of flying!

A third benefit to the airline will be to reduce the number of delayed take-offs (to deplane a fearful flyer), flight diversions, and unpleasant flights associated with a passenger in the throes of an acute episode of anxiety. Recognising that it costs thousands of dollars for a single delay or diversion (Wells, 1991), not to mention the fact that the air carrier's ability to respond becomes more limited when the frightened passenger works himself/herself into the system, the greatest investment of the air carriers' resources are most effectively made in activities for the fearful flyer prior to the check-in process. That said, the airline cannot only train to prevent the pre- and in-flight episodes of anxiety before passenger check-in. Regardless of how effective the effort, some fearful passengers will always find their way to the aircraft and begin to have an anxiety attack after the cabin door is closed. While options to respond may be limited, there are still more effective ways to respond than others. Such responses will be considered under the categories of 'pre-boarding, pre-flight, and in-flight'.

Pre-boarding the Anxious Flyer

While the airline's ability to respond to the fearful flyer is severely limited in comparison to the pre-check-in period, the goal here is still preventive. That is, it is to the advantage of both the fearful flyer and the airline to prevent boarding a passenger that will disrupt a flight once the cabin door is closed and push-back is authorised. Identification of and communication with a nervous/fearful flyer at check-in allows the airline an opportunity to either: 1) provide advance help to the passenger in the form of fundamental coping skills; or 2) provide counsel and referral to the highly frightened passenger who would ask to be deplaned after push-back or require a flight diversion after takeoff. A third and very important consideration for the airline is the handling of a frightened passenger's baggage in the event that deplaning occurs either after push-back or as a flight (fright?) diversion. It is indeed a time-consuming process to sort through all the baggage in the belly of the aircraft. Properly identified, such baggage could be tagged and loaded in an easily accessible section of the luggage compartment.

Is it possible for a ticket agent to spot a fearful flyer at check-in? Even if it were possible, can the ticket agent make any kind of substantive response within the limitations imposed by passenger identification, security check, baggage check, and seat assignment? To both questions the answer is a resounding yes! Any observer of a check-in line will see that considerable interaction occurs between gate agent and passengers. A little enlightened profiling will help the gate agent know where to look and a little extra training will help the gate agent know what to say after the fearful flyer is found.

Profiling the Fearful Flyer

An informal survey conducted by the author reveals the following identifying characteristics of fearful flyers upon arrival at the airport.

1   The fearful flyer rarely travels alone.
2   When the fearful flyer does travel alone, he or she is commonly quite talkative – reflecting the desire to cope with the fear by 'connecting' with airline personnel.
3   Fearful flyers frequently ask questions about the weather, the timeliness of the flight and the flight loads – hoping to receive some type of answer that will calm them. If spotted by a gate agent, this can be an excellent lead in to an open discussion with the fearful flyer (more on this in the discussion of communication).
4   A person travelling alone that appears intoxicated or talks of visiting the airport bar (e.g., 'Where is the bar?' or 'Will I have time for a drink before the flight?') is likely to be experiencing some type of distress.
5   When travelling in groups of two or more, the fearful flyer is never the leader of the group.
6   When the leader of a group talks to a fearful flyer at the ticket counter, the fearful flyer appears withdrawn and distractible or responds in a short-tempered and hostile manner.
7   Children under the age of 10 are almost never fearful flyers. If a young child is a fearful flyer, he or she never even gets to the airport because of his/her outspoken nature about not wanting to fly.

Once tentatively identified, the gate agent must go the final step toward confirming that the observed distress is emanating from the fear of flying. This is where accurate and empathic communication is of the utmost importance.

Communicating with the Fearful Flyer

One might say that Mother Nature is on the side of the gate agent. The fearful flyer is looking for any acceptable and appropriate manner to 'let the cat out of the bag'. All the gate agent has to do is tug (gently please!) on the appropriate string! The social posture of 'benign curiosity' necessary to ask the critical question is easily taught . Consisting of a two part response the fear of flying can be broached at check-in (or other phases of the flight) by: 1) commenting on the behaviour just observed or answering the question asked; and 2) asking the passenger if he/she is afraid (in a curious and friendly manner, please!).

Communication example The following is a sample of an actual communication between the gate agent, the wife (leader) and the fearful husband.

Gate Agent: Welcome to XYZ Airline, what is your destination please?
Wife: We are travelling to Los Angeles.
Gate Agent: May I see your identification and your tickets please.
Wife: Honey, she needs your driver's licence.
Husband: I heard her, I'm listening!
Gate Agent: You didn't look like you were listening, you were looking in the opposite direction.
Husband: Well I was, I was just looking to see how many other passengers were on this flight.
Gate Agent: (while checking tickets and IDs) Were you worried about it?
Husband: Only that full flights are really heavy and the engines have a hard time getting the aeroplane off the ground.
Gate Agent: Actually the wings do most of the work, why don't you take one of these brochures with you to read before boarding, Perhaps it will answer some of your questions.

The husband thanks the gate agent, the check-in process is completed and the couple proceed to the boarding gate with material that answers the husband's question, and explains other aspects of the fear of flying – including the importance of muscle relaxation and controlled deep breathing. With minimal intrusion and maximum efficiency, the gate agent has helped to reduce a fearful flyer's anxiety and perhaps helped to prevent a more disruptive episode aboard the aircraft.

The importance of accurate and empathic communication as illustrated above cannot be under emphasised. Had the gate agent responded to this short-tempered man as if he were just belligerent and spoiled, significant tension would have begun immediately and this man could have been destined for a miserable flight at best or, at worst, a costly interruption of the flight schedule when he finally decided that the aeroplane was too heavy for a safe take-off.

Pre-flight, Increasing Needs – Decreasing Ability to Respond

The aircraft boarding process initiates the pre-flight phase of the mission. With airline personnel increasingly dependent upon formal procedure and concerned about meeting an approaching take-off reservation, every unplanned, individual need of a passenger represents a delay to the process. It is also during the boarding process that the fearful flyer's anxiety and needs for individual attention increases significantly – just what the airline personnel *don't* need!

Fearful flyers separate themselves into two categories at this phase – enlightened and unenlightened. The enlightened group, while anxious, has at least somewhat of a grasp of the task at hand. They understand the air crew dependence upon procedure, they see the orderliness in the boarding and pre-flight process, rather than the chaos in it, and above all, they have some idea about what to do to cope with increasing amounts of anxiety. Focus is upon muscle tension levels, breathing, and identifying the procedures leading to the takeoff. For the most part, air crew personnel cannot even identify these individuals. Occasionally, an enlightened fearful flyer will identify himself/ herself to a member of the air crew as a nervous flyer. Otherwise, enlightened fearful flyers may appear somewhat less talkative and more reserved than most passengers. This is certainly not a distinguishing feature of anxiety. In fact, this is exactly what the air crew wants from all of its passengers!

The unenlightened fearful flyers are hanging by a proverbial emotional thread. Faced with intense feelings of impending disaster, hypervigilance is at its peak. For many, deplaning the aircraft before take-off is still a real possibility. Air crew personnel are likely to encounter this type of passenger in one of two ways. Some passengers will have questions about the weather, the captain of the flight, condition of the aircraft. Embedded in the question will be found a thinly disguised reference to the nature of the fear. For example, questions about the weather reflect fears of turbulence; the captain, fears relating to competence and experience; the aircraft, the timeliness of maintenance, attentiveness to the cargo bay, etc. Not only is the question itself a reflection of high anxiety levels, the time of asking also reveals the emotion. Passengers with questions such as this during busy boarding and pre-flight activity are declaring their needs to be higher than the needs for orderly group movement. Generally, flight crews feel 'put out' or burdened by such an individual request ('Can't they see that I'm busy!'). While it is true that selfish and self-centred individuals will also make individual requests during busy group activity, it is prudent to first presume such behaviour as a sign of fear and treat it as such until other evidence proves the contrary.

The second way a fearful flyer is revealed to the flight crew is through the appearance of belligerence and/or intoxication. Once again, this is not to say that all belligerent or intoxicated individuals aboard an aircraft are fearful – just most of them. Flight crew members who posture themselves to respond to the presumed underlying fear will diffuse more potentially dangerous situations from this perspective than they will by treating such an individual as a behaviour problem about to happen. If the attempt to respond to the underlying fear fails to produce results, crew members can always revise their strategy or response.

Responding to the Fearful Flyer during Pre-flight – a Little Empathy goes a Long Way

With a little practice, including some role playing, flight crews can learn to integrate skilful, individualised responses to nervous flyers within their complex and regimented pre-flight activities. Consider the following example.

Case example – accurate empathy A businessman, travelling alone, boards the aircraft on the final boarding call. The flight attendant notices that Mr A is seated in the centre of the aircraft, suggesting that he purposely waited until last call. The following conversation ensues.

Mr A: (appearing a little nervous and rushed) Hi, how does the weather look for the flight?

FA: I haven't talked to the Captain about it, are you concerned with possible turbulence?

Mr A:	Not too much, I just find that it helps if I kind of know what to expect.
FA:	What seat are you in, I'll ask him and then tell you when I check the aircraft before takeoff.
Mr A:	I'm in 16C. I would really appreciate that!
FA:	Get yourself as relaxed as you can in your seat, I'll see you in a few minutes.

(Ten minutes pass and the FA is walking the aisle. She arrives at Mr A's seat.)

FA:	How are you doing?
Mr A:	Fine thanks – how's the weather?
FA:	The Captain said we would be flying about 75 miles east of a line of thunderstorms for the first hour of our flight. It could be a little bumpy at first but should be smooth after that.
Mr A:	I wish I'd taken the earlier flight.
FA:	There is a lot I could explain about turbulence if I had the time. Right now the main thing is to get your muscles as relaxed as possible before takeoff, and keep them that way until the turbulence passes. When the flight smooths out I'll come back and give you some important information that will help in the future. Do you think you can do that – get your muscles relaxed I mean?
Mr A:	I'll try, I'm pretty tense right now.
FA:	You work on it and I'll check back after takeoff.
Mr A:	Thank you.

In two very brief conversations this FA has: 1) connected in a positive way with a fearful flyer; 2) got to the point of his struggle without unnecessary humiliation or embarrassment; and 3) provided Mr A with an important coping skill that will reduce his anxiety and prevent a 'cycling-up' effect if the turbulence should prove to be worse than forecast.

There is an important postscript to the above example. That is, Mr A frequently requested weather information from the flight crew. He commonly received the standard answer: 'The weather will be fine, there's nothing to worry about'. When the weather was in fact not fine, Mr A would become quite angry, feeling as if the flight crew had lied to him and not taken him seriously. The presence of such dynamics in the passenger cabin are not only completely invisible to the flight crew, they also bring a passenger one step closer to a disruptive episode. The method of communication recommended here not only helps the passenger, it serves a major preventive function as well.

Coping with Deplaning a Passenger

The vast majority of passengers who board the aircraft, frightened or not, will follow through with the trip. Occasionally, however, a frightened passenger asks to be deplaned prior to take-off. The most disruptive request for deplaning is that which occurs after push-back. This type of episode requires a return to the loading gate and a deplaning of the passenger's luggage as well. Frequently, companion travellers will deplane with the fearful individual. Significant flight delay and great expense are the cost to the airline of such an episode.

Airlines can prevent such events by spotting and offering the deplaning option to a severely distressed individual before the cabin door closes. If baggage has been properly identified and loaded last, deplaning can be accomplished with minimal delays. Paradoxically, a severely distressed individual is often relieved by the offer to deplane because FAs are providing the fearful individual with a clear and non-coerced choice. Beyond the offer to deplane, little can be done to convince a fearful flyer who has reached the near psychotically distressed stage of panic that the fear will lessen if he or she can just control their breathing rate (deep and slow) and their muscle tension levels. Identifying such an individual is not difficult. He or she is openly distressed, often expressing visible panic, anger or tears. The person's travel companion is often desperately trying to convince the passenger to 'calm down' – all to no avail. Deplaning such an individual as quickly and efficiently as possible (at their request of course) saves everyone involved much time, money and personal agony. Also, consistent with a complete approach, deplaned fearful flyers should be provided complete information about treatment resources in their area. Such a response not only is good community relations, but it leaves a very frightened and discouraged passenger with a message of personal hope when it is highly needed.

The Fearful Flyer in Flight – Comfort Zone or Danger Zone?

It would be the wish of every air carrier that all fearful passengers aboard have enough self preparation and self control to weather the 'storms' of emotion either alone or with the help of a travel companion. It is also the wish of every airline that there would be no engine problems, no thunderstorms, no sick crew members, no cancelled flights and no empty seats – in fact, no problems whatsoever! In the real world, contingencies are in place to manage these problems. Similarly, training flight crew to work with an unexpected panic stricken fearful flyer to the successful completion of a flight plan, not only provides an important passenger service, but also saves money for the airline, even if it only prevents one diversion per year.

Two important skills are necessary to facilitate work with a panic stricken individual in flight – knowing what to say and knowing what not to say.

Knowing What Not to Say

Generally speaking, FAs should avoid saying anything that could be defined as judgemental, argumentative, authoritarian or persuasive. A judgemental statement would be: 'You know, it is really selfish of you to keep calling me over here like this. I have 100 other passengers that I need to take care of too!'

An argumentative statement sounds like this: 'You keep asking me the same question over and over again. You must not believe what I'm telling you.'

An example of an authoritarian statement is: 'I'm in charge of the passenger cabin and you have to do as I tell you. Please stop your crying and yelling or I will have to report you as being disruptive to the flight!'

A persuasive statement – 'Look, you're safer up here than you are in your own bath tub. You know, the captain wants to live just as much as you do so you are just going to have to trust him.'

The reason to avoid these statements is that they inflict injury upon the already brittle self esteem of the fearful flyer. Such injury creates a very negative emotional atmosphere in an environment that is already terrifying, eroding the fearful flyer's decreasing ability to cope and thus increasing the severity of the anxiety attack in progress.

Training programmes can be made available to pilots and flight attendants to help them explore negative emotional reactions they may have to fearful flyers much the same way therapists must be trained to prevent negative emotional states from intruding on their interactions with patients. It is quite easy to fall prey to the conclusion that 'the passenger is selfish' or 'the passenger is 'just being difficult'. From such negative conclusions, damaging statements are easily made, and further reinforced when the passenger reacts badly to the rebuke. Of course, if flight crew are to be trained about what not to say, it is important to create a training balance by teaching and practising the right things to say in the crisis situation.

Knowing What to Say (and Do)

If a flight crew member is to successfully help a passenger 'cycle down' he or she must: 1) form a 'working bond' with the passenger; and 2) use that bond to help the passenger control their breathing and muscle tension levels until the acute anxiety runs its course (usually in 10 to 20 minutes (Tomaro, 2000 p. 16; Benson, 2000 p. 67)). The working bond is established both verbally (e.g., 'We have work to do', 'Let's try to focus') and non-verbally through some kind of gentle and non-threatening touch. If two adjacent seats are available in the aircraft, the passenger might be removed and seated with the crew member. Alternatively, an adjacent passenger or travelling companion might be temporarily relocated, allowing the crew member to sit next to the frightened passenger.

With the working bond created, the crew member begins slowly to encourage the passenger to focus his or her attention on deep and slow breathing and muscle relaxation. It is difficult work at first, but with gentle persistence, the passenger will work to cooperate. No mention need be made about controlling negative thoughts – it is a waste of time. Emphasis must be placed directly in the area over which the passenger has most control – breathing and muscles (see Tomaro, 2000, pp. 1–8). The work between flight crew member and passenger is greatly facilitated if the crew member reinforces even the smallest achievement of greater muscle and breathing control with compliments and encouragement (e.g., 'Your muscles are a little more relaxed, I knew you could do it'). Narrowing the focus on the passage of time facilitates achieving muscle relaxation and breathing control (e.g., 'Mrs B, I need your attention for the next 15 minutes, we have some work to do'). Passengers who imagine having to sustain high levels of anxiety for a long time actually become more anxious. Giving the passenger a short-term focus and two new coping mechanisms helps him/her to see that if breathing and muscle tension control can be achieved, anxiety will not remain high for the entire flight. After the episode of acute anxiety passes, further coaching of the fearful flyer can be achieved with the help of the travelling companion. The crew member gives specific instructions to the anxious flyer and the travelling companion to keep breathing slow and muscle tension low. Crew members also promise to 'check back' after the passage of a short period of time, usually around 15 minutes. Again, using short time references tends to be an anxiety reducer.

At the completion of a flight where this type of intervention was necessary, the airline should provide literature and referral to the fearful flyer. It is the best preventive of a repeat episode. If a return flight is in the near future, encouragement can be given in the pre-flight preparation that will help prevent a repeat episode.

Summary and Conclusions

Significant numbers of fearful flyers will be boarding aircraft as the airline industry expands its services throughout the world. Since a fearful flyer can severely disrupt flight schedules and flight plans, it behoves the industry to help flight crews identify and work with such individuals throughout all phases of flight, from ticket purchase to completion of the trip.

Recognising that the air carriers' ability to respond to the individual needs of the fearful flyer is inversely proportional to the time before flight, maximal service can be provided between the point of sale and check-in for the flight. Each fearful flyer who is helped prior to check-in lessens the possibility of significant delays due to individual needs of a fearful individual in flight.

After check-in and throughout the flight, the airlines' ability to respond to the fearful flyer narrows. Flight crew can be trained to integrate personal communications with the fearful flyer with the myriad of other tasks that must be completed throughout the flight process. It is important that air crew avoid any communication with the fearful flyer that contain messages of: 1) judgement; 2) authoritarian control; 3) argument; or 4) persuasion. Instead, flight crew should seek to: 1) form a 'working bond' with the fearful flyer through empathic communication and appropriate touch; and 2) work with the fearful flyer to control breathing and muscle tension levels until the acute episode passes. This task is supported by narrowing the fearful flyer's time perspective through planned 'check backs' every 15 to 30 minutes. Supported by informational brochures and community referral resources, airlines should not only increase the overall comfort of its flights but also create significant goodwill throughout its consuming public.

References

Anxiety Disorders Association of America (2002) Rockville, MD (www.adaa.org).
Benson, H. (2000), *The Relaxation Response*, New York: Avon Books.

Bandura, A. (1977), *Social Learning Theory*, Englewood Cliffs, NJ: Prentice Hall.

Cummings, T.W. and White, R. (1987), *Freedom from Fear of Flying*, New York: Pocket Books.

Hawkins, F.H. (1987), *Human Factors in Flight*, Brookfield, VT: Gower Technical Press.

Dean, R.D. and Whitaker, K.M. (1983), 'Fear of Flying: Impact on the US travel industry', *Journal of Travel Research*, Summer, pp. 7–17.

Selye, H. (1980), 'The Stress Concept Today', in Kutash, I.L. and Schlesinger, L.B. (eds), *Handbook on Stress and Anxiety*, San Francisco, CA: Jossey-Bass Inc.

Tomaro, M. (2000), *Flying in the Comfort Zone*, Milwaukee, WI: Institute for Human Factors.

Wells, A.T. (1991), *Commercial Aviation Safety*, TAB Books: Division of McGraw Hill, Inc., Blue Ridge Summit, PA.

Chapter 15

Putting Fear to Flight: Cases in Psychological Treatment

Elaine Iljon Foreman

I stood holding the phone! I was shaking! What had I done?

This was the reaction of a lady in her 50s who had just booked a place on a course to overcome her fear of flying. She had steadfastly refused to apply for a passport until this time, as in her words: 'That meant I was definitely unable to go abroad'. Her difficulties were far more widespread than just being unable to travel by air. 'I was unable to drive a car up higher than the third floor of a multi-storey car park. I was unable to go down the escalators in those modern shopping centres. I did not like lifts, and so it continued.'

Though this particular lady had never flown before, she noted that to her surprise, on taking the 'terrifying step' of undertaking therapy for her problem, there were other people on the course, and 'some of the others had flown many times, and it was amazing to see how at the start of the course they were just as scared as me'. When people pluck up the courage to find out about the help that is available, many do not know either the range of options, or their own preferences. They can also be concerned that seeking psychological therapy in some ways marks them out as being 'weak', or 'stupid', or even 'crazy'.

Fear of flying is classified in the *Diagnostic and Statistical Manual of Mental Disorders* (DSM-IV) (APA, 1994), as a specific phobia, characterised by a marked, persistent, excessive fear that is precipitated by the experience or immediate prospect of air travel. Exposure to this phobic stimulus almost invariably provokes an anxiety response – sometimes to the point of a panic attack – which the individual recognises as unreasonable, and which produces significant interference or distress. Treatment for fear of flying has been offered based on various models of psychological therapy, as well as pharmacotherapy, the latter requiring a medical prescription, usually from general practitioners and psychiatrists.

Even a cursory glance at the range of vastly different psychological therapy approaches available shows such a breadth that it can make even the experienced clinician wonder whether all of these can indeed be subsumed under the same heading. Of these different forms of psychological therapy, a number have been utilised specifically to enable people to overcome their fear of flying. The nature of the interventions has usually been dictated by the model hypothesised to describe the underlying cause of the fear of flying. Thus for those who believe in an unconscious cause, psychodynamic therapy would be the treatment of choice. Carr (1978) reported that before 1965, the standard treatment was indeed psychodynamic psychotherapy and the success rate of treatments was on average 18 per cent. After the development of behavioural treatment, however, Carr (1978) reported an increase in the success rate to 77 per cent. In a review of psychological treatment of a fear of flying Bor, Parker and Papadopoulos (2000) confirm that long-term explorative psychoanalytic therapy has not been shown to be effective in the treatment of a fear of flying. More recent results from treatments based on cognitive behavioural principles have however shown success in 70–98 per cent of cases (van Gerwen and Diekstra, 2000).

Other treatment interventions such as systemic therapy, hypnosis, virtual reality, reattributional training, systematic desensitisation, stress inoculation training, coping self-talk, cognitive preparation, flooding, implosion, *in vivo* exposure and relaxation training and cognitive behaviour therapy have all been described in the literature (Denholtz and Mann, 1975; Roberts, 1989; Rothbaum, Hodges and Kooper, 1997; Capafons, Sosa and Vina, 1999; Beckham et al., 1990; Haug et al., 1987). Howard, Murphy and Clarke (1983) compared systematic desensitisation, flooding, implosive therapy and relaxation training, and found that all were equally effective compared to no treatment control. The most common and successful treatments reported have included various forms of *in vivo* exposure and cognitive restructuring, (Beckham et al., 1990; Roberts, 1989). It is interesting to note that in one of the more recent therapeutic developments, Anderson, Rothbaum and Hodges (2001) carried out a randomised control study, comparing virtual reality (VR), a technique which allows individuals to become active participants, interacting through sight, sound and touch, in a computer generated three-dimensional world, to standard exposure and to a control group. They found that VR and standard exposure were better than controls, with no difference between the two treatment groups at two and six month follow up. Further development of this work can be found in Chapters 12 and 13.

Even when reviews indicate that of all the differing forms of psychological therapy, cognitive behaviour therapy has proved the most successful (Andrews, 1993), a summary by van Gerwen and Diekstra (2000) highlighted a considerable range in the duration and content of courses specifically designed to enable people to overcome fear of flying. Thus though most of the courses employed many of the principles of cognitive behaviour therapy, each did so in either a slightly, or sometimes quite substantially, different way to the others.

Cognitive behaviour therapy proposes the supposition that people's behaviour and emotions depend to a large extent on what they understand to be happening. What a person thinks and feels can greatly affect their reaction to events and people. Cognitive behaviour therapy involves understanding what one is thinking, acknowledging how this affects one's feelings and behaviour, and then training oneself to respond in a different way. The new behaviour can lead to a potentially more satisfying way of life and become part of the person's normal pattern of existence. Cognitive behaviour therapy therefore examines and modifies the relationship between what people think, feel, say and do (Iljon Foreman and Iljon, 1994).

The results of 15 different international courses on overcoming fear of flying all showed high levels of success. However, knowing that something works does not always mean knowing how or why. Thus clinicians and researchers increasingly need to focus their efforts on maximizing effects and minimizing costs, and on specifying variables that facilitate or impede treatment outcome (Foa and Kozak, 1986).

At the First International Fear of Flying Conference in Tarrytown, New York (February 1996), research was presented which indicated that people's fears fell into two categories – those whose fear was of a loss of external control – in other words something happening to the plane, and those who were afraid of a loss of internal control (Iljon Foreman and Borrill, 1993). The very worst case for both these scenarios is death. In both groups, the central core of the problem can be summed up by the early adverts for the British National Lottery, '*It COULD be YOU!*'.

Therapy for fear of flying aims to enable the individual to change their perception of risk, such that they then decide that on balance it is more worthwhile to undertake the flight, than to continue with the pattern of overt avoidance (not flying), or covert avoidance (using 'props' such as alcohol). The significance of such a change in perception was neatly summarized many years ago by Shakespeare as: 'Nothing is either good or bad, but thinking makes it so.' This change in the perception of risk is one of the central aims of cognitive behaviour therapy (Clark, 1999; Salkovskis and Clark, 1992; Beck and Emery, 1985; Greenberger and Padesky, 1995; Wells, 1997).

How does this change in perception actually happen? Are there differences between successful clients in what they learn from a course, perhaps as a result of their differing prior experiences? In addition, how can we explain why a small proportion of people fail to overcome their fears?

This chapter began by alluding to the range of people who can be affected by a fear of flying, from those who had never flown before to frequent flyers, including civilian and even military aircrew (Dyregrov et al., 1992; Goorney, 1970). The consequences of the fear can be far-reaching. It can limit the person's professional opportunities, affect leisure options, and even mean that one person may decide to take holidays without their partner on a regular basis, if the partner will not fly. There are implications for long-term relationships, and likewise difficulties in family holidays if children refuse to travel. The problem can have a substantial impact on professional, social and family life, (van Gerwen, 1988), and can affect marital or relationship satisfaction because fear of flying hampers or restricts either partner's freedom of movement. When considering the range of the population who suffer from fear of flying, Ekeberg, Seeberg and Ellertsen (1989) propose that individuals affected can be divided into three groups – those who avoid all flights, those who restrict flying to an absolute minimum, and experience considerable discomfort prior to and/or during each flight, and those who display continuous mild or moderate apprehension about flying, but do not avoid it, even though it remains an unpleasant experience.

Clinically, it can be challenging to elucidate the detail of people's fears. Frequently clients will say that they do not know what would happen if they stayed in the feared situation, but they are sure they could not tolerate it, and that it is too much of a risk to try and find out any more. This terror of the unknown is reminiscent of the words of Coleridge, from 'The Ancient Mariner' :

> Like one that on a lonesome road,
> Doth walk in fear and dread,
> And having once turned round, walks on,
> And turns no more his head
> Because he knows a frightful fiend,
> Doth close behind him tread (Coleridge, 1798).

In order to begin to understand the nature of the cognitive change wrought by therapy, the chapter now describes a model which, it is proposed, underlies the process of cognitive change. The model is presented, and then interrogated regarding whether it can account for the change observed in two clients, both of whom had flown many times prior to treatment. One client had tried several different therapy courses and therapists over a period of years, while for the second, this was a first attempt.

The course that these clients undertook was the 'Freedom to Fly' course based in London. Given the differences between courses outlined by van Gerwen and Diekstra (2000), the structure of the course is worth noting. It consists of three stages: a telephone assessment, one session in the consulting room, and then, a week later, a return flight to Europe on a scheduled plane.

The telephone assessment enables assessment of suitability – there may be some people for whom it seems that the treatment is unlikely to be of benefit. It is clearly best that they do not join the course in the first place – for their sake – for that of the therapist, and for the others in the group! Once accepted onto the course, people are seen either individually, or as a maximum of four per group. The first session involves taking a detailed history. An explanation for the development of the fear for each individual is explored, and the nature of anxiety explained. The maintaining factors are considered, and clients are encouraged to test out their fears regarding the consequences of their anxiety. The second session involves meeting at the airport, and taking a scheduled return flight to Continental Europe. Technical information provided is minimal. The rationale is that one does not necessarily need to understand how something works in order to be comfortable in using it. Many people who have a fear of flying will nevertheless happily use other forms of travel that have equal disaster potential, which they have neither any idea of how it works, nor any control over it, and yet not feel at risk. This view is supported in the conclusion of Wilhelm and Roth (1997), who suggest that informational aspects of a technical nature may be unnecessary.

Trying to understand how therapy can change this perception of risk led Borrill and Iljon Foreman to carry out in-depth interviews of patients, to ascertain what had changed, and to try and understand the process. This paper, 'Understanding Cognitive Change: A qualitative study of the impact of cognitive-behavioural therapy on fear of flying' (1996), proposed a model to describe the process of achieving control and overcoming fear.

The model was developed following in-depth interviews with ten people who had successfully completed the 'Freedom to Fly' course. The interviews were taped and transcribed, and then analysed using the method of grounded theory (Glaser and Strauss, 1967). Common themes regarding the process of change were extracted from the interviews, and led to the development of the model. Though it appears quite complex, essentially it can be broken down into four stages, each with their component parts: i) relinquish control; ii) accept control; iii) experience control; and iv) achieve self-control.

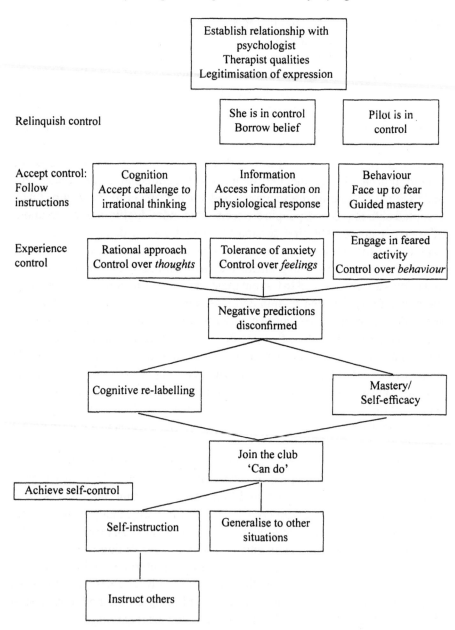

Figure 15.1   Model of the process of achieving control

The Relinquish Control Phase

For this to take place successfully, the person needs to establish a relationship with the therapist, and to have their experience legitimised. They then move towards trusting that the therapist is in control. This has been described by some as 'borrowing the belief of the therapist that they can do it' – one client said 'it's like borrowing someone's belief in you to actually believe in yourself, and also learning to leave the flying itself to the pilot!' The trust and establishment of the 'therapeutic relationship' appears central to the success of the therapy.

Most people appeared to have a good rapport with the therapist, felt understood, and also said that they felt that they could trust the therapist. Given that the person undertaking therapy is concerned that they may be risking their actual life, plus risking an emotional and social catastrophe should the therapy not succeed, the vital importance of trust and a good rapport is clearly apparent. Acknowledgement of the potential danger which forms the basis of some people's fear can facilitate the development of a good rapport. As one client said of the therapist, 'she didn't say "It isn't dangerous", and it so obviously is dangerous, potentially, that if some one says black is white you can't believe it'. It is interesting to note that one lady who did not make any progress with the therapy appears to have felt that she was not well understood by the therapist. She felt that the questionnaires she was asked to fill out, rather than being for her own benefit to enable her to understand her difficulties in greater depth, were primarily for the benefit of the therapist and for 'research'. Although she described the therapist as 'a nice person and very dedicated', there is no evidence from her account of any sense of trust or confidence, and hence no possibility of her 'borrowing belief'.

Whisman (1993) noted that, in comparison with other theoretical models, cognitive therapy has tended to place less emphasis on the therapeutic relationship and more on techniques. Nevertheless, this model suggests that the therapeutic alliance is vital if therapy is to be maximally effective. This view is supported by a recent review of the literature (Waddington, 2002). Roth and Fonagy (1996) concluded from the analysis of 100 research reports on the therapeutic alliance that there was a 'robust relationship between alliance and outcome'. Further support is found in the work of Castonguay et al. (1996) and Muran et al. (1995). It is interesting to note that the work of Krupnick et al. (1996) raises the possibility that the therapy relationship has an impact not only on the outcome of psychological therapies, including cognitive behaviour therapy, but also the outcome of pharmacotherapy. Current thinking by such practitioners as Beck and Freeman (1990), Burns and Auerbach (1996) and Wright and Davis (1994) all support the view of the importance of the therapeutic alliance.

Accepting Control

This stage includes following the instructions regarding identifying and challenging the person's 'irrational' thinking, accessing information about the normal physiological responses to anxiety, and engaging in behaviour which directly challenges their fears. This guided mastery includes undoing the seatbelt, eating the meal, walking about the cabin and going to the toilet. When clients were asked what they remembered from the first session of treatment, they frequently recalled being given explanations of how the body responded to threat and the physiological mechanisms underlying the fear response. 'She was able to tell me what fear was ... and how things are triggered off, and the feelings and sensations that you get. And then you can relate ... when you are going through this you know what's happening.' The client who did not benefit from therapy had no recollection of any discussion of the physiology of anxiety, a critical part of the therapy. She also rejected the suggestions which would have lead to guided mastery, 'She said I had to walk about, because I never do. But I didn't ... she can't force me'. The stage of guided mastery was seen as particularly important by clients who had a range of in-flight avoidance patterns.

Experience Control

Clients adopt a rational approach to questioning the irrational thoughts, thus discovering a certain control over the thoughts. They learn that they are able to tolerate anxiety and find that they can in this way control their feelings, plus discovering through guided mastery that they can be in charge of their own behaviour.

The fear that one will lose control over one's behaviour is graphically illustrated by a gentleman who experienced such intense claustrophobia that he would not sit by the emergency exit in case he became overwhelmed by his feelings, and found that against his will, he would somehow be forced to try and open the emergency exit door while in flight. A critical part of this stage is learning that the experience of high anxiety, whilst extremely uncomfortable, is not dangerous and can be tolerated. It is reported that through tolerating anxiety symptoms, people feel that they can exert control over them, and they can use this in other situations of emotional arousal. As one lady put it 'through conquering my fear of flying, I conquered everything else that I feared … it's just the fact that you have to look at everything logically and I'm doing that in my whole life now'.

Once the person has had their catastrophic negative predictions disconfirmed, this leads to the final part of experiencing control, when they begin to employ cognitive relabelling of the arousal symptoms and of the movements of the plane, and develop mastery and a belief in self-efficacy. The symptoms can be relabelled as 'discomfort', or even 'excitement', but are no longer seen as dangerous, and to be feared and avoided. The benefit of relabelling seems to be particularly apparent for those clients who suffered from agoraphobia, 'Since I've got over the fear of flying, I can do anything that I couldn't do; it really is amazing, the change'. Understanding the symptoms, tolerating and relabelling them therefore provides a sense of control over the feelings, so that they no longer get in the way of logical argument and judgement. Thus when clients describe themselves as being rational, they are saying that they feel in control of their decision making, rather than being overwhelmed by (irrational) feelings. An important component of this stage is 'facing up to the fear', and actively engaging in the experience, rather than using distraction and disengagement strategies. It is interesting to note that a study by Wilhelm and Roth (1997) compared cognitive behaviour therapy with and without medication, and found that the latter was superior. This study suggests that the medication prevented clients from fully experiencing the anxiety, and so they did not learn that they could tolerate and hence conquer their fear.

Achieving Self-control

The final stage, is that of 'joining the club'. The person now sees themselves as one of those who 'can do'. They now can generalise their techniques to other situations, employ the newly-learned techniques of self-instruction, and even begin to instruct others! 'Joining the club' of 'normal' flyers does not mean experiencing no fear; rather it means experiencing no more fear than anyone else in the circumstances: 'I'm probably normal. I find it no worse than anyone else now, whereas before it was something I wouldn't even contemplate'. 'I felt like I was a proper passenger because I behaved like one.' This is also the basis for generalisation to other fears, since clients perceive themselves belonging to the group of people who 'can do' whatever they want to do.

In summary, the detailed interviews indicated that the 'trick' of the therapist lies in convincing clients that it is the therapist who is in control, and that the client is therefore safe, thus giving 'permission' for clients to challenge cognitions, engage in experiences, access knowledge, tolerate feelings and achieve mastery. Assuming the person makes the desired choice, and does indeed test out their catastrophic fears, this results in the disconfirmation of uncontrollable outcomes, cognitive relabelling of uncontrollable symptoms and feelings, and substitution of controlled behaviour for uncontrollable avoidance. Clients no longer feel at the mercy of unknown fears, but in control of known, ordinary and understandable feelings. Client success is consequently attributed to self-control, not to a crutch, and can therefore be generalised to other feared situations. Successful clients were not only able to fly without fear, but also reported such changes as being able to drive, go through tunnels, face crowds, learn to swim and even take up sub aqua diving, assert themselves in business situations, make decisions, and change many habits of a lifetime.

The model described, developed in 1996 and derived entirely from qualitative analysis of detailed individual interviews from a number of patients often elicits the response from clinicians of: 'that's so obvious!' This parallels the experience many a clinician has had with clients, where once something which has taken painstaking refinement is explained to them in a simple and digestible form, say: 'that's so obvious!' In order to establish whether the model really does encompass the core factors within the process of cognitive change, it was decided to put the model to the test using data from other patients, whose experiences had not been part of the development of the original model, in order to check out if the stages did hold, and whether they held for different clients, in different ways.

Case Vignettes

The detailed interviews were carried out by Paul De Ponte in the client's home, using the guided interview protocol developed by Jo Borrill in 1996. Two clients, Mandy and Emma, were interviewed. Mandy was in her mid-30s, and was a bubbly extrovert. She had refused to let her fear of four year's duration stop her from flying. She took Valium, cried throughout, constantly sought reassurance, and had tried two airline-run courses, one of them twice, as well having had hypnotherapy and various alternative therapies. The family had recently bought a house abroad, and the prospect of continuing to fly with her level of terror was overwhelming for her. She said of the 'Freedom to Fly' course: 'this is the last thing I'm doing. I'm not doing anything else because it's cost me a fortune and I can't afford any more. I'll just have to face the fact that I'll always have to take Valium, and that I'll always be terrified, and that's just the way it is'.

Emma was in her mid-20s, and needed to fly for professional reasons, to enable international expansion of her theatre company. She had begun to avoid flying altogether, and felt that she could not start limiting her professional and personal life at this stage.

It became apparent that both clients did go through the four stages of the model: relinquish control, accept control, experience control and achieve self-control

A few quotes illustrate the flavour of the various stages, from forming the relationship with the therapist through the different levels of control.

> I think she's a mixture of ... a great guru, and then someone you're just going on a flight with.

> She talked about us and about how we felt ourselves – It was definitely more about yourself with Elaine.

> She made me feel really confident that I could do it, really positive that I could definitely do it.

> Now I know if I do have an anxiety attack, it's not so bad. I'm not going to die.

> So many pilots have said to me 'There's nothing to worry about and I fly all the time'. But it's different if somebody like Elaine is talking to you, isn't it? She's just a normal person.

Looking for the key elements supplied within the 'Freedom to Fly' programme which were missing from Mandy's previous attempts, one can identify a number of omissions:

Beginning with establishing rapport, the previously attempted airline courses had 45 and 250 people respectively, making it impossible for the close connection which Mandy found so helpful to be established. The smaller of the two courses, with 45 people was 'more successful' than the larger, in that Mandy felt more able to ask some questions. However, this course did not include a flight. This element is generally agreed to be crucial by those working in the field (van Gerwen and Diekstra, 2000), and it would seem to be of considerable significance in progressing through the stages of the model.

The technical information, rather than providing reassurance and knowledge, made Mandy feel more anxious by becoming aware in detail of the things that could go wrong. She said 'I don't get in my car in the morning and think "how does it work?" I just get in'. In line with this, Wilhelm and Roth (1997) postulate from their analysis that informational aspects of treatment programmes to do with how a plane flies may be unnecessary.

The stage of mastery and relabelling requires that the client actually engages in the feared behaviours. Mandy reported that the extra care, attention and 'molly coddling' that she received on the trial flight of her previous course meant that she did not do it herself. She described how even after these earlier courses, whenever she flew, she had frequent visits to the cockpit, constant questions from the crew as to how she was feeling, and repeated reassurance that everything was alright. This meant that she could never achieve the stage of mastery.

Mandy said that the previous focus on learning to relax proved less helpful than learning to experience the anxiety and to deal directly with it by challenging her terrifying thoughts. She felt that the other courses had aimed to protect people from their fears – one trying to treat the anxiety through relaxation, rather than dealing with the causal, catastrophic thoughts, and the other actually encouraging sedatives and alcohol, if she thought it was necessary. Both of these lead to avoidance, and appear to prevent the stages of mastery, self-efficacy and joining the club being reached. Foa and Kozak (1986) strongly support this view, concluding from both a theoretical and a clinical perspective that successful exposure requires experiencing of substantial anxiety.

With regard to Emma, analysis of her interview showed that she went through all the stages, in the order outlined by the model. For instance, she was able to re-label symptoms of anxiety as excitement – 'It was fun. There was a sense of adventure'. And for the more frightening parts, the relabelling was still employed: 'This is something I don't like, not something I'm scared of. I'm excited, not scared'. 'It was very empowering'. At the stage of achieving control: 'there are elements of flying that I can actually enjoy ... I can fly on any airline'. Given that Emma had not undertaken any therapy before this, it is apparent that previous failure is not a prerequisite to the success of the treatment programme. It would also appear that the effectiveness of the 'Freedom to Fly' programme is indeed linked to the four stages of the model of cognitive change.

In a review paper by van Gerwen and Diekstra (2000), 15 well-established courses for overcoming fear of flying were described. While there were certain common elements upon which all clinicians agreed, there were nevertheless notable differences in content, length and professional background of course leaders and tutors. Highly successful outcomes were reported by all the courses. Given the differences between courses, it therefore seems that there are many routes to the 'top of the mountain'. The therapeutic journey can thus be construed as a way of climbing to the top of the 'mountain of fear'. It would be valuable if data across clients from different courses could be compared, to test out whether despite the different routes, the way stations, those four sequential staging posts described above, are all the same. Likewise, for those clients who do not succeed, perhaps it is because they have missed out on one or more of the way stations, and are still scrambling about precariously, somewhere on the mountain of fear, looking for a route that will take them through the four staging posts. Another interesting aspect to investigate is whether internationally the staging posts are reached in the same order for all clients.

It is exciting to work in the field of the treatment of fear of flying, as the rewards that clients experience can be as great as the limitations from which they previously suffered.

Both Emma and Mandy have flown since the course, and both report highly successful experiences. Emma laconically described it as 'no big deal' while Mandy exuberantly declared that she 'was brilliant'. Turbulence was encountered on both their flights, and both reported that they dealt extremely well with it. Assessing themselves, Mandy and Emma described their progress as follows.

Firstly Mandy:

> I feel now like I used to feel before when we went on holiday. You know, just looking forward to the holiday and looking forward to getting on the plane and to relax, to read, to have a meal that's done for me, sit and have a nice gin and tonic. You know, and that's how I used to feel about it. And that's how I feel now about it!

Emma concluded:

> All feelings of dread have gone and I can fly on any airline. It's amazing. Loads of places have opened up to me, and I'm finding myself looking at holidays all the time. I do feel like my confidence has been restored. It's like having my freedom back.

Some therapists working in different parts of the world are seeking to refine the interventions that are offered to those whose wings have been clipped by their fears, and many people with a fear of flying are either seeking help, or attempting to overcome their difficulties on their own. It is the ultimate aim of all these endeavours that people are enabled to move from fear of flying and to achieve the freedom to fly.

As can be seen from the wealth of studies reviewed in this chapter, there is a wide range of clinical interventions available for fear of flying, which are both varied and creative. However, it can be clearly surmised from the literature that the intention of all those working on this fascinating and complex problem is that, with the increasing refinement of the treatment available, in the words of Jonathon Livingston Seagull: 'We can be free. We can learn to fly'.

References

American Psychiatric Association (1994), *Diagnostic and Statistical Manual of Mental Disorders*, 4th edn, Washington, DC: American Psychiatric Association.

Anderson, P., Rothbaum, B. and Hodges, L. (2001), 'Virtual Reality: Using the virtual world to improve quality of life in the real world', *Bulletin of the Menninger Clinic*, Vol. 65, No. 1, pp. 78–91.

Andrews, G. (1993), 'The Essential Psychotherapies', *British Journal of Psychiatry*, Vol. 162, pp. 447–51.

Bach, R. (1972), *Jonathon Livingston Seagull*, Turnstone Press Ltd: Great Britain.

Beck, A., Freeman, A. and Associates (1990), *Cognitive Therapy of Personality Disorders*, New York: Guilford Press.

Beck, A. and Emery, G. (1985), *Anxiety Disorders and Phobias: A cognitive perspective*, Basic Books: New York.

Beckham, J., Vrana, S., May, J., Gustafson, D. and Smith, G. (1990), 'Emotional Processing and Fear Measurement Synchrony as Indicators of Treatment Outcome in Fear of Flying', *Journal of Behavior Therapy and Experimental Psychiatry*, Vol. 21, No. 3, pp. 153–62.

Bor, R., Parker, J. and Padadopoulos, L. (2000), 'Psychological Treatment of a Fear of Flying: A review', *Journal of the British Travel Health Association*, Vol. 1, pp. 21–6.

Borrill, J. and Iljon Foreman, E. (1996), 'Understanding Cognitive Change: A qualitative study of the impact of cognitive-behavioural therapy on fear of flying', *Clinical Psychology and Psychotherapy*, Vol. 3, No. 1, pp. 62–74.

Burns, D. and Auerbach, A. (1996), 'Therapeutic Empathy in Cognitive Behavioural Therapy: Does it really make a difference?', in Salkovskis, P. (ed.), *Frontiers of Cognitive Therapy*, New York: Guildford Press.

Capafons, J., Sosa, C. and Vina, C. (1999), 'A Reattributional Training Program as a Therapeutic Strategy for Fear of Flying', *Journal of Behavior Therapy and Experimental Psychiatry*, Vol. 30, pp. 259–72.

Carr, J. (1978), 'Behaviour Therapy and the Treatment of Flight Phobia', *Aviation, Space and Environmental Medicine*, Sept., pp. 115–18.

Castonguay, C., Goldfried, M., Wiser, S., Raue, P. and Hayes, J. (1996), 'Predicting the Effect of Cognitive Therapy for Depression', *Journal of Consulting and Clinical Psychology*, Vol. 64, pp. 497–504.

Clark, D. (1999), 'Anxiety Disorders: Why they persist and how to treat them', *Behavior Research and Therapy*, Vol. 37, No. 1, S5–S27.

Coleridge, S. (1969 [1798]), 'The Ancient Mariner', in *Coleridge's Poetical Works*, ed. H. Coleridge, Oxford University Press: Oxford.

Denholtz, M. and Mann, E. (1975), 'An Automated Audiovisual Treatment of Phobias Administered by Non-professionals', *Journal of Behavior Therapy and Experimental Psychiatry*, Vol. 4, pp. 111–15.

Dyregrov, A., Skogstad, A., Hellesoy, O. and Haugli, L. (1992), 'Fear of Flying in Civil Aviation Personnel', *Aviation, Space and Environmental Medicine*, Vol. 63, No. 9, pp. 831–8.

Ekeberg, Ø., Seeberg, I. and Ellertsen, B. (1989), 'The Prevalence of Flight Anxiety in Norway', *Norsk Psykiatrisk Tidsskrist*, Vol. 43, pp. 443–8.

Foa, E. and Kozak, M. (1986), 'Emotional Processing of Fear: Exposure to corrective information', *Psychological Bulletin*, Vol. 99, No. 1, pp. 20–35.

Glaser, B. and Strauss, A. (1967), *The Discovery of Grounded Theory: Strategies for qualitative research*, New York: Aldine.

Goorney, A. (1970), 'Psychological Measures in Aircrew – Normative Data', *Aerospace Medicine*, Vol. 41, pp. 87–91.

Greenberger, D. and Padesky, C. (1995), *Mind Over Mood*, New York: The Guilford Press.

Haug, T., Brenne, L., Johnson, B., Bentzen, D., Gotestam, K. and Hugdahl, K. (1987), 'A Three System Analysis of Fear of Flying: A comparison of a consonant vs a non-consonant treatment method', *Behavior Research and Therapy*, Vol. 25, pp. 187–94.

Howard, W., Murphy, S. and Clarke, J. (1983), 'The Nature and Treatment of Fear of Flying: A controlled investigation', *Behavior Therapy*, Vol. 14, pp. 557–67.

Iljon Foreman, E. (forthcoming), 'Just Plane Scared? An Overview of Fear of Flying', in Bor, R. (ed.), *Passenger Behaviour*, Aldershot: Ashgate.

Iljon Foreman, E. and Borrill, J. (1993), 'Plane Scared: Brief cognitive therapy for fear of flying', *Scottish Medicine*, Vol. 13, No. 4, pp. 6–8.

Iljon Foreman, E. and Iljon, Z. (1994), 'Highwaymen to Hijackers: A survey of travel fears', *Travel Medicine International*, Vol. 12, No. 4, pp. 145–52.

Krupnick, J., Sotsky, S., Simmons, S., Moyer, J., Elkin, I., Watkins, J. and Pilkonis, P. (1996), 'The Role of the Therapeutic Alliance in Psychotherapy and Pharmacotherapy Outcome. Findings in the National Institute of Mental Health Treatment of Depression Collaborative Research Program', *Journal of Consulting and Clinical Psychology*, Vol. 64, pp. 532–9.

Muran, J., Gorman, B., Safran, J. and Twining, L. (1995), 'Linking In-session Change to Overall Outcome in Short Term Cognitive Therapy', *Journal of Consulting and Clinical Psychology*, Vol. 63, pp. 651–7.

Roberts, R.J. (1989), 'Passenger Fear of Flying: Behavioral treatment with extensive *in-vivo* exposure and group support', *Aviation, Space and Environmental Medicine*, Vol. 60, pp. 342–8.

Roth, A. and Fonagy, P. (1996), *What Works for Whom? A Critical Review of Psychotherapy Research*, London: Guilford Press.

Rothbaum, B., Hodges, L. and Kooper, R. (1997), 'Virtual Reality Exposure Therapy', *Journal of Psychotherapy Practice and Research*, Vol. 6, No. 3, pp. 219–26.

Salkovskis, P. and Clark, D. (1992), 'Cognitive Therapy for Panic Attacks', *Journal of Cognitive Psychotherapy*, Vol. 5, No. 3, pp. 215–26.

Shakespeare, W. (1994), 'Hamlet', *The Oxford Shakespeare. The Complete Works*, ed. S. Wallis and G. Taylor, Oxford: Oxford University Press, Act 2, Scene 2.

van Gerwen, L. (1988), 'Fear of Flying: Reasons, effects and remedy', in van Gerwen, L., Spinhoven, P., Diekstra, R. and Van Dyck, R. (1997), 'People who Seek Help for Fear of Flying: Typology of flying phobics', *Behavior Therapy*, Vol. 28, pp. 237–51.

van Gerwen, L. and Diekstra, R. (2000), 'Fear of Flying Treatment Programs for Passengers: An international review', *Aviation, Space and Environmental Medicine*, Vol. 71, No. 4, pp. 430–37.

Waddington, L. (2002), 'The Therapy Relationship in Cognitive Therapy: A review', *Behavioural and Cognitive Psychotherapy*, Vol. 30, pp. 179–91.

Wells, A. (1997), *Cognitive Therapy of Anxiety Disorders: A practical manual and conceptual guide*, Chichester: Wiley & Sons.

Whisman, M. (1993), 'Mediators and Moderators of Change in Cognitive Therapy of Depression', *Psychological Bulletin*, Vol. 114, pp. 248–65.

Wilhelm, F. and Roth, W. (1997), 'Acute and Delayed Effects of Alprazolam on Flight Phobics during Exposure', *Behavior Research and Therapy*, Vol. 35, No. 9, pp. 831–41.

Wilhelm, F. and Roth, W. (1997), 'Clinical Characteristics of Flight Phobia', *Journal of Anxiety Disorders*, Vol. 11, No. 3, pp. 241–61.

Wright, J. and Davis, D. (1994), 'The Therapeutic Relationship in Cognitive Behavioural Therapy: Patient perception and therapist responses', *Cognitive and Behavioural Practice*, Vol. 1, pp. 25–45.

Index